Love From Both Sides

Love From Both Sides

A True Story of Soul Survival and Sacred Sexuality

By
Stephanie Riseley

FINDHORN PRESS

First published by Findhorn Press 2008

ISBN: 978-1-84409-139-3

British Library Cataloguing-in-Publication Data.
A catalogue record for this book is available from the British Library.

Edited by Shari Mueller
Front cover photograph by Nancy Santullo
Cover design by Bernard Lescure
Layout by e-BookServices.com
Printed and bound in America

1 2 3 4 5 6 7 8 9 10 11 12 13 14 13 12 11 09 08

Published by
Findhorn Press
305A The Park,
Findhorn, Forres
Scotland IV36 3TE

Tel +44(0)1309 690582
Fax +44(0)1309 690036
eMail info@findhornpress.com
www.findhornpress.com

Table of Contents

Acknowledgements

To my teachers:

Brian Weiss, M.D.,

    for his skilled teaching and generous kindness.

Raymond Moody, M.D.,

    for leading the way.

Lew Hunter,

    UCLA School of Theater, Film and TV, who teaches never to give up.

Hayes B. Jacobs, Stella Adler, and Harold Clurman

    for their fierce dedication to their students and crafts.

To my friends who were kind enough to read and edit:

Alice Folcke Yensen, Lorelle Patterson, Lynn Pounian, Grace Brina, Ada Shaw, Joan Gordon and Jan Onofrio.

To:

Jayne Howarth at the Birmingham Post, without whose kindness, this book would never have found its way out of my computer.

To:

Thierry Bogliolo at Findhorn Press, who said, "Yes!" Thank you.

To:

Mark Bruce Rosin for enthusiastic encouragement, help and suggestions.

Daniel Allen Butler for his sea-faring insights.

Dan Pearson, for his solid friendship.

Dave Ursin for always lending a helping hand, and Christopher Vogler.

To the Iyengar Yoga Community in Los Angeles.

To my sister Melanie.

And finally,

To Jonathan...

I love you.

Chapter One

Free at Last!

I had my hand on my husband's heart when it stopped beating. To feel his big, strong heart come to a complete and utter stop under my hand was so shocking, I didn't have time to even think or react; because, just as his heart stopped, I felt "him" whoosh through me like a wind, and then from behind I heard, "Free at last! Free at last! Thank God Almighty, I'm free at last!" What? Had Dan become Martin Luther King? I turned to look behind me. Was he on the ceiling? No. Where then? What? Free? Free! Free of me…of our life?

This is not what you want to hear after you've just spent six manic, exhausting months doing everything possible to save a man. I turned back to look at the face I loved. The man that I'd married just twelve years before, the love of my life, the man I'd waited for so long to come. That man. The man who asked me to marry him on the fourth date, the man who worshiped my body when he made love to me, the man who could make me scream. The man whose soul I thought I knew so well. The man I fought with, the man I hated sometimes, the man who hated me. The man whose smell I couldn't get enough of. That man? And the asshole died? He died! How could that be? He'd leave me? I wanted to scream, "No! Don't go! Come back!" But all I could do was whisper, "No, no, no. Please, no."

Samuel, my straight-arrow, twenty-eight-year-old stepson, who stood stock still next to the bed in the Intensive Care Unit at Kaiser, would say later that Dan, my husband, had whipped into him and said, "Sam! Sam! I know it looks like I'm dead, but it's okay! It's really okay. I mean, I'm dead, but it's all right."

That night as I roamed the rooms of our little duplex, just screaming in the unbelievable pain of loss (thank God, my neighbors are Russians because they understand wailing grief), I thought that this was the end of our particular "love story." But I was wrong. Completely wrong, for it was really only a beginning. It was a reclaiming of our own authentic love, and a reconnecting to a love story that began a very long time ago.

It took me months to understand and to trust that what I experienced that night in the ICU wasn't just shock, grief, and utter craziness. It is why I write this book. My experience with my husband after he died was very specific, but was as real to me as oxygen. Can you see oxygen? No. But you know it's there because you continue to breathe and you continue to live. And so it is with your own "connection" to the source. You may not see it, acknowledge it, but you know it's there just the same.

If you were drawn to pick up this book, then these words were meant for you to hear. You have a love – a husband, a wife, a lover, a sacred sex partner – and it is my job to share what I *thought* was the reality of our own love story and then to tell the "truth" of what was really going on. For what was going on with us might just help you to understand and appreciate more about your own sacred, sexual, eternal relationship. Unfortunately, don't think for a moment that it means un-eventful and blissful. When you meet the love of your life, you've got business together and Sacred Agreements that need to be fulfilled.

I started out to write a book called *The Married Girl's Guide to Hot and Sacred Sex*. The book you're reading is still about the sacredness of sex, but it's also about death and our connection with the "In Between," as the Buddhists call it. Sex and death go hand-in-hand: one creates life, one takes it away. When sex is good, we feel connected with "a oneness"; we feel connected with the "All That Is," the Godhead, the Sacred. Since bookshelves at Barnes and Noble's and Borders book store simply overflow with how-to sex books, I realized I didn't need to write an-other one. Anyone can tell you what goes where, how to have multiple orgasms or how to give great head – all valuable information.

My book is different, because my experience is different. In the months after Dan died, he gave me first-hand, personal awareness that a specific consciousness survives after death, at least for awhile. If I can share my own experience, it might help to remind you that it's the relationship with that sometimes exasperating, challenging, frustrating mate who shares your bed that counts. It counts now, and it counts in the "In Between."

My own journey to awareness began the night Dan died and continued for more than a year. In that year, I discovered what agreements we made with each other, what we were meant to achieve together, what we managed to ac-complish, what we didn't and why. Yes, my husband died that night, but truth be told, he died so that our love would live. For in the months before his dying, we'd almost lost each other and we'd almost lost our love. We simply weren't "paying attention."

Since I wasn't paying attention, it's amazing how much I knew yet refused to acknowledge. The morning Dan died, for instance, I woke up at four a.m. with the bitter taste of adrenalin in my mouth. I knew this day was different. It was Wednesday, the day after Christmas 2001 and Dan was in the hospital at Kaiser

Permanente in Los Angeles. Some things you get used to, and I'd gotten used to Dan being in the hospital. He'd had a "nasty" case of acute leukemia for more than six months by then. Lots of people get leukemia and they get over it, right? I was sure that Dan, my big, strong husband, would get over it too. I, myself, had gotten over a condition that the doctors fully expected me to die of and I assumed that Dan would get over this. I knew he would.

He'd gone in on Saturday with just another case of pneumonia (if you don't have platelets, you're prone to infection). So today they were going to do a thoracentisis – a lung tap – to see if they could drain off any of the accumulated fluid. As far as I was concerned, this was a simple procedure. When I was young, I'd had lots of them performed on me, and they were not a big problem. From my memory, I told him they would stick a big needle into his lung and they'd draw out the amber fluid so he could breathe again. It was a snap, and I'd told Dan just that.

But as I dressed that morning, I saw my own blood-shot, red-rimmed eyes in the mirror, and I knew I was terrified. Our two "alternative" doctors said Dan was getting better, but thought that we'd have another six months before he would be well again. Sick people are not always at their best, and Dan was no different. Since I'd once been a very sick person myself, I knew how awful it feels to be in pain all the time. Still, I knew we'd get through this – it was just a matter of time.

Wrong again. By the end of that day, Dan was dead. Death is so final, or that's what I thought. After all the screaming and crying I was capable of, I finally collapsed into bed around four-thirty in the morning. But just two hours later I woke up, startled. It was as if someone screamed in my ear, "Get up! Get up! Go outside!"

Okay! I thought. All right! Stop it! It was barely light, but I got up and dragged myself outside, then looked east. I stood in the chill of dawn, and watched as the sun burst through the clouds, and the horizon filled with streaks of deep reds, blues and golds. Then I heard a disembodied voice say, "It's a new day. You will go on."

It would be an understatement to say that I was not in a good mood. Go on? Why should I? Who'll care? So I sullenly went back to bed and to sleep. Four months of unrelenting hell passed as I mourned the love of my life – the stubborn, immovable, impossible man I'd just lost, but whom I still loved beyond endurance. Grief can be so intense, and I was simply sure I was losing my mind. At least that's what I thought when I woke up climaxing one night and *knowing* that my dead husband had just had sex with me. Sex in the afterlife, you say? You bet. Sex is the "cosmic connection," and weird as it seems, our own sacred, sexual connection didn't end with Dan's death.

That's why in April, I decided to go back to the book I was thinking of writing before he got sick: *The Married Girl's Guide to Hot and Sacred Sex*. I wanted to write it because most of my married girlfriends were either not having any sex at all, or if they were, it certainly wasn't the kind they used to have when they were wild, single babes: the "tear off your clothes, throw you down and fuck you silly" kind of sex. I wanted to find out why, and then figure out how, and even *if* we could reclaim our "authentic" sex life.

I'd gotten married late, and I had my own very specific opinions on how to keep the home fires burning. I felt the "wife job" had to be taken seriously. I fussed with dinners and we ate together whenever possible. I insisted that Dan and I take time for one another; we scheduled "dates," time spent just talking. We'd light a fire, sit on the couch, talk and laugh. Sometimes we'd have sex, sometimes we wouldn't – but at least we had the option and the energy.

So I gathered a group of friends together – mostly over-extended, professional working moms – at a friend's house. They would be my focus group. We all sat around talking about how hard marriage was in the first place, but when kids come along? Sex? Forget it! "Lying down is enough of an orgasm for me," one friend said.

I asked them questions like, "How do you deal with grievances?" "Do you schedule sex?" "Dates?" As they bitched, moaned, and complained about their husbands, I realized that of the fourteen women there, I was the only one who wasn't married and was *never*, ever having sex – at least with anyone still among the living. And it hit me like a ton of bricks once again – Dan's dead? My husband's dead? I filled up with an achy heaviness and I simply had to go lie down. By now I knew that this was what "physical mourning" felt like, so I just went to bed and left everyone else to chat away about their sex lives and marriages.

The next day was a Sunday, and Sundays were the worst – no husband, no hugging, no sex. I'd endured four hard months without Dan, and once again, mourning crashed into me like a tsunami and I went down. As I sat in bed crying, I picked up a journal and started writing:

Sunday, April 14, 2002 – It's 12:30 daytime.

I'm in bed. Crying and crying because my heart still aches. My insides heave and I miss Dan.

But I miss the Dan that "might have been" more than the Dan that was actually here. It's Sunday, if he were really here, face it, he'd be watching a God-damned football/baseball/basketball game on TV or staring at his stupid computer. He'd ignore me – make me furious!

Humph! I thought, That'll teach him to die! Finally, I got mad, and because I got angry, my energy shifted.

I sat there thinking about the night before and my book, when something like a focused buzz drilled into my ear and someone yelled: "Put the pen in the other hand! Put the pen in the other hand!" I looked around, Oh, God! I'm going crazy. But I did it anyway. I put the pen in my left hand and it slowly started to move, first forming letters, and then words:

From Dan the man –
You are my goddess now and forever. We walked a life together that allowed me to experience my own ability to love so profoundly and deeply because of you. You must honor what we had together and forget the *rest*.
I was an idiot much of the time and for that I am truly sorry. Please forgive me. And forgive yourself for not being superwoman.

I stopped and stared at the awkward writing. I could feel "Dan," his energy, blasting through me. I could feel his delight and relief that he could finally reach me. I knew it was Dan and not just my longing for him.

Samuel, his son, had been "hearing" from Dan for months. Actually, to hear Sam tell it, Dan was simply chatting up a storm. "Dad's trying to explain how it all works. He can speak to me, but I have to provide the words. I don't hear his voice, but it's him. I know it's him." So if Samuel – logical, practical Samuel who unlike me had no experience in "alternative" anything, could hear Dan – maybe I wasn't going crazy after all.

Actually, Sam and I both experienced Dan's "coming back" at the same time when we had to go to Callanan's Mortuary and Funeral Home to arrange for his cremation. It was as if Dan just tagged along.

In real life, Dan's favorite TV show was the first season of "Six Feet Under," which was about a struggling mortuary owned by a dysfunctional family. The first season's villain was a Big Corporation that was trying to drive them out of business. The show always started out with a death and the Dead Person usually had a speaking part.

When Sam and I got to Callanan's, the funeral director, Cindy, was blasting the top tunes of 2001 throughout the place, but that seemed fitting. Cindy sat us down in her office and started to explain our options. I told Cindy that Dan's favorite show was "Six Feet Under."

"Oh, mine too," she laughed. "Some funeral directors hate it, but they just have no sense of humor."

"We must be in the right place. How accurate is the show?"

"Oh, it's spot on. Whoever writes it must have worked in a funeral home."

"Dan would want to be with a small, family-owned mortuary just like on the show," I said.

"Sorry, you're too late for that," Cindy said. "We were bought out three years ago. If you want a privately-owned mortuary, you'll have to go outside Los Angeles; everyone else has been bought out. Of course, the corporations can't break into the black mortuaries. You could go to Inglewood, Compton or Watts if that's what you really want."

Suddenly, Dan yelled out, "Okay! Let's go to Watts! I've really always been a black person. I need to be with my people!"

Sam squeezed my hand – he heard him too. We were about to stand up and head off to Watts. Obviously Cindy couldn't hear Dan, because she was still talking, telling us that this mortuary was now owned by the Catholic something or others.

"The Catholics?" Dan said, "Okay, I'll be with the Catholics."

Since Dan was Jewish that might seem odd, but we both adored the women (and former nuns) who run the Immaculate Heart Center for Spiritual Renewal in Montecito, Calif., just south of Santa Barbara. It's a beautiful estate that once served as their novitiate, and Dan and I loved it there.

So Dan stayed at Callanan's.

A few days later, I decided to head to Immaculate Heart and get myself renewed. As I drove along the coast toward Santa Barbara, glancing at the sparkling blue Pacific, I could hear Dan "chatting" to me. It felt as if he could see the beauty of the ocean through my eyes. I heard him wondering why in the hell he was so damned depressed all the time. He simply couldn't understand it; I felt his sheer frustration and annoyance. But because his chatting merged with my addle-brained grief, I didn't know if it was actually Dan or my own inner monologue. His real voice was so fresh in my consciousness that I couldn't separate it out.

While I stayed at the Retreat Center, I continued to "hear" Dan, but like many people, I discounted it. For all I knew, it could have just been my own hallucinating mind. When I hiked to a waterfall we both loved, only days after he died, I felt him there with me. When I walked through the library, I passed a book about Chartres, the cathedral in France, and it was as if Dan screamed, "Stop! Look! The book! Take my ashes to Chartres. I need to be in Chartres. I want to be mixed with the stones."

Okay, fine. I knew he loved Chartres. He'd been a blacksmith in the 70s, and talked about its magnificent stained glass windows and its bells and ironwork. Since I'd always wanted to go to France, I thought, "Great, I'll go to Chartres. Someday."

But on that day, his body hadn't even been cremated.

A few mornings later, however, when I was still in bed, it felt as if I were standing next to Dan, holding his hand, as we watched his body being cremated. He just wanted me to be there with him. So I stayed put, ethereally, and held his hand as we watched his body burn. Still, as far as I was concerned, it was all up for grabs. I wanted to stay grounded in "reality," but my reality was pretty shaky since losing a husband completely undoes you. My brain was in shock and it stayed that way for months – until that Sunday in April, when I got sick and tired of being in so much pain, and I finally just let his energy move my hand.

I began to ask him questions. I asked about a dream I'd had the night before where a disembodied penis came floating toward me, trying to pat my cheek. He wrote:

I tried to reach you but couldn't.

That would be my Dan, thinking a "floating penis" just might appeal to me. It's not as if people change. Then I burst into tears again, because I felt his presence so intensely. All at once, a rush of frustration shot through me and the pen began to move again:

> **Cry as much as you want my beautiful, you won't bring me back. The only thing you can do to communicate with me is this. Believe it is *authentic*. Because it is.**
> **We are on the same team now. What's really amusing about the whole little drama is that I am better off dead. I had lost my reason to live and you knew it was killing you. You have your own time frame, babe and you ain't through yet.**

Later, I asked him about what happened on the night he died.

> **When you crawled into bed with me, I knew I could let go and to show you how much I loved you – and to *make up* – I let your hand feel my last heartbeat. Then I whooshed past you. You felt it – I knew you'd felt me go through you. But then your own *shock* kicked in and that horrid night…I was there, unable to get through until you fell asleep – I saw the sunrise and woke you up. I screamed.**

This is from my journal:

> *Dan? I miss you so much. The pain feels unbearable sometimes. The deep hole in my heart…but why, I try to ask myself, why wasn't I happier with you? Was it me? Was it you? Was it us?*

> **You forget our perfect moments – the moments when we loved each other beyond the limits of our world.**

(I started to cry and I felt him get frustrated again.)

Don't go being crazy. My best times were with you. You gave me much joy. Don't dwell on all we didn't give to each other. We did a great job being married. The problem for you now is to find the course you want to follow from now on. You need to honor the emptiness of your life. Embrace the quiet. Sit in silence. Believe that you can communicate with me, or at least the familiar part of me. We have more business together.

That was the beginning of my "Dan channeling." It continued for almost a year, and in that time he led me on a journey through the In Between like my own personal Virgil.

Fortunately, I learned to channel on the computer, which was much less draining, although Dan's "presence" did take an energetic toll every time he "came in." In more than two hundred pages, Dan narrates his way through his "re-education." I meet his "oversoul," and I meet my own. Dan tells me about viewing his "soul progressions," and then like a kid, he wants to show me mine, but my own "guides" stop him. He tells me about our pre-planned "agreements," which, much to my chagrin, he stubbornly refused to fulfill. He makes amends, and more amends. He makes me laugh – something he loved to do in life – and he makes me cry. He yearns for sex, which seems strange since he has no body. He longs for my body and he longs for his own.

Finally, he chooses his next adventure and he takes flight. He's conceived into a new body and he tells me about his altogether new and challenging situation.

Yes, Dan died that night. But ultimately what I discovered and understood deeply was that my husband died so that I would live. He died because he betrayed himself, he betrayed me, and he betrayed *us*. That's why he had to come back to make things right. And he did. He gave me back the love of my life – his true, authentic self.

He encouraged me to tell this story – our story – because it is a story of true love. As it turns out, it's also a story of unrequited love that began more than four hundred years ago in a tiny town in France. And that town has a cathedral, and the cathedral has a bell. So in December of 2002, when I found my way back to France, to Chartres, and threw Dan's ashes onto that bell, it rang for a full ten minutes.

I hope that by sharing this journey with you, the processing and postmortem of our hard fought marriage, it just might help you to pay attention to how deeply you and your mate – your *sacred* sexual partner – are connected…connected to each other and connected to the "In Between."

Chapter Two

Welcome to the In Between

D an's dying was not my first experience with the "In Between." I'd had others, but since I desperately wanted to be normal, I chose to ignore them.

My first happened when I was 19. I had pericarditis with bilateral lung effusions, or in English, the sack around my heart, the pericardium, got inflamed and both my lungs filled with fluid. As one doctor would say, "You've got a literally weeping heart. It's actually very poetic." Poetic perhaps, but it made it so painful to breathe that I couldn't lie down flat. My parents had no interest in my health or anything besides their own passionate dance of destruction; so consequently, I sat alone and upright in a darkened room for almost two weeks. When one of my mother's friends opened my door, looked in and saw me, it was almost too late. They rushed me to the hospital, but after the nurses got me settled into bed, I simply wanted "out." I remember closing my eyes, and it felt as if my hands were holding onto a bar just overhead, then I simply let go. Like magic, I slid easily down toward a warm, amber light. I knew exactly what was happening; I was dying and I felt relieved. But then out of nowhere, something grabbed me by the scruff of the neck and yanked me back. It felt as if my body screamed, "Hey, wait just a damned minute! You're nineteen. You may not want to live, but all of us hundred-twenty trillion cells do! So get a grip, girl!"

As it turns out, according to "Dan," it wasn't just my body, it was my "oversoul" and my "guides." It didn't matter to me who or what brought me back, because there I was, in searing pain, and knowing that I would live, which at the time was not good news.

That was in April of 1967, long before Elisabeth Kübler-Ross published her book on death and dying, so like many people, I kept that experience to myself. But it changed me; it gave me the courage to ignore the doctors who told me I had five years to live. So I had systemic lupus…so what? People got over worse things, and somehow I knew I'd get over this. The following March, I managed to get myself into University of California, Berkeley, which still amazes me, since I'd barely bothered to show up at Hollywood High School. After three years in Berkeley, I moved to New York City to study acting. I lived there eleven years, moved back to Los Angeles for seven, then back to Berkeley to finish up my degree in 1988, so UCLA would be kind enough to let me into their graduate school of film.

In the twenty years in between, I flirted with the alternative world, but kept my distance. It seemed too flaky, airy-fairy, and filled with far too many spiritually smug people. Although, to be honest, Jane Roberts's channeled books, *Seth Speaks* and *The Nature of Personal Reality* changed my life. Her books not only gave me doable exercises that helped me heal my damaged body; they also gave me a dynamically different perspective on day-to-day living.

Looking back on it now, I was connected to the alternative realm whether I wanted to be or not. For instance, while I still lived in New York, I heard a man on the radio talk about past life regressions. So I sat right down, followed his instructions, and wham! I saw myself as a nun – an ugly, French nun – sitting in my little cell, writing and looking out onto a beautiful garden. I knew the time period was late Middle Ages and I saw her life then, but I didn't take it seriously.

Besides, I was too busy supporting my acting addiction, so on weekend nights I drove a taxi to pay for the acting, dancing, and singing classes that went along with it. One snowy, slippery night, when I got home at three a.m., completely exhausted, I put Beethoven's Ninth on the stereo and curled up on the couch to unwind. I was still in my twenties, so I sat there wondering, "What was life all about? What was its purpose: to do good work? Be a success? Find happiness?" When suddenly my whole insides filled up with that same radiant, amber light. Only this time a voice – a distinctly male voice – boomed out, "Life is to be loved." Implicit in that message was the realization, the deep understanding, that life wasn't to be figured out or fretted over (my own unending "inner monologue") – life was simply to be *loved*. Since I come from a background steeped in American Protestant self-denial, "life is to be loved" was real news to me. I thought life was simply to be suffered through. I assumed my ability to stoically withstand pain was the path to spiritual redemption. It's the "Brownie Points in Heaven" view of reality that most good little Christian girls are taught.

Did the "life is to be loved" message solve any problems? Did I pay attention? No, I had more important things to worry about. I studied acting with the amazing Stella Adler, and so I only asked the Big Questions, the questions that mattered – What is Art? Truth? Beauty?

Life goes on (unless, of course, it doesn't) and mine continued for years without any more nudges from the "In Between." Then in June of 1988, my baby sister Gheri-Llynn committed suicide. She was eleven years younger and only twenty-nine. During her downward spiral into despair, I tried desperately to get her help. I finally managed to get her into UCLA's Neuropsychiatric Institute

(NPI), where I'd worked for four years, but all they could do was drug her into a shaky-handed stupidity. She hated how that made her feel and consequently, she was determined to do what she wanted. And she wanted "out."

The month before she died, while I still lived in Berkeley, finishing off twenty-eight units of undergraduate work, Gheri-Llynn drove up to say good-bye. It was my birthday and she handed me a beautiful pair of blue teardrop earrings and said, "These stones are three million years old. Some things last and some things don't."

I'm five-foot-eight and she was just barely five-three; I grabbed her by the shoulders, looked down into her deep brown eyes and said, "Gheri-Llynn, if you do this, I will never forgive you. I swear. I will hunt you down in the afterlife. I'm serious. You cannot do this." She looked away, hugged me and kissed me good-bye.

The night before I was due to drive back down to LA, (where I was going to try to get more help for her) my father called at one a.m. All he said was, "Steph?" and I knew she was dead. I threw the phone across the room and started screaming, "My baby! My baby! My baby!" I screamed for five hours.

I drove back to Los Angeles and stayed in a friend's guest house the next night. As I lay there in the stunned disbelief that goes along with death, I turned and looked through two tall French glass doors out into the darkness. Suddenly, amorphous, scary figures of black men began to sail through the doors toward me. One held a knife, the next one held a gun, the next a rope, but they evaporated just before they reached me. Each one looked so real, so threatening; they were very specific people. I knew they weren't real – I knew it, yet I didn't know it.

I'm not afraid of black men. As I said, I drove a cab in New York City for seven years, and since I was just out of Berkeley, I drove with my belief system in tact. Which means that I was one of the few taxi drivers who would pick up black people – black men in particular – and take them to more challenging areas of the city: to Harlem, the South Bronx, Bed-Sty, East New York, to the places where many African American people lived. And believe me, in the late 70s at the height of the drug epidemic, those were dangerous destinations. But I drove in and out of these places all the time, so fear of black men was not an issue for me.

Gheri-Llynn, on the other hand, had been raped by a black man. She was only twenty-one when he climbed through her bedroom window at three a.m., and held a knife to her throat while he raped her.

As I continued to watch these flying black men, I wondered what the hell they could be. Since I did field research evaluating the incidence of mental illness in the population at large when I worked at NPI, I knew that one of the key indicators of schizophrenia was seeing things that aren't there. I kept my eye on these black phantoms, these threatening men, trying to think clinically, unemotionally. "Well, this is interesting. This must be what it's like to be crazy." Until finally it hit me. I'd finally broken. I *was* crazy. Then I filled with fear. I would be like Lily Tomlin's character Trudy, in the stage play "The Search for Signs of Intelligent Life in the Universe" – one of the crazy people who roam the streets, chatting to the phantoms who keep them company.

And that's when the leaping stream of black men stopped. They simply evaporated. Then Gheri-Llynn "came through." In real life, she was a tiny, determined, fireball of energy with a wicked sense of humor, and it was Gheri-Llynn, all right. "Wow! This is nothing like what I expected. You were right, damn it! That was so stupid of me. Nothing to do about it now. But those black guys? I just needed you to experience my reality. I needed you to understand why I couldn't go on living. I was too scared – all the time." This happened in a flash, not in words, but in images and feeling tones. I tried to ask her what the Other Side was like, but she couldn't tell me. "Too complicated," she said. This was all she could do now.

Then she wanted to be held. I was lying still, my arms at my sides, and yet it felt as if I held my chubby, cuddly three-year-old baby sister. I hugged her and she hugged me. My body filled to the brim with so much love that I felt throbbing love-tingles in my fingernails, and then she was gone.

I didn't hear from her again or directly from anyone else, even though my mother died just a few years later. My father died in 1999, and then my older sister, Valrie, died the February just before Dan. But I didn't hear from any of them.

When Dan died, I dropped into the deep despair of mourning. I'd fill up with an intense energy, and all I could do was cry. But I kept getting strong urges to turn on his computer and pick up his e-mail. Finally, I sat down at his desk, got his e-mail, and found some old e-mails to me. One reminded me of our life when Dan would be in the front room at his desk, and I'd be working in my office in the back, trying to finish a script.

He wrote this one while the Democratic National Convention of 2000 was in session:

----- *Original Message* -----
From: Daniel Wax
To: Stephanie Riseley
Sent: Monday, August 14, 2000 9:48 AM
Subject: Date
The Bcc is for your subconscious.
I just wanted to tell you in a non-verbal way (sometimes the medium does get in the way
*   of the message) how much I still am so madly in love with you (most of the time - the*
*   lil' imp speaks) and speak into your ear sweet whisperings of love and invitation - to*
*   a date tonight, starting right after Yoga. The date will take on the meanderings it*

freely must do for it must not be too scripted, but it will definitely involve a massage from my hands on your beautiful body, should you desire it. I would suggest that you select a snack of your choice, light and preparatory to love. I will cool the glasses and open the champagne and toast you, about 7:50 PM. Depending on the heat factor, we will commence the evening at our usual locale, the couch.

This message is brought to you in part by the Democratic National Committee of Hope, betting that we can enhance our ability to live in the moment, (the one seeming constant purveyed by all the sages and sagesses thru all cultures and time - as the key to salvation, and probably even fortune) if we can concentrate and so honor these moments of our love. It will get us home just fine, as long as we honor it.

My sweet Stephanie - I love you. Please accept my heartfelt invitation.

Dan

I read that, sitting there at his desk, and just wept. The desk where for almost four years he worked on "Conflict Solvers," a mediation Internet start-up venture that simply ate up the time of his life – and mine.

And then I found a file, marked "To Steph." I opened it, but it was empty, except for the words, "Twelve years." Dan died four days before our twelfth anniversary, and for our anniversaries, I would always ask for one of his letters. I knew that empty file would have been my "anniversary letter." I closed the file, and went on putting one foot in front of the other, my only expectation of myself during that time. But then a few weeks later, I plunked myself back down at his desk. I opened the file, and rested my fingers on the keyboard. It was as if he just started typing through me.

Anniversary Letter – 2001

Twelve years. When I wrote those words I remember the exhaustion of our life together – the push and pull, the frantic battle to save me – but even though that seems like reality, it wasn't. Reality – our reality – goes on... continues whether I breathe air, fart, annoy you, love you, want you, yearn for you, hold you, fight with you, want to murder you, want to save you, want to leave. It goes on, my sweet Stephanie. It goes on. We are a couple now. We are a team. You gave me your magic and I believe in it now. I have no doubts now because your "magic" is my reality.

The twelve years we spent together as a married couple were the best years of an otherwise unremarkable existence. Your grief is so tangible to me – so painful to me that sometimes I marvel at your ability to feel.

We didn't celebrate our last "first date" or our last anniversary. But we celebrated our love and I continue to feel the love you have for me. You

must believe this…you are not crazy…even though if it weren't for the fact that you were channeling _me_, I'd be sure – completely sure – you were.

Let this not be the last love letter I write to you. Sit with me…let me feel your love. It will do us both more good than you understand. Forgive me for not letting you love me more. Forgive me for pushing you away. Forgive me the pain I caused you. I can't undo that…I can only love you now, and truthfully forever. We have many lifetimes to annoy each other, to fight with each other, to love each other. I only wish I could do the dishes for you…me.

And so did I, because I hate doing dishes.

* * *

That was in March. I knew that was Dan, yet it seemed way too strange for my taste. Maybe it was just the mourning. Maybe I was delusional. But by mid-April, when the channeling just flooded my circuits, I connected with him quite easily. Sometimes, however, it drained my energy so completely that I would just conk out. Dan urged me to go back to his computer and type there, rather than do the left-handed channeling. But I hated sitting at his machine, for all kinds of reasons. I didn't like his chair, and there was an anger in me about how many hours of our life together he spent focused on more important things. When I finally sat down and put my fingers on the keys, I could feel his frustration with me. It was just like in life – he was downright annoyed with me. This is what he said:

April 25, 2002

We need a schedule to talk. Cannot be called "away," unless it's an emergency. Let us decide when it is you want to communicate and I will make the time for it. I suggest you do it first thing in the morning when your mind is not filled with the events of the day. But you know this already. I just wanted to reinforce your own beliefs. Your body is still in mourning, which I find amazing. As I said, I had no idea how deeply you loved me. Of course, there is a part of you that didn't understand that as well. We were both pretty unconscious. But still, we did a damned good job of it! And I will be _eternally_ (underline that) grateful to you for standing up to me as best as you could. I was a knuckle-headed dope for much of our marriage.

Now, re: your book. Yes, you will write it. And I will help. I always was such a writer. Thank you for insisting I write you those letters. My god, to be forced to say on paper what you meant to me. That was the gift. That was your gift to me. And don't think it didn't pass my awareness that I gave you anniversary presents, but you never gave them to me. And we both understood why. You celebrated our marriage everyday, in every way. From the flowers you fussed with, to the shopping and dinners you insisted we eat together. I am so grateful that you cared enough for me to continue to do that all the days of our lives together. No one else – and I mean no one else – would have had the determination to continue on with me.

So from that April on, I couldn't pretend that the channeling wasn't real and I couldn't ignore the In Between any longer. It screamed too loudly for me not to pay attention. I started out to write a book to help married girls get more sex into their harried lives. The real quest for all of us, however, is to connect with our own "core selves" – the sacred. And here's the good news: sex *is* sacred. Your relationship is sacred. Here's what Dan said to his newly widowed wife while trying to encourage her to write:

In your book, if you can communicate the beauty of animal, smelly, joyous sexual expression to only _one other_ soul on this plane of reality, your effort will be worthwhile. But your time, once again, is limited. I don't say this to scare you. Only to make you focus on what is important to you. The book, and the information contained in the book, will help many, many other souls who are in the same kind of pain.

It will lead them to make the journey to connect with their lost loves, children, parents and then connect with their own source. And that, my dear, is your _true mission_. You are part, a small part, of the working whole that is set in place. But you have to commit to do the work. If you don't do the work, it won't get done. No one up here can type!

But I could type, and so I did.

Melvin Morse, M.D., the pediatrician who wrote *Closer to the Light, Transformed by the Light, Parting Visions*, and *Where God Lives*, scientifically documents experiences like mine, as have Raymond Moody, M.D., and the late Elisabeth Kübler-Ross. Still, I feel it's a bit like trying to explain blue to a blind person, but since you're still reading, you probably know what "blue" is.

Chapter Three

"When Harry Met Sally"

I f this were a movie, this would be the flashback. For to make sense of what Dan reveals about our marriage and "agreements," you need to see where we started. How Dan asked me to marry him on the fourth date – only two weeks after we met – used to be my favorite story, and I'd tell it at the drop of a hat. I was forty-two and terminally single, so it was an extremely popular story with single girls over forty, because it filled them with such hope. If I could find the love of my life after forty, then maybe they could too. It's still a good story, but now it doesn't seem like the great leap of faith it once did. Back then I thought that I married a complete stranger. As it turned out, Dan was anything but a stranger.

***

In the summer of 1987, I read Shakti Gawain's *Living in the Light*, and I decided it was time to take Joseph Campbell's advice seriously and "follow my bliss." I wanted to be a screenwriter, so I decided to get myself into UCLA's graduate film school. I filled myself with "determined optimism," overcame obstacle after obstacle, and I got myself in. When I met Dan in October of 1989, I was doing exactly what I wanted – at long last. I had just started my second year at UCLA and I loved my life. I lived with the wonderful, acerbic character actress, Eve Arden, or "Our Miss Brooks," for anyone old enough to remember her TV show. My job with Eve was to relieve Ana, her longtime, devoted housekeeper on Sundays and Mondays, which meant cooking a couple of meals, taking Eve to church on Sunday mornings, then out to lunch and to the movies. It was a great job, because as we drove around Beverly Hills, Eve would tell me all the Old Hollywood gossip, like how she'd go dancing with Greg Peck, or how she turned down Clark Gable because he had bad breath. ("Eve! You turned down Clark Gable?")

I also headed up my own goddess group, where once a month I gathered a bunch of girlfriends together and led them through a guided visualization based on the "Seth" book exercises and *Living in the Light*. For those of you who know those books, we sent our "pink bubbles up into Framework Two." My "pink bubble" always included my winning an Academy Award, finding "the love of my life," and having a baby girl. I filled my heart with big dreams and quite magically, they seemed to be coming true.

I'd just won "The Women in Film" screenwriting award and finished a rewrite on a "Made for TV" movie, but I longed to meet the love of my life; I _knew_ he was out there somewhere. In early July, I'd met a sexy, talented art director named Jim, who was out of town working on "Back to the Future III," the Western. He drank too much for my taste, and told me straight out he would never marry again, but hey, no one's perfect. The movie was shooting up in California's gold country near Jamestown, and I drove back and forth all summer long. Now it was mid-fall, and I hadn't heard from Jim in weeks and weeks. Finally, I decided that it was only a summer romance, so when Dan called, I agreed to go out with him.

Dan was forty-nine the night he showed up on my doorstep. He'd just finished law school, and as I used to say, "had just stepped off the boat from Mendocino." For even though it was 1989, to Dan it was still the Sixties. He'd met my tall, beautiful friend Valerie at a party and asked her out. She was engaged to her future ex-husband, but told Dan that she knew someone he'd like. She called me, told me about him and I said, "I don't want to go out with a lawyer."

"But he's an _environmental_ lawyer. He wants to save the redwoods. Besides, he's cute and when's the last time you heard from Jim?"

"Okay, give him my number." A girl has to keep her options open, especially at forty-two.

We went to dinner – nothing fancy – we split a pizza and a salad. When I worked for the Neuropsychiatric Institute, I interviewed people to determine the incidence of mental illness in the population at large, and I still tend to interview everyone. So I interviewed Dan. He was from Brooklyn – a "red diaper" baby. Both of his parents, a postal worker and grade school teacher, had been idealistic Trotskyite Communists in the 30s, as a lot of New Yorkers were in the Depression years. Did they know Stalin was on his way to killing 30 million people? No. They believed that the Soviet Union was the most advanced society to ever grace the face of planet Earth. Dan told me about how his mother worshiped him, and how his younger sister resented him because of it.

"I peaked at eight," he said, and smiled. "I was president of my first, second and third grade classes. But then, I don't know what the hell happened. I got really shy."

In 1948, when Joseph McCarthy's House Un-American Activities Committee (HUAC) hearings were in full swing, and the great Red Scare swept the nation, both his parents came under suspicion and surveillance.

"My dad had to sign a loyalty oath to keep his job," Dan said. "My mom made me promise I would never tell _anything_ I heard at home,"

As he talked, I could picture the cramped, row house street he grew up on, because I knew Brooklyn cold. I also knew his mom. Brooklyn overflowed with feisty, opinionated little dynamos who ruled their own private universes.

Dan said he moved to Berkeley in 1969.

"Really?" I said. "I was there then. Where'd you live?"

"Parker and Ellsworth."

"That's weird. I lived just around the corner."

"No kidding. We must have passed each other all the time on the way to campus."

"You couldn't have missed me," I said. "I'm allergic to the sun, so I had to wear big hats all the time. And since I wouldn't wear hats with jeans, I wore dresses – short dresses – up to my ass. In that world of jeans and blue work shirts, I stood out like a sore thumb."

"Oh, my God! You're the girl in the hat? Of course, I remember you."

We both laughed, because of how funny I must have looked.

"Me?" he said. "I went for the big, earth mother types – they didn't wear make-up or bras."

"That would have left me out. I wouldn't be caught dead without either. You must have been, what? Twenty-nine then," I said. "Were you still in school?"

"Briefly," he said. "I'd transferred from a Ph.D. program in Philosophy at Santa Barbara to Berkeley. I mean, Berkeley was the only place to be, wasn't it? I spent a couple half-hearted semesters in grad school studying Maoist thought, but I was really just waiting for the Revolution to begin." He laughed and shook his head. "When the Revolution refused to begin on schedule, I quit school to become a welder. I wanted to be part of the proletariat. And then I met Maggie – my ex-wife – and we got married. I was thirty-two."

"How long were you married?"

"Depends on what you call married. We were legally married eight years, but our marriage fell apart pretty soon after my son, Sam, was born."

"How come?"

"I was her fourth husband – she was five years older – she didn't have a whole lot of patience. And do you remember the O'Neil book? _Open Marriage?_"

"Where everyone sleeps with everyone else?"

"Total nonsense, of course. But, we tried it." He turned away, and stiffened. "That's not quite true. What really happened was that Maggie fell in love with her pottery student. He was only seventeen. A shy kid whose mother asked her to bring him out of his shell. She brought him out, all right."

He tried to smile, but his eyes shot away – the pain of that memory.

"You got divorced then?"

"No," he said, "Maggie kept telling me that she still loved me. She convinced me that if I really loved her, I'd let this passion burn itself out. I wanted to be 'leading edge, far out,' so I went along. I mean, what was I going to do? I didn't want to take Sam away from his mother. I was bored stiff working for General Electric anyway, so we sold our house in Livermore and moved to Mendocino. Together. As a unit."

"Excuse me?" I put my fork down and stared at him.

"I know it sounds strange now, but it was the Seventies. What can I say? When I realized she was never going to love me again, I finally moved out."

"Wait. Stop the presses. You lived with your wife while she was sleeping with another man?"

"Look," he said, suddenly defensive, "I was an idiot. But our little household was nothing out of the ordinary in Mendocino. People experimented with everything, pushed the envelope over the edge. I mean, Jim Jones was the superintendent of the school district, for Pete's sake."

"The guy who moved his flock to Guyana and then Kool-Aided everyone to death? That Jim Jones?"

"Right. You see? We were almost conservative by Mendocino standards."

"When did you leave New York?"

"Sixty-seven. Everyone was heading to California in the Sixties, and I knew I had to be a part of it. I had friends in grad school at UC Santa Barbara, and they said, 'Come on down!' So I applied and got in. What heaven! I lived way high up in the hills, near Painted Cave. I rode my Harley down this wild, windy road toward the Pacific Ocean every single day. I had a big bushy beard with hair down to my shoulders that blew straight back behind me in the wind. I got to study philosophy with Huston Smith. Man, how sweet does it get?" He smiled at the memory.

And so did I. He lived the quintessential "California Dreamin'" ideal. But "The Times, They Were a-Changin'," and then we both sighed, because things had certainly changed, but not in the direction we'd once hoped for. By the late Eighties the size of your bank account was what mattered most, and on that score, Dan and I were pretty much in the same boat – neither of us had a spare nickel.

When the check came, Dan fumbled with it. I could see that he expected me to pay for half, but I just smiled at him. He'd asked me out on a date, and I'd be damned if I wouldn't be treated like a girl – finally. The Sixties were over in my book.

After dinner I took Dan up to the bar at the Bel Air Hotel for a drink. It's a cozy piano bar with wood paneled walls done up in hunter greens, rich reds and when it's cool enough, there's a fire burning. We sat next to the fire and talked some more, then I paid for the drinks with my American Express card. (I didn't know it then, but I would be married by the time I paid the bill.)

Then, under a full harvest moon, I led Dan through the hotel's lush gardens, and it was so romantic, he tried to kiss me. But his bushy mustache felt like a brush, so it was just a peck.

As he drove me back to Eve's, he said, "Do you want to come to my place?"

I turned toward him, "Are you out of your mind?"

"Oh, right. I didn't want to insult you by not at least asking."

And that might have been all she wrote. Dan said later that he wouldn't have called me again, since he thought I wasn't interested. (Read: I didn't want to sleep with him.) The following night though, I had tickets to go see a guitarist perform in Pasadena. My friend Valerie was supposed to go with me, but she wanted to stay home, so I called Dan instead. After the concert, I decided I would show him my Los Angeles – I'm a native, and I like the place. New Yorkers and Northern Californians, on the other hand, seem to hate LA on sheer principle, and since Dan was both, he was no exception. I wanted him to see how beautiful the city looks at night, so I took him up to the Griffith Park Observatory.

The entrance off Los Feliz was blocked, but I know LA, and I still had my taxi-driver's heart. So I whipped my little Nissan around the barricades and took the back way up through the hills.

It was a clear, gusty October night and the city looked like a blanket of sparkling lights stretched out before us. I pointed to a long, straight-arrow street just below.

"That's Western," I said, "it goes almost to the harbor."

"Look at that." He pointed to where the street jogged to the right. "See? The engineers made a mistake."

"That's not a mistake. That's just how it goes."

When I got home that night, I wrote in my journal, "How anyone could find fault with all that beauty is simply beyond me. This guy isn't for me."

But up there under the stars, I continued to interview him.

"How old were you when you had your first sexual experience?"

Dan looked away, somewhat embarrassed.

"Hey, not fair," he said. "I went to an all men's college – Brooklyn Polytechnic. No girls. I graduated in 1961 – things were different back then. No birth control pills, and good girls didn't. Well, they did, but not with me. I was really shy."

"So what happened?"

"Three buddies and I swore we weren't going to graduate as virgins. So the night before graduation, we got on the subway, came into the city, got off near Times Square and found Consuelo – or rather she found us. She walked up to us, and said, 'I fuck, I suck, I do everything.' She took us back to a seedy little room, and she did us one by one."

"You stood around and watched?"

"No, the other two stayed in the bathroom with her boyfriend. It was pretty creepy. Hey, but what did we know? We had a professor who always called us 'fuzzy puppies,' and that's what we were. Big fuzzy puppies. But oh, my God! When she lowered herself down on me? Man! I must have lasted all of ten seconds, and all I could think was, 'Yes! Yes! Yes! What have I been missing?'"

"And you were…?"

"Twenty-one."

We laughed and turned back to look out over the city lights as the warm Santa Ana winds blew around us.

"How about you?" he asked. "How old were you?"

"Seventeen. That's the average age for girls. First boyfriend. Still know him, and he's still a teenager."

"What'd you do about the draft?" I asked.

"I applied for Conscientious Objector status, but they denied my petition. I turned twenty-seven just before my draft board hearing, and that was the end of it. Of course, I've always wondered if it wouldn't have been a good thing to have just enlisted."

"And have your legs shot off?" I told him how I'd spent four months in a military hospital in San Francisco's Presidio, surrounded by boys with no beards and no legs.

"Yeah," he said, "but men go to war. And I'll never know if the C.O. stuff was bullshit, and I wasn't just afraid."

Dan told me that after Samuel was born, he took the job at General Electric as a nuclear engineer, and I remember thinking, "Well, that can't be a good thing." So when the French oncologist-hematologist said, "Your blood, it looks like you've lived in Chernobyl," I knew the reason why.

In Mendocino, Dan became a blacksmith, and then worked as a wine maker. When I asked him why he stayed living in such a crazy-making situation for so many years, he shrugged. "To stay near Sam."

"Why did you become a lawyer?"

"I'm Jewish. Jewish boys become doctors or lawyers, everyone knows that. Besides, when I was cellar boss at Fetzer, I only made six bucks an hour. I knew I couldn't send Sam to college making six bucks an hour."

What a good man, I thought. He did everything for his son.

Dan lived in Burbank at the time, so for convenience, I'd met him in the valley, in Toluca Lake, close to where I grew up. When I drove him back to his car, we stopped in a parking lot. And now he interviewed me, or rather, he cross-examined me for more than two hours. I was still infatuated with Jim, so I didn't care what Dan thought of me. I was absolutely honest about everything: This is me, who I am. Take it or leave it. We talked for a couple hours, until I finally said, "Well, this must be getting pretty tiresome."

"Nope," he said. "Only game in town."

As I drove back to Eve's that night, I realized that Dan knew more about me than Jim did, and I'd been seeing Jim for more than three months.

Dan called me during the week, but I was too busy. Besides my "Eve job," I worked in the film school production store twenty hours a week and I had a script due. I couldn't go out until the following Saturday night. When Saturday came, Eve told me that her daughter Connie (whom Eve had adopted because Joan Crawford was having such a good time with her own adopted daughter, Christine) was coming to visit and she was bringing a new boyfriend. Connie was my age, and wanted any possible competition out of the house. Luckily, my friend Valerie had just moved in with her boyfriend, so her little house up in Laurel Canyon would be empty until January. I figured I'd move in there on Sunday, and work out what to do next, later.

When Dan arrived that night, I said, "Why don't we just go out to the beach and have a picnic?"

"Fine," he said. Since his Brooklyn driving sent my heart into my throat, I drove. But as we headed out Sunset Boulevard toward the beach, the fog rolled in. Okay, no picnic? No problem. I made a fast left turn, and we wound up at the old Aero Theater in Santa Monica, where they still played double bills. That night it was, "When Harry Met Sally," and "Parenthood," both movies about love and relationships. In "When Harry Met Sally," during the scenes when all the old married couples talk about how they met and fell in love, Dan took my hand and kept squeezing it.

I knew I had to tell him about Jim.

On the way home, Dan said, "You know, I talk to you all the time in my head."

"Oh, yeah? And what exactly do you say?"

"Mostly I say, I love you."

What? But before I could say anything, Dan asked what I was doing Sunday.

"I have to move," I said, and I told him why.

"Let me help you."

He wanted to help? "Great, thanks."

So the next afternoon, our fourth date, Dan came over and moved me to Valerie's, but once I got settled, I said, "There's something I've got to tell you."

He looked at me as if I were going to tell him I had AIDS, so I quickly said, "There's another man."

He nodded, and then slowly sat down at the table. "I thought so." He waited, and then looked up at me. "How long you been seeing him?"

"About three months."

"So why are you going out with me?"

"I'm not married, he's out of town, and I haven't heard from him in almost a month."

"Sorry. This isn't going to work for me. I'm falling in love here."

I knew I didn't want to close the book on this one, so I grabbed a yellow legal pad and said, "Look. Do me a favor. Take a test for me?"

I gave him what I call the "container test." It's an association game that exposes a person's inner self in about fifteen minutes. It consists of visualizing three different sized containers, then placing inanimate objects inside each one, and imbuing each object with an emotion.

Dan took the test. He chose a dumpster for his large container and he put a wine goblet inside. So I asked, "As the wine goblet inside the dumpster, you wish...?"

"I had a mate," he said.

"You will...?"

"Do what I'm made to do."

"You fear ...?"

"Being broken."

The test went on, and I looked down at the results. I'd done a lot of these, and I'd never seen such a genuinely good-hearted result. He had a strong ego, wanted to do the right thing, be of service, and be mated. Who could ask for more in a guy? I looked up at him – he seemed too good to be true.

I explained the results, and how the test worked. Then Dan said, "Okay, now you take it."

So I did. For my large object, I chose a big glass bowl, and placed an imaginary Teddy bear inside it.

Dan said, "So as the Teddy Bear inside the glass bowl, you feel...."

"Protected."

"You need...?"

"To be cuddled."

"You want...?"

"To make a baby laugh," I said.

Dan stopped and looked up at me. "Hey, you really want to have a kid, don't you?"

"I used to. But I'm forty-two. It's too late."

"No, it's not. Marry me. We'll do that."

Marry him? I barely knew him! I was stunned speechless, but at that exact moment the phone rang. I looked at Dan and picked it up. It was Jim, calling from Jamestown. "Hey, Babe!" he said, "I'm done! I'm coming home!"

"Jim," I said, nodding to Dan.

Dan stood up, walked outside and sat down on the porch.

I walked into the kitchen. "I haven't heard from you in weeks and weeks."

"I know, it's been crazy here. I've been working fifteen hours a day since Zemekis left. I was first in charge, and..."

I knew I'd have to make a choice right then. And I did.

"Look, Jim, when you didn't call, I figured it was over and I went out on a blind date. And, well... he just asked me to marry him."

"What?" he yelled.

"I can't talk now. Bye." And I hung up.

Dan came back inside. "What do you want to do?"

"Before I can make any decisions, I'm going to have to try out the merchandise."

Dan's eyes lit up and, guy that he was, he made a step toward me.

"Not now. I've got to go direct a scene, but you wait right here. I'll be back by ten."

"Okay." Then we hugged for the first time. And as we hugged, we both made the same guttural animal-like sound, simultaneously. We pulled back and looked at one another.

"That was weird," I said.

Dan explained that sound after he died:

That funny noise we both made? That was our _code_. You remembered.

But that night I was late for a rehearsal and I rushed off to UCLA.

When I got back, I was still in director's mode. "Come with me," I said. I took him by the hand and led him into the bedroom, sat myself down at the head of the bed, pulled my knees up to my chest and said, "Okay, you're on. You undress first."

He laughed. I still remember watching as he yanked off his sweater, then like a stripper, he unbuttoned his shirt, stepped out of his pants, and kicked them into a corner. He turned around, peeled off his underwear, twirled them over his head and tossed them over his shoulder.

I sat there in awe, marveling at what I saw. Who knew this could be hidden under a suit? He had massive shoulders and perfectly chiseled strong, long legs. I'd never seen such an amazing body.

"Wait a minute; I don't need to sleep with you. I should sculpt you. Where's my clay? You look like Atlas. Turn around."

I was serious. I couldn't believe how perfect he was. When he'd worked for Fetzer, he said that all the guys would toss huge, heavy wine barrels back and forth all day, and he had the back and shoulders to prove it. But still, he looked so shy, as he stood there naked with nothing on but a pair of glasses.

"So take off those glasses," I said.

"No way. Now you."

So I pulled off my sweater and jeans, and he crawled into bed next to me. When his lips met mine, he trembled, he was so nervous.

"So what did you think?" he asked afterward.

"Well, to be honest," I said, "you were kind of tentative and I like wild."

"Wild? Honey, I can do wild. I just didn't want to scare you."

And, bless his heart, he could do wild.

"Wow," I said, luxuriating in the sweaty afterglow of sex. "I knew you were out there. What the hell took you so long?"

***

That question and many others would be answered – but not for a very long time.

Chapter Four

"Moonstruck"
or
"Meet the Parents"

Falling in love is a lot like dying – you just have to let go. So I let go and fell in love. The night after Dan proposed, a newly married girlfriend flew in from New York to show off her husband. She gathered her LA crew together, and I brought Dan along. He sat down among a roomful of complete strangers and was chatty, charming and adorable. My friend Nancy pulled me aside and said, "He's great! Who is this guy?"

"I don't know, but he asked me to marry him last night."

"Wow! What did you say?"

"I didn't say anything. I mean, I only met him two weeks ago."

She grabbed me by the shoulders. "Oh, just do it!"

"If we were to get married," I said, thinking out loud, "we'd have to do it between now and January."

"If you do, I'll fly back out – and you can wear my wedding dress." That would solve the wardrobe problem.

By the following week, Dan and I were in the glorious delirium of "hot, new, never-get-out-of-bed lust/love." When it became clear he was never going home again, I said, "Okay, I've decided I can marry you. But first I want a real proposal – the real thing. On your knee – the whole nine yards. And I want a ring."

I wasn't in film school for nothing. I'd seen "Moonstruck," so I knew I needed a ring, or it would bring bad luck.

"A ring?" he said, as if this were big news.

"Didn't you ask me to marry you?"

"Yes."

"Okay then, I need a ring. I've waited a long time for this." I extended my empty ring finger.

"I can't afford a ring."

"Wait a minute," I said. "How much money do you make?"

"Right now? About thirty thousand a year."

"Thirty thousand? Good grief! You can't afford to marry me or anyone else."

"It's my first lawyer job," he said. "I'll make more. You'll see. Trust me." He shrugged his shoulders, like "What's to worry?"

"I've got another year-and-a-half of grad school," I said. "I don't pay for food or rent now, so I don't expect to if we get married. Will that be okay with you?"

He looked me over, and mock stroked his chin. "I think you might be worth it," he said. "Let's go find you your ring." And we fell back into bed.

The following Thursday was Thanksgiving and I wanted him to meet my family. Everyone knows that when you get married, you don't just marry a person, you marry the person's family too. If he survived that ordeal and still wanted to marry me, then I'd plan the wedding. Considering my family, I knew it was an iffy proposition. I figured I'd just better get it over with. As we drove down to my sister Melanie's house in Long Beach, I gave Dan a fast thumbnail sketch: Dad was a womanizing lawyer and Mom drank to deaden the pain. If I were to use my NPI lingo they would "code out" as narcissistic personality disorders. Big time.

My older, ex-hippie sister Valrie (not to be confused with my friend, Valerie) would be down from San Francisco. I told Dan that she and I had never been close because the night I was born, when she was not quite three, my father left her all alone, locked in a parked car, asleep on a dark street. She woke up terrified and screamed until dawn. Consequently, she never forgave me for being born. To make matters worse, my mother, who wasn't particularly interested in parenting, made her my primary caretaker. I was an extremely busy baby, got into mischief constantly, and my mother punished my poor sister because of it. So Valrie simply hated me, and who could blame her?

As Val, Dan and I sat outside Melanie's house in the warm November sun, I watched her size Dan up. He was closer to her age than to mine, and she wanted to make sure he knew that she was cooler, hipper and "farther out" than I was or would ever be. We sat side by side on a narrow brick ledge, with me in the middle. Val leaned into me, asking him questions until finally she said, "And when are you two love-birds getting married?"

Dan got that "deer caught in headlights" look, so I answered, "Well, it's got to be between December fourteenth and January fourth, because that's when school starts up again."

"What?" said Dan, "I thought we'd live together a while first."

I could feel my sister's glee from beside me. She stood up to face him directly. "Now, don't you let her talk you into anything. She always gets everything she wants."

Excuse me? I sat there, stunned. I turned to Dan. "We don't need to get married at all," I said. "But we will not discuss it now, okay?" I knew enough to close down the topic and get us out of enemy territory fast.

As soon as we pulled onto the freeway to head back to Los Angeles, I calmly said, "There must be some confusion. You asked me to marry you, right? And I said I would, right? So I thought we'd just do it."

"I assumed we'd live together first," he said, "for at least six months."

"Oh," I said and focused on the sea of red tail-lights straight ahead. "I didn't understand. I lived with a man for eleven years and I won't ever make that mistake again."

"But I want you to get to know Sam first."

"Why?" I said. "He's sixteen. He'll either like me or he won't. And if we do get married, he'll never live with us. It's how you feel about me that counts."

Dan was silent.

"Look," I said finally, "why don't we just date until June? We can make the decision then. That's fine with me, but once again, I will not live with you."

"Okay," Dan said, "then we'll get married."

He had survived my family – but now it was my turn. The following day he called his mother, Riva, the little Brooklyn dynamo. I stood next to him, ready to say "Hi" to my soon-to-be-mother-in-law. "Guess what, Mom," he said, "I've fallen in love and I'm getting married."

"Is she Jewish?" I heard her say.

"No," he said, and walked away with the phone gripped tightly in his hand.

"Another *shicksa* you're marrying? Maybe on your fifth marriage, you'll ask your mother's permission first." That's everything you need to know about Riva Goldberg Wax – Empress of Ocean Parkway, iron-fisted ruler of her tiny fiefdom.

His face turned red. "I'm forty-nine years old. I don't need anyone's permission to get married!" He slammed the phone down. "She's not coming to our wedding."

He stormed away, brooding and angry. When he calmed down, he said, "Why don't we just go to Las Vegas?"

"No. I want a wedding. If we're going to get married, I want the ceremony of it. I want to know I'm getting married. I want you to know it. But again, we do not need to get married. I'm not Jewish, and I'm never going to be Jewish."

"She ruined my first marriage," he said. "She won't ruin this one."

Not the best way to begin our journey, was it? But since I didn't take my own parents' craziness seriously, I certainly wasn't going to let someone else's nutty mother ruin my day. I figured she was his problem; I was utterly wrong about that, of course.

Okay. We'd get married. I had two weeks to plan the wedding after I turned in my final script. I wrote out the invitations by hand and mailed them off. A good friend's mom said we could have the wedding reception at her house; another dear friend offered to cater the reception as her wedding gift, and Nancy sent me her gorgeous "Paris 1900s" antique lace dress. Since I'd spent a year-and-a-half taking Eve to what I've come to think of as the Church of Old Character Actors on Sunset Boulevard, I called Reverend Dominique, the gay, defrocked Catholic priest who presided there, and asked if he would marry us. "No problem," he said.

I found a rent-controlled apartment in West Hollywood, got the gas, lights, telephone and water turned on, so that as soon as we got back from our honey-moon we could move right in.

Christmas came and went. Things happened very fast, and suddenly I noticed that Dan was eating like a lunatic – he'd gained almost ten pounds. What was that about? Nerves? But I was too busy to think about it.

Samuel flew down from Mendocino three days before the wedding, and I fell in love with him at once. He was whip smart, cute and funny, and since I'd just recently been a college undergraduate myself, I felt completely comfortable with him; he felt like an old friend.

All went well except for one telltale glitch. The following day, what with all the wedding preparations, my nerves and body just needed a time-out, and took it in the form of a vomiting migraine. Charming, but back then I was used to them. (I no longer get migraines because I do Iyengar yoga.) Dan wanted me to come to a party at his cousin's in Glendale, but I said, "No. You two go. I'll be fine."

He called from the party around seven and asked if I needed anything. "If I sleep," I said, "it'll go away." He pressed. "Well," I said, "if you're leaving soon, you could bring me some Matzo ball soup. It makes the vomiting stop."

"Fine, then we'll leave in a couple minutes."

"Great. Thanks." In my taxi-driver's brain, that put him at my front door at about eight. So instead of going back to sleep – the only form of pain relief – I waited for my soup. Eight came and went – nine o'clock came and went. By ten-thirty, I was in pain, hungry, and now furious. So when he knocked on the door with the soup in hand, instead of being grateful, I exploded.

"I thought you'd be here by eight. No one forced you to come! You offered."

"I got to talking. We got sidetracked."

"Sidetracked? Your only excuse would be you got hit by a train!"

Then I saw Sam, standing on the steep steps below, cowering in the shadows. Clearly, he didn't want to hear anyone yell at his father like that. He turned and darted down the stairs.

"Perfect." I looked at Dan. "You go inside. Let me deal with him," I said.

I ran down the stairs, and found Sam sitting in the car, in tears. "I'm sorry you saw that," I said. "But Dan said he'd be here and I waited and waited."

"You don't know my dad well enough to marry him," he said, wiping his eyes. "He does this stuff all the time. It's just how he is!"

"You're absolutely right. I don't know him well enough to marry him, and if that's really the way he is, then I won't. But we're going to walk upstairs and we'll talk this over. If he's going to continue to do this, I can't marry him. I'll tell him that."

We walked back upstairs, and I told Dan that if this is the way he ran his life – said one thing, and then did another – I couldn't marry him. We were both adults, right? He promised it would never happen again, and I believed him.

So on December 30, 1989, when Reverend Dominique said, "I now pronounce you husband and wife," I turned around to all my assembled friends and said, "Hey, I'm a _wife_!" My new job had begun, and I was ready to attack it with the same determined optimism, energy and enthusiasm that had worked so well for me up to that moment.

But first, we would go off to Huntington Lake, just on the western slope of the Sierras, for our three-day honeymoon. When we got there, the place was completely deserted. In winter the lake's a skiing resort, but California was in the final year of a five-year drought; there'd been no snow so far, and none was expected. We stayed in a funky, old-fashioned cabin, with no phone, no TV, nothing to distract us from our exhausting job of being newlyweds. It seemed odd to me, however, that if we weren't actively involved in honeymoon activities, Dan kept hiking down to a pay phone to "call home."

Then on New Year's Eve, like magic, the skies opened up and snow began to fall. The moon was full that night, so I wanted to go and walk in the falling snow. We walked along an old logging road, under the tall pine trees in the moonlight. The only problem with this romantic scene was that suddenly Dan just wasn't "there." His body was there, but he simply didn't respond to anything I said. He completely shut down. I remember my own sudden anxiety. I didn't understand what was going on, so I thought, Well, you did just marry a stranger. Maybe he's nervous.

***

Almost a month after I started the channeling, that scene popped vividly into my mind. Dan explained that he was "in session" and was forced to "watch" the major events of his life in order to understand his own decisions. He said that our honeymoon walk was a pivotal moment, for in that instant, he chose not to give me what he had "agreed to."

May 10, 2002

You just went back to our honeymoon. You were right. I wasn't even completely present there. I wanted everyone to know what a good time I was having,

that's why I kept calling home. Made you feel second fiddle intentionally. That walk? Preoccupied with my own bullshit. I'd won you, now I could ignore you. Crazy isn't the word I would choose. There's another one I know you won't want to hear – that was evil, my darling.

They made me watch that scene: you and me walking in that beauty – the first snowfall. You wanting so desperately to love this _stranger_ you'd just married – and there I am, pulled back, pulled in – not responding to you. No wonder you loved Sam more at first.

Oh yes, I knew. But since I loved him more too, that was okay. It was only later that it drove me crazy. The easy way you had with each other; the way he made you laugh, the _direct_, clear communication...

Now do you see why I need to clean this up? I don't especially want to face you here – exposed – without being honest first.

When Dan and I got back from our honeymoon, I made him carry me over the threshold of our new apartment. I wanted to do everything right. I'd finally become "Sadie, Sadie, Married Lady," and I was ready to start my new wife job. I was determined to create a marriage filled with love and lots of hot and sacred sex. I was also looking forward to getting what Dan had offered to me: a baby and a family all my own.

According to "Dan the Man," that baby was looking forward to being a part of our family too. Unfortunately, Dan had other plans.

Chapter Five

"War of the Roses"
or
"Philadelphia Story"

Those plans, however, didn't include me. Of course, my darling Dan didn't realize that then and neither did I.

* * *

After the honeymoon, Dan went straight back to work at his lawyer job with a small environmental firm. He'd only been there since late September and felt completely overwhelmed by the demands of his new career.

I, on the other hand, got to go back to film school – a place I adored. I couldn't believe I'd gotten so lucky. I remember telling my screenwriting instructor that I wouldn't be able to write what had just happened because no one would believe it. I felt like the heroine of my own inner movie – I'd done it. Against all odds, I'd found my guy, had the wedding I'd been planning since I was six, and now, as far as I was concerned, my _real life_ could begin. Romantic comedies usually end with a wedding – it's a dramatic convention – so I was looking forward to my own "And they lived happily ever after" ending. I would get pregnant and have my baby girl. I would get my "pink bubble." I was positive it would all happen.

Back at UCLA, my first assignment for a Film Structure class was to go see the "War of the Roses," not once, but twice, then write up a two-page analysis of the movie. The film is about a couple, played by Kathleen Turner and Michael Douglas, who "meet cute," marry fast, then descend into marriage hell. She winds up despising him, and especially hates the way he eats. Yet her husband seems oblivious to everything except his own demanding law career. Ultimately, they kill each other in a magnificent fight, swatting at each other while swinging from a high crystal chandelier, until it finally gives way under their weight and careens down, shattering their bodies and ending their lives.

In the final moments, as they lay splattered on the floor, amidst shards of broken crystal, Michael Douglas reaches over to take Kathleen Turner's hand, as if to say, "Despite it all, I still love you." But she swats his hand away. She's almost dead, and she's still angry at him.

A chill shot up my spine. Oh, my God! I'd just married a lawyer. A lawyer? My father was a lawyer, not to mention my grandfather, my uncle and a cousin – all lawyers. And I just married one? What was I thinking?

As I wrote my paper I asked myself, "How did their love die? What was it? Did they stop listening to one another? Talking? Having sex?" I analyzed the movie and resolved that what happened to their marriage would not happen to mine. Marriage, I decided, was a serious "job," and all jobs take work. I would do the work it took to make mine succeed.

I knew I didn't have a healthy example from my own parents' marriage, but I remembered the research I did at NPI. Whenever I interviewed a person who said they were happily married, I stopped the interview and talked to them about their marriage. I asked them to tell me what the secret of their happiness was. Invariably they would say that their husband or wife was their best friend, that they had good sex, and that they laughed a lot.

Okay, that didn't seem too difficult. 1. Make your husband your best friend. 2. Have lots of good sex. 3. And laugh a lot. Great. We could do that. We liked each other. We loved having sex. And Dan did back flips to make me laugh, something that endeared him to me. Especially after he died.

I told Dan my fears about the lawyer in the movie, and I asked him to go see it. He did, and he swore up and down that could never happen to us; he would never make his work more important than our life together.

Unfortunately, in the first few months of our marriage, Dan discovered he hated being a lawyer. Needing to make more than six bucks an hour is not the best reason for choosing your life's work. He hated the adversarial nature of the job, he hated being a rookie at forty-nine, but mostly he hated the long hours being "an associate" demanded and was desperately unhappy because of it.

On top of that or because of that, Dan started to eat like an insane person. He'd wolf down food so fast, making noises I won't describe out of respect for the dead, until I wanted to tear my hair out. I sat across the dinner table in stunned disbelief. Finally I said, "So when did you get out of the pen? You eat like an inmate."

"Really?" He looked up, surprised, and then explained that table manners never mattered around his house. Riva, he said, was one of thirteen, all raised in the teeming ghetto on Manhattan's Lower East Side. Food was simply thrown onto the table, so the kids would have to fight to get their share of it. Since Riva was one of the youngest, she never got enough to eat. According to Dan, as an adult she took a perverse pride in her unladylike table manners because it outraged his far more refined father. Her refusal to adhere to "bourgeois rules of etiquette" was yet another expression of her proletariat class consciousness.

Great.

His own table manners were pitch perfect in the six weeks we lived together before we got married, but now that we were legally wed this educated, elegant man ate like a stevedore. Finally, when I could not stand one more second of it, I looked him in the eye and said with no emotion, "You have to stop eating like you're at a trough. If you don't, I simply won't love you anymore. Do you understand me?"

A flash of awareness flickered across his eyes. You mean I wouldn't love him "no matter what?" I would leave him for his table manners? When I assured him that men had been left for less, he understood I wasn't kidding, and promised he would do better.

Still, by the end of our first year together, he managed to take the exquisite body I'd married and turn it into a different body altogether. He'd gained more than forty pounds. He went from looking like Atlas to resembling Rodin's rendition of "Balzac." Dan was still tall, with massive shoulders and a broad chest, only now he looked as if he'd just swallowed a big beach ball.

Because of his weight gain having sex became a little problematic, to say the least. I'd try to joke and say, "Hey, where'd your penis go?" But we both knew I wasn't exactly kidding. He'd put five inches of fat between me and his darling penis, and ladies, let's do the math here – unless a guy has a twelve-inch member – and mercifully Dan didn't – you're in trouble. Don't forget, I was a goddess in my own mind, and in the language of the *Kama Sutra* I loved his "flaming sword," his lingam. I loved everything about it: I'd barely touch it – it got big. How fun is that? I loved giving head – I swooned for the smell of his maleness. His penis was the source of a great deal of pleasure, but it seemed to be disappearing at a breakneck pace.

Besides needing his penis if I were to going to get pregnant, I was also addicted to screaming orgasms. And Dan, bless his heart, could make me scream. The rapture of making love to him – that straight hit from the divine – was one reason I married him. Hot and sacred sex with the man I loved, who could ask for more?

But little by little, instead of being his lover, he began to treat me like "a wife." He'd be done, jump right up and rush off to do more important things.

"Hey! Wait a minute!" I'd yell, to his fleeing behind. "Get back here! My date's not over!"

I'd sit there in bed wondering: was this what being married was like? Was this why my married girlfriends were all so angry? Did every husband do this? Or just mine? I began to feel an undercurrent of "annoyance" all the time.

I didn't have the advantage of hearing from my newly dead husband who would explain the _real_ source of my annoyance, so I did what any sensible girl would do – I talked to my girlfriends.

One friend, who had an adorable, big-bellied husband, told me how much she loved his oversized gut. She found it incredibly sexy.

"Really?" I said.

"You love Dan, right?"

"Yeah."

"Well, there's just more of him to love now."

That was the "glass half full" way to look at it, and I decided if she could do it, so could I.

"But," she said, "you just always have to be on top – that way their stomachs don't get in the way of their dicks."

Good advice, but it didn't exactly fix things. I still couldn't make sense out of my constant uneasiness, so I talked to my therapist, Louise. I'd been seeing Louise since the December before my sister Gheri-Llynn committed suicide. When I took Gheri-Llynn to a place offering free counseling – the California Graduate Institute – a student-psychologist insisted on interviewing me along with my sister. She asked how I was doing. "Fine," I said, "I quit my job because I want to go to film school, but first I have to move up to Berkeley and finish college. I'm sort of homeless just now, but aside from that? I'm perfectly fine."

The interviewer nodded and put down her pen. "We'll be happy to treat your sister, but we'd like to see you as well." And so I got Louise.

Louise warned me that in all new marriages people push for boundaries, and shadow sides come out to play. Shadow sides? She also warned that as I began to feel safer in the marriage, my own "abandonment issues" might bubble to the surface and I should be aware of that. Perhaps that's what those feelings of unease and annoyance were about – my own fear. Okay, I would wait and see.

Still, it felt as if my internal tectonic plates were shifting, dissolving. I remember sitting at the table, wondering, Were all marriages this hard? I loved this man; I knew I did. But we'd get agreement on simple roommate behavior, as in, "Your dirty underwear goes in the hamper," or the ever popular, "Please, put the toilet seat down," and I might just as well have been talking to the plants. The *pitzicaca* stuff was driving me nuts.

All my married girlfriends assured me that the first year was the toughest – the shakedown year. I didn't _need_ to stay married – I wanted to stay married; I wanted to learn to love in a committed relationship. What did that mean? Just take care of him? Shop, cook, vacuum? What did I need to learn? Maybe it was me? Louise helped me understand that when I got angry at Dan, it didn't mean that I didn't love him. She said I had to learn to hold two opposing emotions at the same time – like an apple in one hand and an orange in the other.

No matter what happened during the day, when we crawled into bed at night, I got to hug my big bear of a man. And there in the warmth of his arms, I was home. I was happy just to smell his neck. Although sometimes he'd wake up in the morning, pull me close, tell me how much he loved me, then tell me I was still way too independent. He wanted me to need him more.

"Okay," I'd say, "I'll work on it."

* * *

By March, Dan made up with his mother and Riva was ready to reclaim her son. One night he was on the phone with her and I heard him talking about me. I'd just won a screenwriting award, so he told her how proud he was and how he was sure I would be successful. Then I heard him laugh.

Later, I asked him what she said that was so funny.

"I wouldn't hold my breath if I were you," he said.

"And you thought that was funny, Dan?" It felt as if he'd socked me in the solar plexus.

Sure, it was a long shot I'd be successful as a screenwriter – that goes without saying. Only crazy people want to be screenwriters in the first place; only truly delusional people have the guts – it's part of the package, comes with the territory – literally. Here in Los Angeles you can ask almost anyone – the tattooed girl gyrating around a dance pole, the guy bagging your groceries at Trader Joe's – "Hey, how's your screenplay coming?" And the response will be, "How'd you know I was writing one?"

But Dan was my husband. Why didn't he defend me? Wasn't that his job? When I told him how much his laughing hurt me, he said, "You're being over-reactive and hypersensitive."

"So? And your point is?"

I asked him to come and see my therapist, Louise, with me, but he refused. We all know getting a guy to see a therapist is never easy, so finally I just said, "We either clear this up right now or we get a divorce. Your choice." So he went.

Louise explained to him that I was trying to protect what I felt was sacred: our marriage. I had learned to protect myself in order to survive and that I expected him, as my husband, to protect me from abuse – abuse of any kind. Louise cautioned him that his mother was trying to undermine our marriage by making him side with her against me. Skillful triangulation, she called it. She told Dan that he needed better boundaries with her. Basic therapy 101.

"Oh," he said. "I guess she did ruin my first marriage." Then he told us the classic mother-in-law-from-hell story. Just after Samuel was born, Riva came out from New York to help. One afternoon while Maggie went shopping, Riva rearranged Maggie's entire kitchen. When Maggie got home and saw what Riva had done, she was furious. Who wouldn't be? But Dan couldn't see what all the fuss was about and took his mother's side against his wife.

I sat there stunned. "Jesus, Dan! No wonder she fell in love with a teenager."

After the session, we went home and I fell into bed, exhausted. The night before I'd watched a movie called "Always," with Richard Dreyfuss and Holly Hunter. Steven Spielberg wrote and directed it, and it's about a daredevil flyer, a smoke jumper, who gets killed because he's so cocky. After he dies, he comes back to the love of his life, Holly Hunter, to say he's sorry for being such a jerk.

When I saw it, I thought it was sheer fantasy. Still, it didn't stop me from crying my eyes out in a scene where Holly Hunter dances alone – and Richard Dreyfuss "dances" along with her – only he's dead.

Dan turned on the movie and I fell fast asleep beside him. When his sobbing woke me with a start, I looked up at the movie and saw the dance scene between the two lovers. Dan hugged me tight, and swore he'd do better with the marriage.

As it turns out, it was no coincidence we watched that movie. Dan's "oversoul" was trying to get him to pay attention to his life. And he must have, because months go by and I didn't write a word in my journal, except to say how happy we were.

In April, Samuel had to choose the college he wanted to go to. He'd been accepted to UC Berkeley but he chose to go to Haverford, a small Quaker college just outside Philadelphia. The only problem with that choice was Dan had saved no money for college, and the price tag for Haverford was about twenty-five thousand a year. As I said, Dan was making about thirty.

I was a little confused. "How do you plan to pay for this?"

Dan said that he owned a small apartment building in Sacramento, where he'd lived while in law school and that he would sell it.

"Oh, okay." I didn't think much more about it, since I wasn't included in the decision. For Dan, Sam's needs always came first and that seemed fine. It was, after all, the reason I could marry so fast – he was such a good dad.

Dan had borrowed more than sixty-thousand to send himself through law school, and was about to add on four years at twenty-five thousand per year to that burdensome debt. He did sell the building, and made about fifteen-thousand on it. That paid for some of Sam's first year of college, but the following year, because of all the depreciations he'd taken on the property to make it through law school, we – as a couple – wound up owing the IRS more than twenty-five thousand. And Sam had three more years to go.

Someone had to make money fast, and I hoped that someone would be me.

* * *

When August came, it was time for Sam to go off to Haverford. He hadn't quite turned seventeen yet – young to go off to college – so Dan wanted us to take him. Dan also decided to piggyback a trip to New York City; he wanted me to finally meet his mother. Sam came down a week early so he could spend some time with his dad, but Dan worked those long lawyer hours, so I'm the one who got to hang out with Sam. Fun for me, because Sam was a great kid, but unfortunately, Dan would come home exhausted, be jealous that we'd had such a good time together and feel excluded. Another case of triangulation. Consequently, by week's end things around our little apartment got a bit tense. Dan brooded, Sam was nervous, and I didn't know what was going on.

And it only got worse.

What I've come to think of as the vacation from hell began at five a.m., with the hurried confusion of getting three people to the airport before seven. We would fly to Dallas, where we had a two-hour layover and then on to Philadelphia.

Things started to head downhill in Dallas. We had to change planes, and for some reason I had to carry my luggage from one plane to the next. I remember struggling with my bags, and feeling extremely resentful that my big strong husband wouldn't help me. He was mono-focused on Sam. He and Sam were the team and now I stood on the outside.

By the time we landed in Philadelphia at five, we'd been traveling all day, and we were all cranky. As we waited for the luggage to spill out onto the carousel, I looked at Dan and said, "I know airports. When we get outside, let me choose the taxi, okay?"

Big mistake – never tell a man what to do. But I figured seven years of taxi driving gave me some expertise here. We were heading outside the city, and I wanted to get a driver who was familiar with the town we were going to. I also wanted to make sure we got an English-speaking person who had maps.

Dan's and Sam's bags tumbled out first. I watched bewildered as Dan plucked them all off the conveyor, then both he and Sam just zoomed away. He'd show me – he'd be damned if he'd be told what to do.

When my bags finally appeared, I looked down at them feeling completely abandoned. Where was the guy who wanted me to need him? Okay, I needed him now, so where was he? I hoisted the bags onto my shoulders and headed off toward the exit signs. As the airport's glass doors slid open, a blast of hot, waterlogged air hit me full force, and now I remembered – this was why I hated the east coast in summer – air so thick you can see it. Just at that moment, lightning flashed across the horizon, followed by a rumbling crack of thunder and the skies opened up. I stood there, shards of piercing rain pelting me, and wondered, *Why had I come? And where the hell did they go?*

I looked left toward the cab stand, and its row of waiting taxis, and to my complete dismay, I saw Dan throwing Sam's luggage into the first car in line – an old dilapidated cab. Then he climbed inside, leaving me standing alone in the rain.

I hurried toward the driver, a jittery Middle-Eastern man; he grabbed my bags and tossed them into the trunk, then motioned me inside. I climbed into the front passenger seat, and automatically looked for his hack license – it wasn't on display. Never a good sign. As he started the car, the worn-out wipers smeared grease across the windshield. It was raining so hard, I couldn't see five feet in front of me. And neither could the driver.

"So where are you from?" I asked, squinting out the window.

He didn't answer; he looked totally panicked. I understood why once we passed our terminal a second time – the driver didn't know how to get out of the airport. I shot a frustrated look to my soon-to-be-ex-husband. Why had he ignored me? The poor driver went around the airport another time, before I finally just read the exit signs to him, and freed us all from the traffic loop.

Once we got into rush hour traffic, I asked again where he was from and still he didn't answer. In August of 1990 the U.S. was involved in the first war with Iraq, and I finally said, "Are you by any chance from Iraq?"

He looked away, "How you know?"

"Just a guess. Do you know where Merton is?"

"Sure. Sure," he said, his eyes darting back and forth.

"Do you have a map?"

"No maps."

Great. I shot another frustrated look to the back seat, but both Dan and Sam stared out opposite side windows. Fine. Here we were with a scared Iraqi, heading into rush hour traffic, under a torrential downpour toward parts unknown.

Ladies? A question – was it just me? Or would you want to kill your husband, too?

After forty minutes in the cab, I asked the completely flummoxed driver to pull over. By this time, I'd discovered that this was his brother-in-law's cab and he was only filling in as a favor. I felt so sorry for him.

"Let me call and get directions," I said. We were staying at the home of a woman who rented rooms during the times when the three local colleges needed them; both Swarthmore and Bryn Mawr are within a couple miles of Haverford, just off Philly's famous "Main Line."

To save sixty bucks, instead of ordering two rooms, Dan decided it would be okay for all of us to share one room. I tried to talk him out of it, but he was intractable. You've got to pick your battles, right? And I chose not to fight that one. Another big mistake.

When we finally arrived at our destination, and I was out of Sam's earshot, I asked Dan, "Why did you do that? Did you forget that I drove a cab for seven years?"

Dan ignored me, turned on his heels, grabbed Sam's luggage, and left me to pick up my own heavy bags. Okay, I figured I'd just have to get through the night, the next day's welcoming activities at Haverford, and then we'd have time to ourselves again. We'd talk things out then.

But first we had to eat. All the tables in a tiny Chinese restaurant were filled with happy, chatting little families – everyone taking their own extremely privileged child off to college. The three of us, however, ate in absolute silence. Occasionally, people at the other tables would surreptitiously glance our way, wondering perhaps who those poor miserable souls were.

When we left the restaurant – rain still pouring down – Sam and Dan both walked ahead of me sharing the only umbrella. I trudged along behind, trying to figure out: How did this happen? How had my life gone from being so happy, to this moment of utter hell – in only eight short months?

Up in our room, when Sam went down the hall to brush his teeth, I turned to Dan and whispered, "Next time we're at an airport…"

Dan looked at me with cold distain. "There's not going to be 'a next time.' We're getting a divorce. You're flying home tomorrow, and I'm going on to New York without you – I don't want you to meet my mother."

He was dead serious. I was so shocked, I couldn't say a word.

Sam came back from brushing his teeth and I looked at Dan, but he turned away from me.

Not much I could do, so I headed downstairs.

Maybe Dan was right. Maybe this wasn't going to work out after all – I wasn't happy and neither was he. I walked into the living room and sat down on a couch to think. I looked up at the bookshelves behind me and I realized this must be the home of a psychologist. The shelves were packed with academic psychology books. There sat the DSM III (Revised), the book I did the field research for at UCLA, and just below it I saw *The Dance of Anger* by Harriet Goldhor Lerner, Ph.D. I plucked the book off the shelf and read it through. It explained everything. The annoyance. The triangulation. Everything.

Something fierce rose up inside me and screamed, "No! He can't do this. We're married! I won't give up without a fight." In film school, it's called "The Sixty Minute Moment." It's the moment when the hero takes control of her own destiny. The moment when Scarlett O'Hara stands silhouetted against the sunset, fist to the sky and says, "As God is my witness…I'll never be hungry again." Or in "The Godfather," when Michael Corleone hides his father in the hospital and says, "I'm here Dad. I'm with you."

I marched back up the stairs, tiptoed over to my husband's sleeping ear and calmly whispered, "If you don't want a scene, you will come downstairs with me right now. We need to talk this through. If you refuse, I will stand here and scream my lungs out. Those are your options."

Dan knew I wasn't kidding. He got up and followed me downstairs.

We sat down on the couch together, and we thrashed through the week with Samuel. Dan told me how he'd felt excluded and how he wanted to get even with me. I made him see how he'd set it up – what did he expect me to do? Ignore Sam? Not have fun? How would that have helped?

I saw a glimmer of understanding, then he shook his head and smiled. He reached out, took my hand and kissed it.

"I'm sorry about the taxi, too. God! I hate it when you're right."

We laughed, and hugged each other tight. And there on that couch in Philadelphia, we fell in love all over again. We chose to stay married and we both understood that it was a choice.

* * *

Two months into my channeling Dan, I kept getting urges to pick up an old dream journal that I used at the time I met Dan. On December 23, 1989 – five days before we were married – I had a dream where a fat, fleshy man steals my identity card while Dan just stands back and watches. In the dream, I'm frantic, and I woke up wanting to cancel the wedding.

So now that I was communicating with him, I wanted his perspective on this:

Wednesday, June 19, 2002 – 5:30 a.m.
Last night I picked up an old journal – Wow! Amazing what some dreams know.
Dan? What was that all about? Looks like you wanted "out" almost immediately. You were "acting out." Driving me nuts.

Dan here – all I can say is learn to trust yourself more. That dream was fear, and a sense of what lay ahead for "us." If you had acted on it – called off the wedding, we both would have gone our separate ways. But you still would have missed me, and I, my darling Stephanie, would have missed you.

(In that same journal I read an entry from our wedding reception where a friend thought it was so cute that Dan kept telling everyone what good "prospects" he had.)

The "fear" that I lived with was so _overwhelming_ – I was so tortured. My "prospects" were grim in my own mind. It's why I needed you so much.

Your own ability to live on the edge is what attracted me to you, not to mention everything else.

Keep in mind the great times, which for us was just around the house; the days when we cleaned together and loved each other.

My own insanity should serve as a beacon of how to be brave for you. When "fear" takes over, nothing else can be heard. So much sorrow and grief comes from fear.

You can read that journal through – I led you to it – but not today. Philadelphia was a turning point for both of us. I was determined to leave you and yet you held on to the marriage – and that one single act, your courage in coming up to that room, and standing up for what you wanted – made me fall so deeply in love with you. I knew you loved me. And _you_ knew you loved me.

He was right. In that one moment I understood how deeply I loved him – I thought that would be enough to see us through, because as he would say after he died, ""When we were good, we were great."

Chapter Six

"No Way Out"

The year after Sam graduated high school, I won a couple more screenwriting awards and graduated film school. One award, Disney's Touchstone Fellowship, paid $30,000 for a year-long stint with Touchstone Pictures. The cash helped pay for Sam's college and it was great for my own self-esteem. To me, it all seemed to be working out according to my own little plan.

Since the only thing left on my "to do" list was "get pregnant," I threw away the diaphragm, and bingo! I got pregnant.

I was on the phone with one of my film school buddies when the doctor's office clicked in to tell me the amazing news. I told my friend, Ramin and he screamed, "Yes! You did it! Congratulations!" We both jumped with joy.

I hung up to call Dan. "Guess what? We did it! I'm pregnant!"

But instead of his being excited, I heard a pause, then he said, "Oh, good. Great."

My stomach clinched. "Why aren't you excited? Don't you want the baby?"

"Of course, I do. I've already had a baby, that's why I'm not as excited as you are."

My heart broke – was he lying to me? I asked him more questions, but he swore he wasn't lying. Pregnancy is iffy in your forties, and at eleven weeks I began to "spot." I went straight to the doctor. As he did an ultrasound, he said, "Look, you've got a heartbeat here! You're home free. No way you'll miscarry now." Unfortunately, he was wrong, and by the end of that weekend, I lost the baby.

A few weeks later, because I was working on a script about Voodoo for Touchstone, I invited a Hougan – a Voodoo Priest – from New Orleans, over to dinner with some of my writer friends. A wiry, wild man from Belize with no front teeth, he regaled us with stories of snakes, poisons, and how he was tested and trained as a Hougan. Possibly because he lacked teeth, he ate not a single bite of food, but swilled down six beers fast and got riotously drunk. He looked at my slightly *zaftig* friend, Barbara, and said, "I see many tears. You will wind up a spinster lesbian." Not your usual dinner table conversation, and as a group, we simply laughed until he narrowed his beady little eyes at me and said, "The baby left because your husband didn't want it – he thought it would cost too much money."

Those words hit my gut like a bolt of lightning. They felt completely true. The next day, however, when my "rational mind" took back control, I chose to dismiss what a drunken, demented Voodoo priest had said. Wouldn't you?

I'd gotten married specifically so I could create a family all my own, and I'd be damned if I'd let a little thing like a miscarriage stand in my way. I wanted a baby and I would do whatever it took to get one. Many women who came of age when I did, in the late sixties, early seventies, were persuaded that being a woman simply wasn't good enough. We were essentially hypnotized into believing that motherhood and the nasty fuss of having children was trivial and worthless. When it dawned on the dimmer bunch of us how self-loathing that world view was, we were well into our thirties, making it far more challenging to conceive. Consequently, because there were so many us – we were Baby Boomers after all – we spawned an entire industry. The infertility industry.

I went to see George Weinberger, a hip, clog-wearing Beverly Hills infertility specialist. He said, "No time to waste, dear. Better get you on Clomid or Perganol, pronto." I told him that I'd had lupus as a young woman, that it was in remission now, but since lupus was fairly specific to females, didn't he think it was risky for me to take these powerful female hormones?

"Don't be ridiculous. You'll do just fine," he said, with supreme confidence.

Unfortunately, I didn't do fine at all. I took Clomid, then Pergonal, month after crazy-making month, but I never got pregnant again. Instead, I got more and more exhausted. It began to feel as if I were dragging my own dead body around behind me; I simply had no energy an hour after crawling out of bed in the morning.

My career, however, was picking up. After I left Disney, my script, "Virgins," was optioned by a production company and was now in "development hell." Which means that every time a new director became attached, I took notes and would re-write to each director's "vision," while the production company scrambled for enough money to shoot it.

By late '93, Dan despised his work so much, he was desperate to get out. Sam was almost done with college, and in Dan's mind, as soon as Sam was done with college, Dan could be done with being a lawyer. Dan's weight kept creeping higher, so he went to see Jerry Rosenberg, a cardiologist, for help. I think he wanted to hear, "If you don't stop stuffing your face, you will surely die."

Dr. Jerry, as Dan called him, embraced the new medical paradigm of energetic medicine that focuses not so much on what goes into your body as on what goes into your mind. So after seeing Dan a few times, Jerry discovered that he felt overwhelmed with his work and completely put upon by my desire to have a child. So he asked if he could see me.

"Sure," I said.

He started our conversation with, "I guess you're a really good cook, huh?"

"If you're about to blame me for Dan's weight problem, you can look someplace else. I cook steamed vegetables, broiled chicken and fish."

Then I told him that when I was twenty-one, because I was so sick, my regular doctors gave me about five years to live.

Instead of dying according to their schedule, I found a "health food" doctor named Henry Bieler, who wrote *Food Is Your Best Medicine*. I drove from Berkeley to Capistrano to see this tall, rail thin, ninety-year-old man (in his bright green house) and did exactly what he asked me do. I ate his famous Bieler Broth made of string beans, zucchini, parsley and celery, along with rare meat, raw milk and blueberries, for years. I did what it took to get myself off sixty milligrams of prednisone per day. I told Dr. Jerry that I had fought hard to regain my health, and that if he thought I was responsible for my husband's weight problems, he was entirely mistaken.

Dr. Jerry was taken aback by my directness. "Do you realize how much Dan doesn't want to have a child?"

I gasped. "Excuse me? He said that? Did Dan bother to tell you that was _why_ we got married?"

"No," he said, narrowing his eyes, "he didn't."

I saw his face change. He asked how I was feeling, and I said, "Not great. I'm exhausted and everything aches. I'm sure it's these damned fertility drugs."

He took some blood, and said he wanted to see me again. I went home and told Dan what he'd said. Dan was furious.

"That's not what I said at all! Jesus! The guy thinks he's a shrink and he's simply a quack."

When I saw Dr. Jerry again, he said, "I have bad news. The anti-DNA tests came back high, which means your lupus is active."

"Oh, I see," I said. "That explains the exhaustion and the achy joints, doesn't it? I should have known better. I gambled and I lost. Guess it's Bieler Broth until this clears up. But first, I'll stop taking these drugs."

"You do that," Dr. Jerry said, "But it might not be enough."

"What do you mean?"

"Your husband is the strongest man I've ever met – but he's strong like a cement wall. He's negatively bonded with me, so I won't be able to work with him any longer. My fear is that he's negatively bonded with you, too."

"I don't understand."

"He's using me to rebel against, and I don't have the time or patience to deal with him. But it's you I care about now. You're very sick and you better learn how he does this, because he's probably set up the same dynamic with you."

"I still don't get this."

"Give me an example of a problem – a fight you two had recently."

"Okay. Last week Dan overslept and missed a courtroom procedure."

"Then what happened?"

"He totally panicked. He said he'd be fired for sure."

"How did you react?"

"I got scared," I said.

"Then what happened?"

"I got mad. He's an adult. How do you miss a court appearance?"

"Exactly! He got you where he wanted you – angry and out of control. So then he could see himself as the victim. Here, look at this."

Jerry drew a sideways eight and wrote "event," on the top right loop of the eight. "Okay, Dan does something wrong. Instead of taking responsibility and saying, 'Damn! How stupid of me,' he panics."

Jerry drew a line to the right bottom and wrote, "Panic."

"Then he told you he would be fired and that scared you. Fear brings up anger, so you got mad." Jerry drew a diagonal line up to the left top loop of the eight, and wrote "Mad."

"And then what happened?"

"We had a fight."

"Right. He picked a fight so that he could now claim the bottom spot – the victim." He drew a final line straight down to the lower left loop of the eight, and wrote, "Victim."

"Now he can tell himself that he's got a bitch of a wife who expects him to keep a job he hates. In his mind, it's entirely your fault. Are you beginning to understand?"

As I looked at this neat sideways eight, my head began to spin. One, I had lupus again, and two, my husband hated me. Then Dr. Jerry told me that, literally, if I wanted to survive, I would have to leave him.

Leave Dan? How could I leave him? He was my husband. I loved him. Yes, he was nuts. Yes, he was difficult – but so was I. Isn't everyone?

Sometimes the Universe sends us messengers – and instead of listening to their kind advice, we would rather just kill them. Right then, I wanted to kill Dr. Jerry.

I went straight home and confronted the man who said he loved me at least five times a day.

"Is this true?"

"Don't be ridiculous," Dan said. "Jerry's a little man with delusions of guru grandeur. I told him I wouldn't see him again, and he's just getting even. He's jealous I have a girl like you. He probably just wants to sleep with you – he's a guy, first and foremost."

Who should I believe? A man whom I'd seen only twice or the man who wrote me this letter on our fourth anniversary?

December 30, 1993

Dear Sweet Stephanie

I'll write this on legal paper because I'm in this law office and it's available and it's four star Bond – and you are my legal wife, this day, of four years – and we're Bonded. And I keep trying to put into words, legal or not, failing, how much you mean to me...no how much you are to me. The sweet and gritty aliveness of you enlivens me and polishes that mirror in you/me so that I more clearly learn of myself and am able to grow – best only to appreciate you more.

On this fourth anniversary "when the psychological stuff" is supposed to start uh, the subconscious – let it. It's part of the adventure we're doing together and I look forward to whatever – as long as it's with you.

Thank you being my wife

Thank you for living with me.

Thank you for sharing our bed.

Thank you sharing your body with me.

Thank you for being you.

Thank you for being beautiful.

Thank you for being romantic.

My Love. My Goddess. My Friend. My wife. The best is yet to be.

Dan

Do you see my problem? He would say one thing, yet do another. But as Dan reminded me after he died, the man who wrote me those letters was the man who made love to me. That was the "Dan" who held me all night long, and that was the Dan I was ready to die for.

So once again, I chose to stay married. Since I now had lupus again, I knew my body couldn't take the stress of a pregnancy, so I gave up my dream of having a baby of my own. Maybe we could adopt later, but first I had to get well.

I buckled down and forced myself to eat Bieler Broth, rare meat, raw milk and blueberries – the diet that had saved me twenty years before – until they were coming out of my ears. Within six months, I wasn't exactly back to normal, but I was functional enough to go on living.

But strong, never-been-sick-a-day-in-his-life-Dan, began to complain constantly about feeling tired all the time. His glands were swollen, and he'd say, "I'm fighting something off."

I'd say, "Would you stop fighting and just lie down and get it? Then you can get over it." Unfortunately, Dan didn't know how to be sick. I thought he might have a low grade infection, but nothing showed up on tests. This went on for years. He got progressively more and more tired, until one Sunday, six years later, he looked at me, panicked and said, "I can't catch my breath."

Four days after that, he was diagnosed with an aggressive form of leukemia and six months after that, he died in my arms.

Then, I essentially cried for four solid months. I mourned the stubborn, intractable man I'd just lost. I couldn't think, I couldn't do much besides stumble through the house singing old Barbra Streisand songs to myself. One song in particular kept running through my mind, "Have I Stayed Too Long at the Fair?" I'd listen to it and cry, until that Sunday when I finally just got furious with being so miserable. So because my own energetic field shifted, Dan was able to blast through the heaviness of mourning and reach me.

There I was, sitting in bed, feeling his energy coursing through me. I looked down at the barely legible writing. I wanted him to explain – I wanted information. So I asked:

How does this work? Do you see/know about Val, Gheri-Llynn, your mom? (My sister Val had died of breast cancer just the February before, and his mom had died five years before that.)

Too complicated to explain. Stay focused on you and me for a while. I will be here to comfort you as best as I can. No arms to hold your sweet soft skin but feel my love – it's real. Bye.

Wait! Dan? I miss you so much. The pain feels unbearable sometimes. The deep hole in my heart...but why wasn't I happier with you? Was it me? Was it you? Was it us?

You forget our perfect moments – the moments when we loved each other beyond the limits of our world.

I kept crying and I felt him get frustrated with me.

The problem for you now is to find the course you want to follow from now on. You need to honor the emptiness of your life. Embrace the quiet. Sit in silence. Believe that you can communicate with me – or at least the familiar part of me. We have more business together.

Then I got a "love blast," which felt like warm honey tingling throughout my body. I read over the words and wondered what he meant by the "familiar part of him" and "we have more business together."

I would find out, but not for a while.

Chapter Seven

"Truly, Madly, Deeply"

In the movie "Truly, Madly, Deeply," Juliet Stevenson plays a woman beside herself with despair as she mourns the loss of her demanding, opinionated lover, Jamie, played by Alan Rickman. She weeps and tells her therapist that she hears him talking to her all the time. Jamie, she says, tells her to be careful walking alone at night and to remember to lock the back door. She doesn't know if it's really him, but she longs for him.

Then one day, as she sits at the piano, there he is behind her, playing his cello – solidly – all flesh and blood. She turns and can't believe her eyes. Is it really him? She pounds on his chest, testing to see if he's just an illusion. He's not – he's solid – and she collapses into his arms, weeping. She doesn't understand it, but who cares? He's back! She can love him again. He tells her that he simply couldn't bear to see her suffer any longer. And they are happy again – briefly.

Then, little by little, he begins to become the pain in the ass that he was when he was alive. He rearranges her flat to suit his needs. He takes down pictures she loves and pulls up a carpet he doesn't like. He complains constantly that it's too cold, and worries about his own delicate health. (Which is funny, because he's dead.) Then he invites his ghost friends in to watch old movies and have musical recitals. Eventually, he makes such a complete pest of himself, and annoys her so much that she can finally say "good-bye." She understands that she has to choose the living – choose life – over mourning the love she lost. And that realization frees her to live again.

Dan and I loved this movie; we'd even play the funny word game from the film. One person says, "I love you truly, madly, deeply." Then the other person builds on it, "I love you truly, madly, deeply, passionately." Each one topping the other until someone forgets and misses the progression. Once again, that was no coincidence.

So now it felt as if I had Dan back (mercifully, not like in the movie), but I had "Dan." And thankfully, it wasn't the Dan I'd lost. I barely recognized that Dan because in his dying, he became someone else entirely. His fear was so intense, and his outrage so palpable that his body could betray him, he pushed me away completely. In the three months before he died, he wouldn't let me hug him, hold him or comfort him. We became roommates, and I became his nurse. To everyone else, however, he pretended everything was just fine. Leukemia? What's that? He was brave – he would beat it. He showed one face to the world and a completely different one to me until it almost drove me mad. So much so, that the night he died, my heart ripped completely open, because I thought he had died hating me.

But now I had the authentic Dan – the core Dan – back, and he wanted to chat with me all the time. The only problem was that I couldn't remember what he'd said. His words seemed to land in a part of my brain where I had no memory cells.

Samuel had been telling me about Dan's "talking to him" for months by then, and now we seemed to be on the same wave length. And since it's such a weird, alternate wave length, I wanted validation, so I typed up the first of the channeling and e-mailed it to him. He shot back an e-mail that said it seemed authentic, so I was relieved.

I wanted to capture what Dan said, so when I felt him near, I would sit, pen in hand, and wait for him to chat.

What follows is the real time progression as Dan begins to explain his new reality, our life together, and I begin to develop my channeling skills. I've put my edited day-to-day journal entries in italics, Dan's channeled words are in bold, and my asides are in regular case.

Wednesday, April 17, 2002
Today I felt so happy – so light – much of the day. I feel Dan wanting to "talk" to me – or just talking almost all the time. Especially in yoga – so now I'll see what he wants to say.

DEW – (Dan's initial's)
Dan the man – I wanted to just tell you that pomegranate juice is good for you.

Okay, but that seemed like an odd thing to say from the "In Between." It felt as if he were trying to gather his thoughts, then:

My life was wonderful and thank you for all your fussing. At the time it drove me crazy, but it gave me real pleasure and joy. I loved that you dressed me like a big doll. I was your Dan doll.

I sat there smiling – it was a part of my "wife job" that I really loved. I bought almost all his clothes. After all, isn't that what we do for our guys? Give them some style?

Go to Yosemite – have a great time. I love you so much. I'm so glad you hear me. It's like I have the best of both worlds.

Later that month, Sam and I were planning to take some of Dan's ashes up to Yosemite – but something was bothering me about going on the trip. My beautiful friend Valerie, who had attracted Dan in the first place, was going with us – but she'd suddenly become jealous of my widowhood status, (yes, that happens) and she was driving me nuts.

Thursday, April 18, 2002
I've felt so much better since Sunday when I channeled Dan. Now I feel him around me all the time. It is like "Truly, Madly, Deeply." Only I hope he won't have to bring in his friends to make me stop missing him.
I don't feel him now that I'm sitting here with a pen in my hand – maybe I need to stop for him. I'm sure he's got more to do than to check on me.

Not necessarily so – I am able to do this easily enough. I knew we were "connected," I just had no idea about the depth of the link.

The Santa Ana winds kicked up and rattled my bedroom window, so I focused on them.

You listened to the wind and so I heard it and I lost focus.
I told you today how much I love you and how much I now know you loved me. I think I never really believed it because you were so annoyed with me so much of the time. But now I understand the source of the annoyance. I reneged on the deal we'd made in the life before – not to mention this life.

I sat there wondering, Deal? What deal? My hand began to move again:

You were right about the baby – and she was mad. I didn't want her. She left. I allowed you to do those drugs even though I didn't want a child. I'm so ashamed – you need to forgive me.

Why didn't you just say it? Oh, Dan, I know how overwhelmed you were – that awful job. I know you hated it. I wish I could have been successful. But there was a fear that you didn't want that?

I was just all over the map. I was terrified you'd become successful and find me too boring. You were so full of sparkle when we first met. I felt like a big country bumpkin who'd just grabbed the brass ring on the merry-go-

round. That's why when you sing, "Have I stayed too long at the fair," it breaks my heart. You haven't even gotten to really ride the rides yet.

(Now, your eyes can read these words quickly. But the words came very slowly at first and the pages are filled with smeared ink, because I would just cry as his energy coursed through me. Then I'd read the channeling and respond.)

Could I see you if I tried an "out-of-body" experience?

No, an out-of-body experience wouldn't put you in the same realm.

It was as if he could hear my thinking, and he completely understood my confusion and fear.

Look, I'm going to stay with you as long as you want me. I owe you that. I really cheated you out of the family you wanted.
We could have met in 1969 or 1970 – but I didn't want to. I wanted to do it my way – the funny noise we both made?

(When we hugged for the very first time.)

That was our _code_. You remembered.
I used to pass you _all the time_ on Ellsworth (in Berkeley) **and you might have been Sam's mom, but I don't think that would have been any better. I had so much growing up to do.**
I'm glad we had the love we had. Thank you for creating the life we had. If you left it to me, we'd have the Barcalounger and the TV tables.

I smiled at his humor. In life Dan always said that if it weren't for me, he'd be happy with a La-Z-Boy, TV tables, and Melmac tableware.

I was really the problem. I lost…(can't read the writing)**…and our joy. Only you couldn't change it or fix it. Although we both know how hard you tried to fix me!**
I was impossible. I'm still in awe of my own stubborn refusal to enjoy life. You will not waste too much time mourning that foolishness. When you pulled the car over that day and cried that I was killing your soul, I knew it was the truth.

During the last few months of his life, in an effort to save him, I drove Dan down the dreaded freeway three times a week to see Dr. Bae, a gifted acupuncturist. Dan would sit in the passenger seat, all pulled-up tight inside himself, hard as a walnut. One foggy morning, a huge tanker truck overturned and traffic came to a complete standstill. I managed to get us off the parking lot of a freeway, and was trying to find an alternate route home in the thick fog, but Dan kept yelling at me, "You're lost! You'll get us lost!"

I snapped back, "We're still in LA, Dan! How lost could we be?" But finally, I pulled the car over, and collapsed onto the steering wheel and wept.

> **I know it seemed like I didn't care about you or what would happen to you at the end. I know everyone else seemed more important, but I was terrified of what was happening to me and my body. I wish I had been kinder. That's why I gave you back those e-mails.**

I feel you now very intensely…

I am here but not here – I am around.

(Another baseball season had begun. In real-life, Dan's and Sam's conversations centered on their fervor and frustrations with the San Francisco Giants. Now, Sam told me that he felt Dan with him at a game.)

Were you at the Giant's game with Sam?

Of course!! Sam is amazing. He hears me! You, I expected to be able to reach. Sam, I wasn't so sure. You are my two big loves. You always love Sam and that…

I could feel him thinking something he couldn't express.

…Let's just say it's an old triangle. You've always loved me too.

I read that dream in your book – where you were afraid I left you? Was that a premonition of your leaving me?

No, dreams are not reliable forms of communication. This is easier. Thought you were going to choose those snails (on TV) **over me tonight.**

(I had turned on a PBS nature show.)

That was interesting and I thought about...remembered the tide pools and Morro Bay...

Yes and my being sullen and withdrawn with you. I saw it too. You deserved more from me. You certainly expected it.

What really happened with your body? Was it the radiation? Or was it just time to go?

It was a planned exit. I knew deep down that I didn't want to get old and I didn't. I have a lot of "time" to plan and evaluate my situation. I wish you would not worry so much. It truly is such a waste.
We are closer now than when we were there together because I wasn't _present_. I was always preoccupied with other things.

(I wish I'd been a better interviewer. I still wonder what "other things" were more important.)

Were you there at Lorelle's for my Married Girl's Guide night?

Wouldn't have missed it – felt your pain when you realized you were no longer married.

Then it just felt as if we were sitting side-by-side chatting.

Weird, isn't it? And yet this is actually the more _normal_ world. The one I'm in now – you're just "out" now on an excursion. We're usually together, that's why we annoy each other. Although next time, I'm going to appreciate you more.

(Dan's first wife, Maggie, and her husband Chris, are potters up in Mendocino, and they'd made two beautiful pots for Dan's ashes.)

Maggie and Chris are old enemies and I allowed them to annihilate my soul; it seems wrong for my ashes to be in their pot – but it doesn't matter. I'm not my ashes. Although I stayed with them while they slept on my side of the bed. I stayed with them when you cried and cried. You're so smart to cry.

I wondered what else I could have done.

No, you could have gone mad.

(Then I thought about the day he died. I'd gotten to the hospital early to be with him for his lung tap, but we were both edgy. So I walked down the street to Xerox some legal papers, but by the time I got back, the procedure was almost over.)

That was my fault – I was angry at you for disappearing before that procedure. Do you know how afraid I was? And you were gone.

(I reminded him that he'd made fun of me when I mispronounced a word.)

Yes, I know I hurt your feelings.

I can't go over that day again. Do we have a future here?

The future is now.

Then I felt his energy drain from my arm, so I turned on the TV to watch Charlie Rose, who talked about the Pope's ordering the Bishops back to Rome because of all the sexual abuse scandals. Dan came back to comment:

The church is safe.

Dan and I always joked about the possibility of a past life together where we might have been in the church. We both had deeply spiritual sides, but neither liked organized religion very much, so I asked.

Yes, we were both in the church in France and the god we served didn't exist. The god that exists doesn't care. The future is now. Sweet dreams, my sweet Stephanie. I love you so much.

The next day, my friend Valerie and I drove up to Yosemite. Valerie, a recovering alcoholic and recent Twelve Step convert, had gone from being an acerbic atheist to a smugly superior Born Again Christian in the blink of an eye. Because of her newfound relationship to God, she had become almost insufferable. When I tried to tell her about Dan's coming back, she humored me with an attitude that oozed contempt, yet managed to be simultaneously bitchy and condescendingly pious – a real achievement. I was sorry I'd asked her to come along.

For a broader view of the spiritual, (and so I wouldn't have to talk), I had brought audio tapes of Carolyn Myss's *Sacred Contracts* to listen to on the way to

Yosemite. I'd never done the drive in the springtime and the foothills were lush and green. As I marveled at the beauty of it all, I could feel Dan's energy in my eyelids. After we got settled in the cabin that overlooked the Merced River, Valerie was driving me nuts, so I sat in the front room and picked up my journal to write:

Friday, April 19, 2002 – Yosemite → The Redwoods
I can hear the rush of the river. Tomorrow we'll spread his ashes, and go to dinner and
toast my Dan, whom I now have back. Makes me happy to feel him with me.

From Dan the man – And how are you doing, as if I didn't know. I want to have some of my ashes spread at the river and the sequoia grove and if you want, you can...

(He said something too rude to write down...)

Yes, of course, I'm angry! The beauty of today seen through your eyes made my soul ache.

Sacred Contracts? What did you think?

Not true. Better material in the soul book you skim. Good night.

Valerie walked into the living room and started to question me about Dan's ex-wife. She asked how Maggie was taking Dan's death, and suddenly I felt a rip of anger shoot through me – I could feel his rage. It shocked me.

Saturday, April 20, 2002 – Yosemite
I couldn't sleep at all. Val snored all through the night and I was upset, and angry at
her condescension.

Dan the man reporting in – Last night was painful for me even here because I felt your pain and anger at Val. Confusing to feel emotion from this vantage point.
The reason you didn't sleep was that I kept trying to reach you again and I couldn't.
You won't be able to reach me in a short time. This seems to be some sort of way station for souls. I love you from here, but I don't miss how I behaved. I made your life so much less filled with joy.
Our contract was to love one another deeply and believe it or not, _we achieved our goals_. I had other contracts left to fulfill. You have a work one left.

Write your book.

The next day Sam, his Korean girlfriend, Ho In, Val and I went to the giant Sequoia Grove to spread some of Dan's ashes. I could feel him tagging along as we hiked up to two huge trees connected at the roots – The Faithful Couple. It was "our tree." I took lots of pictures, envisioning that I'd make a David Hockney-like collage. Sam told me he could feel Dan with him when he lay down under the trees. Later I put the pen in my hand.

Sunday, April 21, 2002
I'm sitting out on the deck surrounded by trees. The rushing river is the only sound.
Sheer bliss… This whole "letting go" process is …

Dan the man checking in – you sweet thing – I love you and wish I could be there in the flesh – yet this way of experiencing life right now is fascinating. I did see the sequoias through Sam's eyes and I saw the waterfall through yours.
Yesterday when you were screaming and crying, I heard you and was momentarily afraid you would jump.

(I'd thought about jumping onto the jagged rocks, then figured it would be just my luck to wind up not dead, but a paralyzed quadriplegic instead. So decided not to.)

I am in training for a while before I move on. I have to decide on my next adventure. I can stay with you as long as you want/need me. Advice? Live to the fullest extent of your energy.
I know you doubt this process, but I don't know why you should – it *is* all Seth stuff – the joke's on me in more ways than one.

(That refers to Jane Roberts' books, *Seth Speaks, The Nature of Reality*, and *The Nature of the Individual and Mass Events*. When I read Plato or Aristotle, I'd say, "It's all Seth stuff," and Dan would just roll his eyes.)

Naptime over – you will write those books that we've been waiting for.

What's the contract with my soul?

Your soul/my soul – contract similar. You're a writer and when you refuse to work it's hard on you – it's why I married you.
You have the time _now_ to do the book. Do it about us. *Married Girl's Guide*

to Hot and Sacred Sex **is the first.**

Go get a calendar and chart it out. You can finish by July.

(Oh, do I wish that were true! As I type these words, it's April of 2004. And it is only now, two years later, that I can read over his words without dissolving into the pain of losing him, not to mention the pain of living with him. No one can predict the future – not even dead husbands or spirit guides – there are too many variables.)

I'm glad you're listening to me – hearing me. I know – can see – you bring up the pain of the last months.

There is no way to vacuum those memories from your soul – there is no way for me to make amends except to say, again, forgive me and let it go. I was terrified.

I loved that you took me up to The Faithful Couple. It's where you will rest too. The only way we lose each other now is to forget.

What happened just after you died?

When you crawled into bed with me, I knew I could let go and to show you how much I loved you – and to _make up_ – I let your hand feel my last heartbeat. Then I whooshed past you. You felt it – I knew you'd felt me go through you. But then your own _shock_ kicked in and that horrid night...I was there, unable to get through until you fell asleep – I saw the sunrise and woke you up. I screamed.

Stay focused on you and me. Other connections too complicated to explain. Your "soul" – my soul are from the teacher pack. You are more...outgoing. I would like to hug you so much. I find it hard to remember the _joy_ of just holding you all night long. My greatest joy. When I said that, I meant that.

I don't have much more to say tonight other than thank you for honoring me and my life the way you have. I would never have believed I was worth it. But that was my lesson.

I know you feel bad about not writing me love letters, but you brought me joy – just being you.

And no, I never hated you – it just felt that way to you because I was so scared. I did become 'the walnut,' just like you said.

At this time, in my day-to-day life, I struggled to survive. When Dan died, he left me in $180,000 worth of debt, no insurance, and no retirement; everything had gone into his failed business. Under that kind of stress, I knew there was a chance that I had gone totally crazy and that I was completely delusional. Like Val, most people just humored me when I told them that Dan had come back, so Dan would try to comfort me. Fortunately, Samuel was still "talking" to Dan all the time, and he told me that sometimes Dan was in a bad mood.

Monday, April 22, 2002

> Believe this is so – don't doubt the process – you are a clear channel. I am, like Sam pointed out, not always in a good "mood." I have bad days when I long to be back with you.
>
> I don't have anything to say now – busy with other things.

What other things, I wondered. But that night, when I got back from yoga, I put the pen in my hand again:

> Dan the man, checking in from afar. You are the love I was waiting for and that is why you waited for so long. It was our agreement with each other. I had problems accepting your determined optimism, but it is why I married you. Then forgive me, because I squandered your energy and enthusiasm. I made fun of you and it – my ego – knew no bounds. That's why you wanted out almost immediately. I showed you one side, and then did 180 degree turn-around. You did the best you could, but you got mad. And I don't blame you.
>
> Re: you and my body – again, I presented you that amazing specimen and then because of my hubris began to destroy it. You longed for that body – I'm amazed you were as tolerant as you were.
>
> Re: you and Val? Too complicated for me to see or understand. But you feel she's not a friend right now and that's authentic.
>
> Dan the man loves you so much – I need to help you as much as I can – as much as I am able. You are a wonder.
>
> Nothing will be as painful for me either – the pain of knowing how much you loved me – and how much I withheld – what was I thinking/feeling? I don't even now understand why I wouldn't just come to bed and hold you. It was all you asked of me, and I refused. I refused and I am so sorry.
>
> I have more, but I feel you want to walk – so go. I made you wait. It's my turn.

So I continued to miss the man that might have been, more than the one that showed up on a day-to-day basis. I wondered about the "mechanics" of it all and he would comment.

Friday, April 26 2002

From Dan the man – I know you wonder what / where / when / why and how I can communicate with you. Where was I the last four months? I wasn't able to reach you because of my own _skill_ and your depth of mourning. When I got close to you, you filled up with so much pain because of the awful last months, that (it) made "talking" to you impossible. Sam could "hear" me but you couldn't.

Hey...

Hey back – you know, in a way, I am the perfect love for you now. You don't have to shop, cook, clean for me – service me – thank you for wanting, longing to smell my scrotum...

When you say I should work on my book, which book? The Married Girl's Guide or "Losing Dan"?

Don't like the title – "Losing Dan." "Gaining Dan" would be better. This is _more_ me than I was with you – don't ask me why – I don't know.

Do you have guides? Teachers?

Yes, everyone does. You definitely do. She was very angry at me when I arrived. Seems I really goofed. Once again, it is the _source_ of much of your frustration over the last 12 years. I agreed to one thing, then reneged.

Now you must not – really cannot – lose any more time. You don't have a great deal of it left. You need to hurry and write the books.

If you want me to help (and of course, I can) you will have to set up a schedule for me to follow. I don't just float around on a cloud all day.

What do you do?

First, set up the schedule – how's:
    5:30 – up
    6:00 – computer / write
    9:30 – 10:30 – walk
    12 – 5 – work

6 – 7:30 – yoga
8 – 9:30 – dinner, bed
I love this – I can be the petty despot you always accused me of being!

That made me laugh – I did accuse him of being a petty despot.

Okay…I hesitate to ask about Val, my sister?

This is a big place – she isn't part of anything I've come into contact with yet. I can only know what happened between you and Val W. from your POV (point of view) – I only have a clear connection with you.

Thank you for those last gentle kisses, they meant the world to me. You looked so "spiffy" that day and I loved and hated you such. I was not in a good mood. I was in unbelievable pain. But when you sat and kissed my chest… the love I felt!

That "last day," the day he died, when I got back from copying some papers, Dan was sitting on the edge of the bed, grimacing in pain. Blood coursed through a tiny tube that dangled from his lower right side and spilled all over the sheets. The young Asian doctor looked panicked. I was sure she'd hit an artery.

"I couldn't tap his lung," she said. "I'll call for the portable x-ray."

Dan and I watched her leave, and then we just stared at each other. I helped him to lie back down, and then sat next to him. Because his chest was bare, I leaned over and covered his heart with kisses. Those would be the last kisses I would give him.

***

I tried to follow his suggestions, but getting up at six on a Sunday wasn't easy.

Sunday, April 28, 2002
Got up @ 5:30 or 6 today. Went to the computer. Felt Dan with me much of the day. Just talked to Sam, and he's getting major jolts of Dan. Very real. Said he got a "big hit of love" when he lay down under the sequoias.

Dan the man. Can't get clear channel tonight. You seem too tired. My machine. Go to my machine.

So, I went and sat down at his desk, but none too happily.

From Dan the man…all right…go back to your own machine, if you must… you're cranky. I just like sitting in my own space, rather than yours…makes

me feel more me…okay, now you've settled down.
For today – what you need to do…

But my own sadness bubbled up again. I couldn't stand thinking of him sitting in that space – trying to get Conflict Solvers, his mediation company, off the ground. Four frustrating years of watching him work, night after night, flashed before my eyes. I'd ask him to come to bed, so I could hug him, comfort him, but he'd refuse. So now, he tried to comfort me.

Sweetie, the poetry of our life was in the living of it. Poetry exists everywhere
in everything. Watching you cook was "rapture" (a little joke) for me.

(As in "Rapture" from the Bible? Was that the joke? His humor was always somewhat obscure.)

I'd like to go back to Yosemite in September and if you don't schedule it now,
your cabin will be all gone…just a thought.
Your work is your work and you can do it from your own space…
But to contact me, it's easier for me to attach myself to the energy here…
And there is so much of "my" energy here at this desk. The tenacity of the "Dan"
who sat here night after night absolutely floors me. He, I, was so determined
– so scared of not succeeding – that I made it impossible to succeed.
My darling Stephanie, I don't know why or how you put up with me… rejecting
you so completely. And you are right about not ever feeling that kind of
pain again. You won't. Forgive me for my behavior in Yosemite…
I think…look back on how I avoided you/your touch…your attempts to
comfort me. There are things you cannot do over, but that is one place that
if you can, go again and be alone with you/me. For we are deeply connected
– it would be healing for both of us.

The September before he died, two days after the September 11th attacks on the World Trade Center and the Pentagon, Dan's sister Bonnie, his cousin Judy, her boyfriend Jerry, Sam and I drove up to Yosemite. The trip was an utter nightmare for me, because Dan was nice to everyone else, yet wouldn't let me touch him, except when pictures were taken.

Our dance together continues…and yes, thank you for trying to get me to dance!
I loved dancing. Go back yourself…make the time…you have the time.
I can't communicate with everyone…you and I aren't "soul mates" as much as

components, pieces of a larger whole. We are connected at the roots...just like
The Faithful Couple and yet there are many more connections...many more.
But make that collage...yes, I saw it as you did.
The love that Sam talked about – producing that feeling – does take a great deal of
effort on my part. You know when you got yours. I felt you sit there and take it
in...and there – I just gave you another jolt. You can help. There is something
to "you can't be depressed with an open chest." Your time is limited...your
energy is finite. You must conserve your energy, which I see you doing.

So to reach him more easily, I'd sit at his desk and wait.

Monday, April 29, 2002
Hey Dan. I'm here. At your machine...

Whether you want to be or not, is how it feels to me. I don't blame you for
having resentments still about the time I spent at this damned machine.
But it's a tool now that I can easily access. I can print through or type
through you. Your typing is faster than your printing.
All right. Just for now, be aware that you pick up "signals" (that should be
in quotes) from others...not just me. So last night, for instance, that most
definitely was not me. I know who it was, as do you, but you don't need
to really talk about it...think about it. There's still much anger. Enough
vibration energy given. (It was my sister Valrie, who had died of breast cancer
the February before Dan died.)

Anything else?

Just that I love you...
I don't seem to be able to block out all the damage I did to your psyche.
Forgiveness happens one chink at a time, and I still can't find it in my heart
to completely forgive myself. So why should you?

*Just having what seems to be a connection with you again gives comfort. Yes, you're
right. I don't always know where it comes from and I'm not sure I completely trust
the process, but I'm here.*
Did you spill something on your computer keys? What did you spill?

Tea with honey...that's why they stick. I am with you now, but I won't be "as
connected."

No wait! What did you do in the last four months? Where were you? Why didn't I hear from you?

I already said that your own pain, your grief was too intense for me to break into, and more to the point, experience. Because I seem to experience what you experience along with you. Like the anger up at Yosemite.

There is a _group of us_ pushing hard to open the lines of communications. But I feel your energy flag. Go for a walk. Think healing thoughts. Your body needs to be strong. That's why I gave you that tee-shirt, my Durga, my goddess warrior.

(The last gift Dan gave me was for my birthday in May: a fuchsia-colored tee-shirt with Durga, the Indian Warrior Goddess, who triumphs over ignorance.)

It was now two weeks into the channeling, I was beginning to understand what had happened to my life.

Tuesday, April 30, 2002
Mourning got me again…my loss. Not only the loss of Dan, but of the career I might have had, a family I might have had…it just hit me. My soul? Get in touch?

Go for a walk.

Dan? I just want you to know how mad I am at you!

I tried. I just was too conflicted with the garbage of my past to live in the joy of the present. Don't continue to make the same mistake I made.
Go walk. You did your time at the computer for today.

What happened between us next is fuzzy in my memory and I didn't write it down. What I remember is that Dan kept wanting to have sex with me.

Even though my doctor had encouraged me to masturbate for the sake of my plummeting hormones, I couldn't; it made me feel even more alone. But now Dan's energy could focus inside of me and he was quite insistent.

I could feel him wanting to have sex, so I "let him have his way with me." I'll leave it to your own imagination, because the reality of it seems bizarre even to me.

A year to the day after Dan died, a friend's husband died too – yet another strong and determinedly stubborn man. A few weeks later, I casually said to her, "So has he had sex with you yet?" She turned beet red, then said, "Yes! He wants to have sex all the time!" It's not like new widows talk about this stuff. It's simply too weird, but it happens a lot.

Here's Dan responding to what he would have called in life, "an afternoon delight."

Tuesday, April 30, 2002

Dan the man needs to talk to you. Thank you for turning off the TV. I know you find it soothing, but I want to talk about what happened today – that was great!

I can't believe you did that for me. I stand in awe of your ability to just _do it_. Wow!

Don't read! Because I lose my train of thought – which is difficult enough as it is. See? This is the real deal – whether you trust it or not.

You've actually been "in training" to do this for 30 years. If I couldn't reach you, I couldn't reach anyone from any lifetime.

Do you see other lifetimes – yours? Mine? Ours?

Yes, I see them all. The one on the steppes of Russia I always talked about where I murder as a job. That wasn't my life. I don't know what that "memory" was, but you and me in France – that was real. No, we weren't homosexuals. You were that nun you see and I was also a nun.

(He refers to the ugly French nun from my spontaneous past life regression.)

I see you're tired. I feel so sad to feel your deep sadness. But I can assure you I am much better off now. It's hard to explain the depth of my despair. But I couldn't move. And my energy _affected_, infected you.

You will begin to pull away and out of it soon. It permeates the house. It's in my desk.

At that point, I conked out. Once again, channeling Dan drained so much energy that I simply fell asleep. Then he woke me up in the middle of the night, and I was grumpy.

3:22 a.m.
What? I need to sleep!

Dan the man can feel the beauty of your soul from here and just wants you to be aware of how much I love you. It's like I didn't tell you enough while I

lived with you. I certainly behaved as if I didn't care.
I am so proud of you for trusting this process and sharing what you did.

Anything else?

Give me Saturday night. Go to sleep now and I'll talk to you in the morning.
Love, me.

Give him Saturday night? Okay. So now he wanted to have a "date," just like when he was alive. We'd light a fire, open a bottle of champagne, and sit on the couch and chat. So I obeyed my dead husband and did what he asked.

My life was becoming exactly like "Truly, Madly, Deeply." My husband was back, gently bossing me around. But what was really strange is that I was getting used to it. Until something even stranger happened.

Chapter Eight

Sex and the Single Widow

As April turned into May, my mourning evaporated off me like vapors from a lagoon. Sam and I chatted almost everyday and we'd compare notes about what Dan would say. Sharing this with Sam made me feel so much less crazy, because if this seemed real to him, then maybe I wasn't simply delusional.

Baseball season was in full swing and their team, the San Francisco Giants, was going gangbusters. Sam told me that he could feel his dad with him at all the games, and since he'd just caught his first fly ball ever, he was sure that Dan had sent it his way.

Dan kept urging me to begin working on *The Married Girl's Guide* so I began to write the "introduction." It was a little premature, but I had to begin somewhere.

Dan said he was "In Session," which meant that he had to watch, then analyze his actions and understand the consequences of his behavior in this last life. In the Hindu and Buddhist traditions, the belief that all action – karma – has consequences seems to be a good representation of Dan's experience in the "In Between." He still had time throughout the day to send me "love blasts" – an attempt to make up for his stubbornness in life.

As I said, I had been determined to make our life together work, but most of the time I felt like Sisyphus with his boulder: I'd shoulder my enormous rock on up that mountain, get it to the top and turn around just in time to watch the damn thing roll back down.

Then Dan told me why:

Thursday, May 2, 2002

Dan the man – reporting in.
The life you created for me is now appreciated so deeply and yet the sorrow I feel is so intense. I didn't realize how much of your life force I wasted with my stupid game – my game of I won't "do it" just out of spite and "do"

whatever. I wouldn't commit fully to our life. Wouldn't commit fully to my
job. Wouldn't commit fully to anything, except Sam. That's why you must
commit completely to your book – it is there for you.

Write the books. Do the work – I am so sorry I actively sabotaged your
creativity – my own needy insecurity kept you in such a state of sheer
exhausted panic that you had no energy left.

I need to let you know how much I love you and once again how sorry I am
I wasted so much time glued to the computer and watching, as you would
say, men chase balls all over a little screen. (Sports on TV.)

Good-bye for today – go be alive in the world – smile like you do. I check in
from time to time. I'm looking forward to Saturday.

Our date night. But that night, I had a vivid dream where Dan and I were in
a museum, so he comments:

Friday, May 3, 2002

From Dan the man – the dream is indeed about your relationship to art, which
you seem to have lost completely. Another apology due to you from me. The
time at the Met stands out for both of us as painful, but for different reasons.

Your love and enthusiasm for special pieces so enraged me that the only way
I could control the situation – and my feelings – was to totally ignore you
and your "favorites."

On the Vacation from Hell, in the first year we were married, after drop-
ping Sam off at Haverford, we headed to New York City. When I lived there, I
used to visit the Metropolitan Museum of Art at least once, sometimes twice a
week. Seems obsessive, yes? But it started out as an assignment from my acting
teacher, Stella Adler, and then just became a habit. So I knew the Metropolitan
Museum quite well, and I'd fallen in love with specific pieces, rooms, and wings:
Rembrandt's self-portrait, the medieval cloister room, the Renoirs in the Lehman
Wing. So now I assumed I would share what I loved with my new husband.

But Dan refused to even look at anything I tried to lead him toward. As he
says, he ignored me completely. I couldn't understand it.

Your pain was so palpable and your anger so intense. I enjoyed the power
I had over you. You were so open and needing of my approval and love,
which I gave when *I* felt like it, but in the clutch plays, I withheld.

Remember my "ducky" story? It's how I lived my emotional life.

His "ducky" story was his first conscious memory. When he was six months old, he was in a playpen while his mother and some friends chatted off to one side. He started baby jabbering to a rubber duck just out of reach. The ladies just "ooed" and "ahhed" over how cute he was, and he understood his power at once. He realized he could totally control the actions of the adults in the room with his cute behavior. It wasn't about the fun of talking to the ducky, it was about controlling the reactions of others. It was a lesson in emotional manipulation, and that one moment – that flash realization – colored his entire life.

> **It's why you had more "fun" with Sam – he felt and you responded. He experienced you directly, authentically.**

I could feel his intense frustration at his own behavior.

> **I can't do it over again – I can only walk through our life together and apologize. Because I did and do love you with all my fucked up heart. Once again, you deserved more.**

So I would read over what he wrote and wonder, Why? Then I'd go about my day. I would hear him chat with me, but couldn't retain any of it. It was only when I wrote or typed it that I could capture what he said.

Saturday, May 4, 2002

> **From Dan the man – I am looking forward to making love to you tonight. It can't be the same of course, but it can be _love_ – and that is what I will send you from here. Don't be _sad_. If I had not died...well, let's just say I _had_ to die.**
> **People do _choose_ their own exits, so when the time comes, embrace it. But you will. You, unlike me, have no _fear_ of death. Your fear is your physical vulnerability. And how sorry _once again_ I am for not comprehending at all – not one iota – how much of your energy I _devoured_, then just wasted... said one thing – meant another.**

You...

> **Not through yet – will you do me a huge favor? Find your own life again. Find your own voice again. That's why you need to be alone now. Now is the time to heal.**

I am so sorry for the pain I caused – the pain that was inflicted intentionally – and you knew it from the beginning – but you couldn't make sense of it – so you just accepted it.

Nothing to do about it now, but just to warn you how easily you can be led astray. The lure, the need – your need – for love is so strong that you don't take enough care. You could have left earlier, but you *insisted* on fixing us. It was *worth it* to me – but not for you. I would have left much sooner without you...

Why?

The pain of my own existential bullshit angst was so ingrained. Please remember that you and I are deeply anchored and that whether you feel me or not, I am here with you for now, you sweet, elegant, funny lady. My joy was simply in the hugging of your body. Why I *starved* us both I understand, but it was such a waste.

(The staying up late at night at the computer, working or just playing chess when I wanted him to come to bed, get naked and hold me.)

Dan the man needs to be free to move on soon – that's why I need to keep you focused on the task at hand: fixing us – fixing the past. I know that sounds insane, but the fixing is in the forgiving and in the realization that what we do in the present can change the past.

Our past?

No, not for "us," but we have alternate selves who will benefit – and you will benefit from them.

What? I don't understand.
There's an "alternate reality" where I lived (i.e., didn't die) – but *together*, you and I choose not to experience that reality.

I read over those words and burst into tears.

Multiple realities? Was this quantum mechanics in action? Some of what he said I understood because I'd read books on quantum physics, not to mention all the "Seth" books, but still the reality of "together you and I choose not to experience that reality" cut me to the bone. I got up from the table and left the house.

***

Okay. So it was Saturday night. And as I said, in our marriage we scheduled dates. We'd block out four hours of "date time," and sex might or might not happen, but at least there was enough time for it. Sometimes we'd sit in front of the fire, read poetry or we'd just talk. And he'd always try to make me laugh. Sometimes I was lucky enough to get a massage from his strong, blacksmith hands, and I would tell him that was the real reason I married him – his massages. Sometimes I believed that it was true.

So now, I lit a fire, turned on the stereo and sat down on the couch, pen in hand and ready to chat.

Saturday, May 4, 2002

Turn off the music – too confusing for you.

He was right; I couldn't block out the music. So I turned it off and sat back down, picked up the pen, then felt him flood into me, as if impatiently waiting.
(The feeling is) **so familiar – thank you.**

> **I know how much you loved our dates and so did I – I cherish the feeling of your laughter, your love. And here on this couch you *loved* me with your whole heart and soul – all the rest doesn't matter.**

Ah, so true. When I read those words, I felt his love.

Then he urged me to read over an old, black ledger-like journal he'd kept. I'd seen it lying around for years, but never opened it until after he died. I sat down on the floor in front of the fire, opened it, and was amazed to see that it spanned the years from 1979 through 1997, and beyond, although the final, frightened entries aren't dated.

The journal mixed dreams with sporadic diary entries. In 1980, he's a forty-year-old man in Mendocino, whose wife is sleeping with another man in their own house and for the life of him, he can't figure out why he's in so much pain. Here's a taste of it:

"April 19, 1980 (2 a.m.) – Reflecting on choosing of moods: freaking out with acceptance of a situation is almost a matter of choice. Is this crazy? Why not flow with it? Freaking just a natural reaction to a crazy situation? But who defines crazy?"

Eight months later he writes:

"January 5, 1981 – My hatred for Maggie – I can ossify it, create it outside my body as a thing that has tentacles attached to my solar plexus. I look at it, examine it, objectively. Then I sometimes understand her or accept her, and all hatred drops away and I feel cleansed."

Then I read the pages marked "The Story of My Life," where he tries to figure out why he's done what he's done. He says: "I loved the idea of greatness. Never wanted to do the work to get there." He's open and vulnerable, yet as I sat there reading about his many jobs, I wondered why he writes nothing of his "real" life. He ends with: "Do I believe in anything? Goddammit! Am I doing exactly what I want to do?"

I read the journal through to the end, then I put the pen in my left hand, and he began:

> **Oh! The pain of reading – hearing that. I was trying so hard to be profound, I forgot to be real. You noticed that I missed writing anything about my "real" life – the birth of Sam – that amazing, agonizing, scary thing – then the meltdown war between Maggie and me – only _jobs_ – only ego – only self-important prattle. I was so silly – and you knew that – you knew that and you loved me.**
>
> **I couldn't have been more selfish – I had no idea – and it's no one's fault but mine.**
>
> **I deprived you of simple pleasures – and I did it constantly and consciously.**
>
> **Let me remind you of not even appreciating the beauty of you...**

> _I lost the connection._

> **You start to argue with me in your head and I lose my train of thought.**

> _Wait...you did appreciate the flowers, the cooking...the everything!_

> **No, that's just it. I took it all for granted. I didn't appreciate – I took it as my due.**

(Then outside the window, I heard our neighbors Ken, Julie and their daughter Lily walk by. Julie's close to my age, and she had Lily at 48.)

> **I just heard Lily – and when she was conceived, I felt your sadness. Lying here on the couch, giving up your dream – not mine – of having a child of your own. I'd had mine; I honestly didn't care if you had that amazing joy or not. That's what I mean when I say I was utterly selfish.**

> _What do we do now, Dan? I don't have a clue. I'm alive, you're dead. So tell me about your death._

My death was easy compared with most hospital deaths – they are the worst. Everyone up here agrees. My death came fast after that last injection. As I said, I waited for you to crawl in bed and then to make up for my horrid behavior, I let you feel my last heartbeats – my heart, my darling Stephanie, was yours.

Your life force is not as fragile as you think it is. Your energy can be a problem, but you have a _fierce_ life force – one to be reckoned with. I think that is not the only reason I want to _clear the air_, but it is certainly one of them. I got back at my mother through you – so stupid!

Have you seen or heard from your mother?

My mother was so furious at me, but she's calmed down. Our relationship has many elements to it. As I said, I can't talk about other things because of the complexity of this dimension.

I can, however, talk to you and tell you that that poem I was so lamely trying to write was the absolute truth of my existence.

On the last page of his journal, he was trying to write a poem to me…perhaps for our anniversary: "I don't quite understand how it happens, but you are simultaneously the ocean in which I swim, and the bedrock on which I stand."

You _are_ the ocean and the shelves of its floor for me to swim/stand on – I swim through your conscious mind and stand on the bedrock of your soul and your life.

You are tired – can you just this once, grant me the pleasure of taking you to bed? You are my most beloved wife from all my lives.

I thought, "I bet you say that to all the girls." He shot back.

And _no I don't_ say that to all the girls!

I read a line from his journal that said, "I want a woman 1st to ask me directions" and I laughed out loud, because Dan had no sense of direction, whatsoever.

You laughed at "the direction," but not as hard as I did.

I smiled, but then conked out on the couch, woke up after two a.m. and dragged myself into bed.

Sunday, May 5, 2002

From Dan the man

You are my love and whenever you share your "present" with me, (it) will be a gift – a gift of love that can heal us both, my sweet Stephanie. I've got to help you fulfill your enormous potential before it turns on you.
It is why you gave up Val. She's toxic, filled with self-important rage. Lynn's a much sweeter soul. Bea is holding on. Know the feeling well.

My friend Lynn was in Chicago just then. Her mother Bea was dying of leukemia and Lynn would report in from the hospital whenever she could.

Sunday night, I'll try to seduce you again. Still can't believe the times you'd strip – I know as a joke – and as a joke, I'd continued to watch a damned game!

He refers to his Sundays of "ballgame watching," which for me were possible date times. I would stand in front of the TV, give him the old "come hither" look, and then begin to strip. He'd smile, but gently push me out of the way.

What was your brooding undercurrent all about?

Tormented expectation – unrealistic expectations. You read that journal. You saw my way of dealing with criticism – I withdrew. I can't and won't blame Riva, (his mother) **although she didn't help much. I acquiesced. I ate it up and when the world proved her wrong, I shunned the world.**

Have you seen Riva? Or a part of her?

Riva's and my relationship is too intense to talk about now. The simple answer is yes, I have "seen" her, but it's _not_ simple. Change the subject.

And so we had a date.

Monday, May 6, 2002
Yesterday was the first Sunday since Dan died that I didn't absolutely have a meltdown. I don't know if that's because I have him "back," or if I'm just…

From Dan the man – your energy is so finite you must marshal it like gold, for indeed it is the source of your wealth. I know you're achy, but that's the

champagne. **Walk now if you must. But be back ready to work. You must work every day to get this done.**

I can come "back." **Thank you for last night – the sweetness of those sensations experienced through you was simply exquisite! No big scream, but we could have gotten there if you weren't concerned with the neighbors.**

Then Aliah, a lovely woman who had helped me through the worst of the mourning, came over and we talked about Dan's core issues: his need to put me through the "will you love me if" test, and his not feeling "worthy enough" to deserve love. She'd lost her son to suicide, and because he'd come back to her, she had access to her own "guides."

Monday, May 6, 2002 – 10:10 p.m.

Dan the man reporting in – Aliah is the real deal if you want help with progressing through the mourning work – through your love stuff – I love you, but your _need_ for my love – your tenacity – even surprised me! You meant "till death do us part."

I don't understand. Are you saying I should have left you?

I'm saying you weren't happy and if you had left, it might have moved us in a different direction. But you believed in my dream – you gave up believing in your own.

Excuse me? I sat there staring at those words.

What would you have me do now?

Live with pride that you gave me everything I could have asked for in a wife / partner / lover and finally, nurse. But you got cheated, and I can't make it up to you except to continue to tell you how grateful I am.

Sweetie, when I loved you, I loved you with everything I had. I'll never do that again, but…

(And then I got bathed in his "love.")

You felt that "love burst" I sent. You are sort of an addict, but so am I. I'm already looking forward to my next date.

Is there anything important you want to say? I'm so tired…

That is important – sleep.

I can tell by my journal entries that we were having a lot of ethereal sex during that time, a veritable explosion of sacred sex, right from the source. It only lasted a couple weeks, but what weeks they were. I could feel his being-ness inside of me, wanting to make me scream again. Here's one of the entries:

Tuesday, May 7, 2002

Dan the man is here and you know it, you vixen. You're still tingling with my vibrations. I'm still vibrating – it's _very_ intense up here. My desire for you physically seems so strange. I mean, really strange.

No wonder – he didn't have a body!

Tuesday night – 9:30 p.m.

I'm in bed, going to sleep. Haven't heard from Sam today. Either he's busy or mad or upset. I'll let him be.

Dan the horn-dog here – as I was saying when you went off to yoga, I am still just vibrating from this afternoon. I want to do that again, and again, and again...

That's a little obsessive. Don't you have classes and things to do?

I was busy this morning, but now I feel like a teenager! Who knew you were even wilder than I thought! And that says something. More. I want to be inside you. Feel you climax. That shot my socks off.

Enough said.

* * *

Earlier that week, I'd sent Sam a few pages of edited channeling. When he didn't respond right away, I realized it might have been a mistake. Especially where Dan talked about his relationship to Maggie and Chris, Sam's mom and stepdad. They were both in town and seemed to be on the verge of separating, so Sam wanted to talk to me about it.

But for the first time in our relationship, I refused to help him process his feelings. It shocked him, and he got mad. The following day was Dan's birthday, and we planned to have a memorial dinner, so I knew we'd have to talk.

Dan comments:

Wednesday, May 8, 2002

Re: Sam – he needs to stay in the illusion I created for him a while longer. He's angry at you for making him look at the truth of that fucked up situation to the north (Maggie and Chris in Mendocino). **Keep out of it! Say no more. He is by no means a young soul, but he is still a young man.**

I can't seem to get through on the subject. But there's no need. You were absolutely right when you said there are no victims. I so totally gave away my power in that situation that now it seems absurd. What was I thinking? Well, that was the problem. I was *thinking*, not feeling.

You're in training now. And do what you want. Rest and see you around 2:30. I love you so much. I hope you *feel* it.

He sent another love blast.

Yes! You did. I can't exactly see your smile, but I felt it.

8:40 p.m.

Dan the man with Sam – go watch West Wing.

Two hours later I felt the familiar "nudge" in my arm, so I put the pen in my hand:

10:28 p.m.

Dan the man, back from Sam's. He finally understands about Maggie and Chris and me. Extremely painful for him to hear. I should have been more honest, authentic about what was actually going on with me. I hid from him almost more than I hid from you. I still don't know what I was so afraid of.

Vis-à-vis you and me – I feel you fear that I am going to leave you again and that you will be devastated all over again. But I won't go for a while. I know I said I have to leave, but I don't – if you want me.

Is that throbbing "you" or just my body?

That is me – that's why you get so tired. The mechanics of all this is pretty tricky…

Thank you for getting me up. I almost said, "Letting me walk," 'cause that's what it felt like…but oh, I don't know…I'm so tired…

Do this on my machine or _yours_ tomorrow – you're too tired. Go to sleep. West Wing wasn't good enough to spend the time on, only my humble opinion.

(He's dead, and still critiquing television shows. Love that.)

Thought you were with Sam.

I was, but he got into his music and rocking.

(Sam soothes himself by rocking in a big chair, listening to music.)

May 9, 2002 – Dan's Birthday
Talked to Sam last night. He said he was mad at me. Or he said that he had to digest what I "wrote" for Dan. He defended his mom and I said, "That's over. There are no victims. Dan chose to participate."

But now I feel anger and I don't know if it's mine or Dan's, because why would I care? I feel Dan…now…

Dan the man reporting in.
I couldn't get "through" over there (at his computer). **Think it might have to do with your anger just being there.**
I don't blame you at all. The _hours, days, weeks, months,_ and finally years of our precious time together that I wasted there. I wouldn't walk, hike, go to the movies, go to the museum, go dancing, go anywhere because of my panic.
It wasn't just my waning energy. It was a conscious need to deprive you of pleasure. It was about my power over you and my need to control the situation. My darling Stephanie, once again – please forgive me.
I thought the road to enlightenment was through self-denial and I denied myself the pleasures you offered me. That's why I had no control over food. It was the only pleasure I had that would also hurt you.

I sat there, stunned. I read over those words, "It was the only pleasure I had that would also hurt you."

I don't know what to say, Dan. That must mean you <u>hated</u> me. You tortured me? No wonder I was so unhappy. Oh well, it's over. I knew I couldn't continue much longer. I felt I was dying…

You <u>were</u> dying. But I stepped up to the plate first. I think because of my deep dishonesty, you were convinced it was all your fault.

There's no way to un-ring the bell. The realization of your – own <u>acute</u> ability to see the truth – the essential reality of any situation – is what makes you strong, yet also makes you vulnerable. It is when one thing is <u>internal</u> and the <u>external</u> presentation is something completely different.

Your intense reaction to Maggie and Chris is only one of <u>many</u> examples. When I first told you how happy I was living in that totally <u>demented</u> situation, your bullshit barometer shot through the roof. You actually experienced <u>my anger</u> for me. But it cost you. My refusal to acknowledge my own "negative" feelings sucked your vitality.

I flashed on our honeymoon.

(I've already written about this, but now it's in context.)

You just went back to our honeymoon. You were right. I wasn't even completely present there. I wanted everyone to know what a good time I was having, that's why I kept calling home. Made you feel second fiddle intentionally. That walk? Preoccupied with my own bullshit. I'd <u>won</u> you, now I could ignore you. Crazy isn't the word I would choose. There's another one I know you won't want to hear – that was evil, my darling. They made me watch that scene: you and me walking in that beauty – the first <u>snowfall</u>. You wanting so desperately to love this <u>stranger</u> you'd just married – and there I am, pulled back, pulled in – not responding to you. No wonder you loved Sam more at first. Oh yes, I knew. But since I loved him more too, that was okay. It was only later that it drove me crazy. The easy way you had with each other; the way he made you laugh, the <u>direct</u>, clear communication. I didn't know then what I know <u>now</u>.

(As I said, it's an old triangle and actually this time we did a nice job. Our agreement with Sam was to nurture a very <u>sensitive</u>, warrior soul to adulthood. Your "finishing school" was just what he needed. Also your acceptance and love – the love from a "stranger" fueled a very fragile 16-year-old ego.)

But back to us – for we are the topic…

(Yet, once again, I stand in awe of your ability and his to work through problems. That you gave him all the time to sit with his anger at you, I find amazing) okay...back to us.

> **Now do you see why I need to clean this up? I don't especially want to face you here – exposed – without being honest first.**

(I yelled, "No!" If he had been unfaithful, I didn't want to know about it now.)

> **Unfaithful? No, not physically. But physically is only one small piece of fidelity. I was faithful "in my fashion." Yes, the lovely Leslie, and I'm amazed you didn't care.**

He always said that if it weren't for me, he'd give Leslie, the smart, sexy director of our yoga center, a run for her money.

> **Dan the man needs to go now. I love you so much. Will be back later. I want you to go and type. This way of communicating takes too much of your energy. Go to your machine...**

I can't get through...very well.

> **You will...sit and be patient. The mechanics are different, but more efficient. The energy conserved will be worth it.**

When I look at the handwritten journals, they're filled with, "Go to the computer" commands along with "sit – be patient." I was trying to make the switch, but it wasn't easy.

May 10, 2002 – 9:16 a.m.
Quick question. I "saw" myself going down Ellsworth, singing "Sadie, Sadie, Married Lady." In 1969? Were you around? I seem to know you're around there. Had I just passed you? Just a thought.

> **Dan the man called back. Yes. You saw that yesterday because I am still trying to understand the reasoning involved in the _major_ decisions of my own life. The choice _not_ to meet you was, as I've said in life, a kind of foolish snobbery I had toward anyone as beautiful as you were. The funny thing is, however, I would _never_ have been attracted to you if you weren't beautiful.**

When you sang that song to yourself, it was precisely when you passed my corner. At one point, you even started doing your laundry in the basement of my building on Parker. And still I wouldn't give you a chance. You'd met Paul by then, and as you suspected, we are two sides of a coin and he got you first.

I chose to face Maggie once again, much to my chagrin now. I lost again and really learned nothing new. It's not as simple or clear cut as that, but in answer to your question, "yes," that was me you called to then. That was me who ignored you.

Go move your beautiful body and talk to me again tonight. Back to session for me.

Friday, May 10, 2002 – 9:45 p.m.

In yoga, I got really mad at Dan. Not only did he keep me waiting 20 years, when he does finally meet me, he totally sets me up. Promised, agrees – no, wait – he suggested it...

"You want to have a baby, don't you?"

"I'm 42, it's too late."

"No, it's not. Marry me, we'll do that."

I'd let the "baby dream" go by then, and he hooked me with it. What I want to know, Dan, is where your guides were? What kind of guidance did you get? And where were mine?

You have every right to be angry. But you know anger only turns on you. You are too tired to receive complicated thought.

The session today focused on between experiences – between is where I am now – or between is where you are. Just depends on how you look at it.

What did it say about it?

Go to sleep. You are too sleepy. Tomorrow let's try your computer again. I need not to take so much of your energy and time to do this.

You asked about your guides. My guide and your guide want us to work this communication stuff out – for the good of all.

Good night, my sweet Stephanie. I mean that. Those pictures of that dying man with your hand always on his heart – my love, my life – the sorrow I feel when I'm faced...

And I conked out, yet again.

Earlier in the day, Sam showed me pictures from Yosemite taken the September before Dan died, when we were in the midst of the frantic run for his life. Dan felt pulled in, hard as a walnut to me, but to everyone else he was perfectly fine. As I said, the only time he would let me touch him was when someone snapped a photo of us, so in every picture, I have my hand over his heart, which is exactly how he would die.

Saturday, May 11, 2002

From Dan the man. I think you've got it. Focus. It's uncomfortable (at the computer), I feel that. But have patience.

....to continue:

The sorrow when I'm faced with my own behavior towards you during that heroic run on your part.

Yes, you were frantic. Yes, you were controlling. Yes, you drove me crazy. But, my god! The love I got from you. The devotion. You made me feel so guilty for my own lack of love toward you. I felt none. I was buried in myself, _scared_. Unable to feel it. So when I see, through your eyes, pictures of us then, it brings it back.

Now, onto the subject of yesterday's session. The place is actually quite lovely. Looks to me like a library that I loved in life. I have no idea what it looks like to the other "people" in the class, because we're not exactly people. We're fuzzy things...fuzzy, lighted things, but we recognize each other. The session itself focused on the "between life," which for us is _now_. What we are learning about ourselves and the way we can improve performance in the next go-round, where we hone our skills and see what we've learned. I didn't do too well, I'm afraid, and I had all the advantages. That's why I'm so upset with myself.

You, on the other hand, gave yourself some pretty steep challenges and you've done amazingly well so far. All things considered. Your body stuff is very impressive. I see you almost checking out at 19, just like you always said. But that was your "guide" that pulled you back into your body...with the help of your body. But it was your guide. She wasn't going to let you lose the opportunity of becoming the hero you became. That's where all your confidence comes from...your inner core. Your father was, in a way, absolutely right when he called you "cold, hard steel." You couldn't have survived those two "killers" if you hadn't been made of steel. (He refers to my

challenging "parental units" here.) **They are not back in the main population yet. Much to learn.**

But for you and me, the work continues. But I see, feel you getting worried about time. But we did it today. This is me, connecting with you. And not draining you...too much. For tonight? Please? Sit with me on the couch again. Think of all the love we shared there. Light a fire. Read poetry. Love me. And I'll be there. Don't cry...

You're still directing me not to feel my feelings! I'm going to go eat and take a shower.

Good-bye, my love. Thanks for filling the bird feeder.

Saturday, May 11, 2002 – 10:50 p.m.

Dan the man back. You need to wait longer for me at the computer. You got impatient and I didn't have time to get "through." You know how much this drains you. And so do I, but you slept tonight.

Yeah, I "feel" you or something "achy" in my legs and hips. What is that? Or do you want to wait until tomorrow when I'm at the computer?

I could wait until tomorrow if you want. I looked forward to our date. But I see it's hard for you to have a date alone.

Dan, this is so hard. Suspended between two...worlds? I don't know if this makes me miss you more or less. <u>More</u> because you're so much more <u>there</u> – <u>present</u>, and you're DEAD! It's enough to make me crazy. I get the perfect husband – finally! And he's <u>DEAD</u> – not here, but talking to me all the time.

I can come back in the morning if you want. But I would like to stay. Be with you a while now. Just feel my love.

(But I was cranky, and he knew it.)
Be back tomorrow. I love you. I know this is hard for you and on you. Good-night my sweet Stephanie. You're made of strong stuff.

Sunday, May 12, 2002 – 6:38 a.m.

Dan the man here...see? It's not so hard.

Back to the session stuff. In the sessions we look – examine the lives we've lived and the challenges we created to test and grow. My challenge this time was to overcome some seriously bad habits. John Hannon (one of the alternative doctors) recognized them.

The blame "bad habit," was my big one. (One that you share, I might add, but you have been more successful in overcoming it.) I blamed you secretly for everything, once I had you. Just like I blamed my mother, and then Maggie.

Another bad habit was not "being present." And I have to work on that one again. Don't know what my "guides" have in store for me. But I have time.

I feel "less connected" doing this on the computer, Dan…

I'm in your legs, hips and stomach now. How connected do you need to be? Just trust it. You're not crazy. It's going to take real determination on your part to finish this book, and then take it out.

As I said, there's a group of us, trying to break down the walls that exist between the "two worlds." That's why there is such an *explosion* of this type of material now. You are not alone in this. The people who need to find this material will find it and it will comfort them and lead them to experience more directly their own source. It's a "tipping point" phenomenon. As I said last night, you're made of strong stuff, and surprise, surprise, you'll need to be.

This information – its accessibility is as old as the Nag Hamadi scrolls. It's what they are. Written in Aramaic. Just trust, my darling Stephanie, that where you need to be, you will be led. By me and by your own guides, who incidentally are less mad with me.

Last night, every time I woke up, I felt you, heard you there. Was that me? Was that you? I can't tell if I'm thinking about you on my own, or you're "with" me.

That was me watching you, wanting to be with you. Finally I did get into a dream. I'm practicing different techniques. I would have had sex with you, but you ran inside. The dream about the husband's basement office was a source of information. You will work with those girls again, and include their "experiences" in your book.

I'm going to go eat. Then come back and type up the Christmas Tree Story. (A children's story, "The Lopsided Little Christmas Tree," about a tree Dan loved.)

And not talk to me? I know it's frustrating to have me want to connect so much with you now that I'm gone. But I will be "gone" a very long time. _I'm here now_. Go eat, but come back. I'll wait. Then we'll go to the lake!

(I used to walk around Lake Hollywood everyday.)

Yes, go to the lake. I feel your body. Just one last thing, know that I love you. It doesn't matter where I am. Where you are. There's no righting the wrongs I've done to "us" just now. You should try to understand that you can forgive me easier if you try to…

My legs, ouch! What? I'm not trying? My heart breaks when I think of what might have been…what more can I do?

A date? Please? Time?

When I get home, maybe…if you're lucky.

There I am, flirting with my dead husband. Jeez.

***

At about this time, _The Lovely Bones_ topped the New York Times best-seller list. When I told people about Dan's "coming back" to me, they would tell me to read the book, because it's narrated by a murdered girl who's in the Inbetween (as she spells it). When I was finally able to read it, more than two years later, I found the book sweet and charming, despite its grisly murder. And then I heard an interview with Alice Siebold, the author, and she said, "The first chapter just came to me. Out of the blue."

That "group trying to break down the walls" seems to work hard.

Monday, May 13, 2002 – 6:27 a.m.
Last night I felt Dan with me, but I was so tired. Didn't even try to "communicate" formally – only heard his "date" request, but I couldn't. Sitting here waiting for Dan…can't hear/him feel him yet, but now my legs are beginning to hurt. Just got a "love blast."

Dan the man here – you felt that! Yes. I'm disappointed that we didn't connect last night, but you had no energy. I loved you all night long, though. And that does your body good. I know you miss my arms and my body.

But, oh baby, not half as much as I do! It breaks my heart when you smell my tee-shirts, yet fills me with wonder at how you still respond to my smell. I had no idea how much pleasure you got out of your nose. No wonder you don't need to eat!

Don't read over this stuff as I'm saying it, I lose my train of thought. It's not easy for me to do this, but we're getting better. I feel less drain on your body now.

Open your book file and work now…get the first part right. The "how this book evolved" part.

Then, out of nowhere, I heard Lynn's mom's voice, sounding very chipper.

Bea's here! I've got session to go to, and Bea welcoming! She's part of our cluster – like we didn't know that. Lynn is part too. I love you, my darling Stephanie.

What? Bea had _died_ and I could hear her?

Chapter Nine

Bea's Here! Death Experienced as Birth

Not only was I channeling my dead husband, but I could hear _other_ dead people? When would the guys in the white coats show up? Had Bea really died? I sat there wondering, filled with sorrow.

Bea was one of the most elegant, loving women I'd ever met – beautiful, with an adorable, impish smile. Her energetic sparkle infused everything she did; she was my idea of the perfect mom. But she'd been battling leukemia for more than five years, and I knew her fight was at its end.

I was only a month into channeling and even though it seemed authentic to me, my clinical, critical mind still stood aloof and whispered, "You might be going crazy, you know." One of the specific markers of schizophrenia is hearing "voices" in one's head, so I needed validation from Lynn. I'd wait for her call.

When Lynn called later on, she told me that Bea had indeed "died" – her heart stopped beating – but they brought her back. I told Lynn about hearing her mom's voice, and Dan's saying, "Bea's here!" We both laughed for the sheer weirdness of it all. "Dan's probably with you," I said, "because he's not with me."

"I know," she said. "I can feel him."

In life, Dan adored Lynn. Two weeks after he died, we threw together a beautiful memorial party. Or rather my friends did, since I was in no condition. I was stunned when more than a hundred people showed up, but there was food and champagne to spare, because Lynn produced the entire event. As Lynn said, "Never have an Armenian plan the food; we plan to feed people for a week – on a forced march." And that's a good thing.

For the memorial, Lynn also created four CDs of music to play. The Beatles' "Magical Mystery Tour" was the first song, followed by the Beach Boys' "Sail On, Sailor,". Each song progressed thematically, and ended with Beethoven's Ninth, followed by the Beatles "The End." Perfect musical choices. The day she chose the songs, Lynn told me that she felt Dan sitting with her. At the time, I thought, Oh, sure. I assumed she was delusional…turns out, she wasn't.

That night, I got into bed and tried to connect with Dan.

May 13, 2002 – 10:01 p.m.
So what happened with Bea?

She crossed. She was _here_. Then she went back. Apparently this happens a lot in hospital deaths.

But that was very interesting to experience from this side – the death, which for us over here is more like a birth. It's fraught with as much fear and trepidation as an "earth birth." Bea was a riot, though. She immediately became a very beatific angel. The outfit! You should have seen it! A fairy princess, Glenda-like get-up. Then she looked around and realized very fast that she was a little "overdressed."

And that in itself was very funny to hear, because for years in our little monthly goddess ceremony, we would do one final healing pink bubble and put Bea inside it, dressed as Glenda, the Good Witch of the North in "The Wizard of Oz." Bea knew about this in life, and apparently thought it the perfect way to dress for meeting her cluster mates. But now, in real time, Bea would stay with the living a few days longer.

In Dan's In Between world, there was a lot going on. Besides Bea's transition, his ex-wife and her husband Chris were in town. Dan said he needed to be with them to process old wounds, so he couldn't be with me. The next day would be my birthday, and I felt completely alone.

I'd lost my live husband, my dead husband was busy, and now it felt as if I was losing my stepson, Samuel, too. Lately, he seemed constantly annoyed with me, and just downright snappy, and it hurt my feelings. We'd never had a regular mother-son relationship; instead we were more like buddies. Our friendship was based on my willingness to listen to his problems, and then offer what I thought to be helpful advice.

After college, when Sam chose to teach English in Japan for two years, like clockwork, he'd call us either around midnight or at seven in the morning. The phone would ring and Dan would just hand it to me. "It's Sam. He needs advice." I was Sam's secret weapon with girls. Dan would listen and say, "I wish I'd had you on my side when I was his age!"

Then after Japan, when he didn't know which way to go career-wise, I called my agent and said, "I've got a tall, handsome stepson. Could he work in the mail room?" And he did for almost a year. Then Sam answered phones for a short, obnoxious agent, learned how to take abuse – an essential skill for working in the entertainment industry – and from there, he moved on to a television network, where he still works.

But now, when Sam called and wanted to talk about his mom's and stepfather's problems, I couldn't help him. He'd mention their names and I would fill up with a weird rage. I didn't understand it at all, since Maggie and Chris were always nice to me.

What was that about? I needed some answers from "Dan the man," so I sat at the front room table with pen in hand, looking out the window at the birds eating from the feeder he'd made.

Tuesday, May 14, 2002 (my birthday)
I feel Dan…now…

Dan the man…

> **Connection difficult. When you read the paper in the morning it fills your head with the pain of the world. It's a horrible thing to do to your system early in the morning.**
> **I would suggest that you cancel the paper, but I know you won't. I understand all too well, the need to "know" what's going on. Only that it's not at all what's going on. The dramas written about are so different from the "actual" dramas, that it's simply a monumental waste of time to read it, not to mention, _think_ about it. And that's not to mention the waste of all those trees! But trees grow again…your time, I keep reminding you, is finite.**
> **I'm in a bad mood. But Happy Birthday, my sweet Stephanie. Sorry I can't be there to cuddle your sweet body. Go write up the story. Work on your book. I can't talk now.**

I sat there miffed. He came back:

> **Oh, re: your reaction to Maggie and Chris? Yes, that was my fury that came through your body. Sorry. Didn't mean to do that to you. I'm not through "processing" all that.**

> **You know, yet you don't _know_ the whole story there. There's _much, much more_ to it than even I understood. You might want to make excuses not to see them.**

I thought, I don't want to make excuses…I'll tell them.

> **No, don't "tell them." They are very entrenched in their own drama right now. Just keep away from them. Especially Maggie.**

I'm worried about Sam. Thank you for picking up the baton. You were right about my competitiveness with him.

Dan constantly compared himself to Sam, as in, "I couldn't have done that at his age," and I would remind him that Sam had more conscious parenting than he'd had. Still, Dan seemed to walk on eggshells whenever he spoke to Sam. He'd hang up the phone, and I'd say, "You can stop auditioning. You got the job – you're his father."

I saw us as rivals. Yet my love for him was so strong, _too_ strong, really. I let his needs become paramount, and in the long run, it hurt me. Especially in relation to Maggie and Chris and me. But I feel you don't want to talk about that. You _feel_ my anger and I'm sorry. It's not yours. It's mine and I haven't finished the processing of it all. But I will. Anger is a tough emotion, and as you know, you literally see red. And when that red – that flash anger – invades your psyche, nothing good comes from it. But it's a dance of emotions, like that book that literally saved our marriage.

I have amends to make to Maggie, too. I'm sorry I didn't learn more from her, but she was less patient with me than you were. Once I became despotic, she let me know who was really the boss. And that's what soured us. But that's my business with her. Sorry...

Back to my business with you. Come back to me tonight. Right now, focus on the book. Write the intro part and spend the next two hours structuring it. It will fill you with a sense of accomplishment.

I am still in session up here. Learning the ways of communicating more clearly through you, with you. As I said, it seems to be a project our "cluster" has taken upon itself. You are only one of the many "teachers" burdened with this phase of delivering the information. I say burdened because, as you know, there is a lot of resistance.

Now go work, and my sweet Stephanie, I'm sorry again for all the time of our short life together I refused to let you "in."

So I went and worked on *The Married Girl's Guide to Hot and Sacred Sex.*

May 15, 2002 – 6:29 a.m.

Dan the man – Did I forget to say Happy Birthday yesterday? Well, I see I didn't. Good.

Back to your year: it depends, of course, entirely on you. But my sweet Stephanie, you listen. I need to focus. You need to get more sleep. I feel

your exhaustion from here. That's why I'm having trouble getting through. The mechanics of all this, as I said, are complicated.

I don't seem to be able to connect clearly. There's too much interference from other sources.

Later, I went to Tustin to see Dr. Bae. I love the Teaching Company's "Super Star Teachers" series and was listening to "The History of Western Thought," as I drove.

May 15, 2002 – evening
I filled up with mourning on the drive home from Dr. Bae's. A huge truck with GRIEF written in black block letters passed me. As I watched it go by, I burst into tears. Magical realism? I was listening to Michael Segrue talk about Meister Eckhart and mysticism, and that only made matters worse. Eckhart says that if you can get close enough to the godhead, the flicker – the spark, the light – then all wanting ceases and you are in commune. God is.

Dan the man feels your pain and I'm so sorry I can't make it better. The last three days have been very intense here. What with Bea's arrival so unsure, yet so assured. She lets go, then is brought back.

I think it will be final soon. I am on the team and need to be focused there. That's why you felt abandoned. (I know you hate that word.)

Oh, Dan. On top of everything else, I don't know that I'm not going crazy. Maybe this is all fantasy. My heart aches for this man who broke my heart.

Go read the letters…the love letters I wrote. That was the *real* me. That was the *me* who held you at night and that was the one who made love to the core of your *soul*. And we were lucky to have had the sheer grace and love that we did.

Ouch, my legs. Okay! I got it. I felt your anger and annoyance for my doubt. But my rational side needs – I don't know – validation of some kind.
Dan? I love you so much and I miss you! I miss you! I miss your smell, your voice….

I'm not gone. I just don't have the arms to hug you or the voice to tell you how much I love you. But now I have something far better. I have sight. *Clear sight*. I see what is real and our love was *real*. It's why you fought so hard for it. It's why you fought so hard for me.

See you in the morning. We're on a Bea Watch. I've been with Lynn a lot. Go walk.

There he was, still bossing me around. The "love letters" he refers to were usually my anniversary letters. He wrote this one for our ninth anniversary:

My Dear Sweet Wife

On this, our ninth year anniversary of our marriage, I've been promising you SOMETHING like this for a long time – over several milestones; and always I think of it amid the sturm und drung of daily frenzy – and I say wow, I don't have time – because to say what it is for me is too, too profound, deep, complex – unsayable, really – unless I have a big block of time to get it right – or just right. "Why," this male asks, "should I have to stop, pause, reflect – anyway. Isn't the fact of our living together and loving ENOUGH?" (This is the reactive /male side of the equation). On the one hand, too profound. On the other, why at all.

Thank you for insisting. You are goddess – privy to certain formal necessities of life of which I am only dimly aware – but without which the thin veneer of meaning-that-separates-us-from-chaos-called-civilization would quickly fade. It is sadly true that women are the keepers of the fire of civilization – which would quickly burn out were it not for you, the Goddess, protecting it.

You are my Goddess – my lover, my muse, my world-lens really, because being, living and, yes even fighting with you is nothing less than my being-lens. I see the world as mediated by you/thru/you – my lens. Hmm. Is that it?

I don't quite like that but it will have to do.

I just want to say "I love you" and "I love you" and really, words cannot say much more. But what can they? Mostly it's the being with you and the discovery of newness and freshness – I'm still amazedly delighted at the freshness of my feeling for you, re-birthed daily. I guess that's love. It's always the new little things, the nuances that constantly surprise me. Those can't be well said. Really unsayable. After nine great years. Thank you, thank you. I am truly blessed.

Do I need a great block of time to write my feelings well, or honor you; or just say how you are for me? No; just the open being necessarily forced from me when I must sit and commemorate you-us – Nine years. A moment. An eon.

Thank you. Thank you. Thank you my love for being with me. For trying. For coming back and staying with it. You are loved, and strong and beautiful and brave, and good and sweet. And cute. And funny...no rambling; only rumbling; humbling....

So You Whose Being is My Love

That illumes what you pass

It trembles with expectation

And possibility, given

Life

And In the Reflection, returned, the
Challenge, read; Fear born of
Self-Awareness – illumed by
You: Opportunity in the Duality
becoming, given
Life.
So, when you move, you are;
Galaxies born and worlds give
Birth. And when you laugh, the
Fear is gay and bright and undone.
And I, a man, am blessed and
Here, I am, I fly, given
Life. You.
Love, Dan 12/30/98

* * *

That was my "live Dan." Now back to our correspondent from the In Between:

May 16, 2002

**Dan the man reporting in. Today is busy. Don't have much time to talk/be
with you. Talk to me later. I am still madly, deeply, weepily in love with
you. You "got" that. Love you…Me.**

That night Lynn called to tell me that Bea had died.

May 16, 2002 – 10 p.m.

Dan the man here with you.
**What a day! To be here to welcome Bea was very intense. She had a team of her
component cluster-mates. I was included because I was most familiar to the
earth entity. The dying was quite elegant. She just let go. Lynn was there at
the end. (You're too tired to do this. Tomorrow, OK?)**
I love you. I don't need to talk now.

May 17, 2002 – 6 a.m.
*Bea finally died yesterday, after going back and forth a few times. Lynn called and said
how really beautiful it was to be with her. She sat and held her hand, and read from
the Tibetan Book of the Dead.*
Listening to the doves now, feel Dan in my legs, in my chest…in my…

Dan the man reporting from the front. Yesterday was so busy! I tried to tell you last night but the sheer enormity of what I had to say was too much for your energy to take in.

Bea's "death" was difficult for us here. But since it is my first, the first one that I directly participated in, it was exhilarating. The process of helping her through and out – very interesting. She is still "focused" on earth now. She'll be there for awhile.

I don't feel a good connection here.

(So I went to the dining room table.)

Friday, May 17, 2002 – 6:30 a.m.

Dan the man here. To continue about Bea. She "stayed" four days longer to give everyone a chance to get used to the idea that she was indeed going. Lynn is now too busy to feel the pain. But she will. As usual, let her lead. You'll help by example.

As for us, my sweet Stephanie, our love life together was only a part of our work together and yet for me, it's what I loved the most. Only part of our life, but the most important aspect. That's *why* I had to come back and make that right again. Because in my dying, I *destroyed* your belief in our love as a couple. Believe now in the truth of what we created.

When we were good, we were great.

I won't leave for a while. But eventually I will need to "move on." That doesn't mean that I won't be with you again. It just means focus.

Is the "colored" stuff in the book correct? Do "spirits" have different color vibrations?

(The book, *Journey of Souls*, arrived on my doorstep two months after Dan died, sent by an old acquaintance. I'd constantly "hear," "Go to the Bodhi Tree," but I couldn't get myself to go.)

Yes and no. Color is a matter of eyes and sight. We "see" differently. I can "see" when I'm "with" you. That is my *energy* you feel in your legs and eyes.

I heard him say, "Go put on your glasses so I can see the birds more clearly." But I didn't want to.

You are so stubborn about glasses.

So I looked up and focused on the birds dive-bombing each other at the feeder.

I stand corrected. You actually see quite clearly when you focus.
Love is eternal and yet so easily ignored.

Friday, May 17, 2002 – 10:38 p.m.

Went to a book signing at the Bodhi Tree book store tonight. Turns out I knew the author; she once took me to her "Dream Weaver" group. Her book: Dreams Are Letters from the Soul.

> **Dreams Are Letters from the Soul – written in a _foreign language_. The soul has other ways to communicate.**

Just before Dan died, he'd done a dissolution of partnership for Suzy Prudden, who owns Positive Changes Hypnosis in Beverly Hills. She'd sent him an e-mail that said she was doing a hypnotherapist training. Dan gave it to me and I started working there as a hypnotherapist, on December 18, 2001. He died eight days later, but I've worked there ever since. The job actually saved my life because it gave me perspective. I was not the only person in pain. I was working with people in just as much pain as I was, only they hadn't just lost their husbands, they'd lost themselves instead. And over the past four years, I've helped many kind souls find themselves again.

Still, at that time, I was in active mourning, but Dan couldn't figure out why. It was just like in our life together, he hated it when I had emotions.

Saturday, May 18, 2002 – 6:15 a.m.

> **Dan the man – needs to talk to you. The point of power really is in the present, and the emotions you manufacture now will affect both your future and your past.**
> **The reason I died so early was a direct result of all those negative emotions.**

Wait a minute. I thought you said it was a "planned exit."

> **It was, but only after I had damaged my healthy body with all that bullshit brooding. Don't make the same mistake and stay in the _sorrow_ of my death**

for too much longer. Your body is fragile and even though you take care of it exceedingly well, the *grief* is so draining.

Flip the grief to gladness. I am not gone. And even though you miss "me," you don't miss the man who died. That wasn't me. I lost myself when I chose to put Sam's best interests over my own.

But I did that many, many years ago. I see a way now that I might have fulfilled my potential, but it would have meant leaving Mendocino years earlier.

Water under the bridge.

My choices were *mine*. And ultimately Sam and you were my big gifts. Sam is a wonder to watch and continues to give me much joy. Your love for him is so pure and strong that it scares him. Your love for me was/is still the source of my life. That concept is difficult to convey.

But love is eternal. As I said last night, and it is the love you feel for me right now, which will help you heal. Knit the huge hole in your soul back together.

I need to walk.

I love you from afar
I love you from near
I love you from deep inside
I love you.

Give me Saturday night. Sit with me on the couch. Let me love you. It's a date, my sweet Stephanie and I will look forward to it.

I sat there and read what he'd said. He might have fulfilled his potential? What did he mean? That if he had chosen to do what was best for him, instead of always putting Sam's needs first, he might have done what?

One of the reasons I could marry Dan as quickly as I did, was that when I asked him about why he'd done anything, he'd answer, "For Sam." Why had he continued to live with Maggie and Chris as a threesome? "For Sam." Why did he go to law school in Sacramento? "For Sam." And I thought, "What a good man, what a good father." But now, what did it all mean?

I didn't have time to think about it since I had to rush off to work, and pretend to be a normal person who wasn't channeling her dead husband.

Later that night, however, something stranger than either hearing from Dan or Bea would happen. Something that would utterly transform my perspective and completely change my life from that moment on.

Chapter Ten

Who the Hell is Enoch?

When I got home from work I was tired and cranky, but since Dan had asked to have a date, I obliged my dead husband, sat down on the couch, pen in hand.

Saturday, May 18, 2002 – 7:30 p.m.
I'm exhausted – worked too hard. Wanted to feel good enough to go to the party, but I don't.

You don't want to go to the party. You're tired because you didn't work on your book today. Dan the man needs to be with you tonight. Light a fire and read poetry.

I must have grumbled to myself, and he shot back…

You can do what you want – I just wanted to sit on the couch with you.

Okay. I'm just tired. Tonight, thought I'd just go to sleep – I'm so sad. I just felt your energy pull back when I thought, "or I could watch TV!"
Did I hurt your feelings? Sorry. But you have to understand how weird this is for me, Dan. To have my husband back, yet not have him.

Look, life's more multi-dimensional than even you suspected. I can enjoy the fire and be close to you and make up for some of the missed opportunities.
The energy in your legs, hips, and stomach is indeed from me. It's focused. The music is too distracting.

(I got up, and turned it off.)

You are truly a kind soul – not a good speller, but a kind soul. Dan humor.

(I can't spell because I'm dyslexic.)

Are you still "Dan?"

To you I am. I am more than Dan, but my Dan-ness is very fresh, and I am still processing it.

I'm processing our Dan and Stephanie "ness" – and trying to gain more clarity on my own determined resolve not to let you affect or change me. When it was precisely because I _needed_ your energy – enthusiasm – that I married you. Go figure.

To "make up" is impossible, but to make it better is not. It's why you need to let me continue to bug you about the book and the schedule.

I don't mind. I just seem more tired lately. Don't know if it's the schedule change or just me.

There was a long pause, and I thought I'd lost connection.

Are you still here?

I'm here. I'm just sad, too. I'm so afraid you won't give me another chance.

Dan, I never thought of marrying anyone else but you…

Suddenly, I felt my energy shift, and then my handwriting changed completely. It got fast, slanted, determined, and I felt a sharp rip of anger.

My oversoul steps up to the plate here:

__There are no guarantees.__ The betrayal of our agreement was so profoundly dismaying to me that I didn't know what to do. I almost couldn't believe it. I had waited all those years for you to finally arrive, and then you come with all that infantile behavior and attitude.

We could have been sheer bliss together. We had the goods, Enoch. We had the goods!

I sat there, stunned, looking down at the writing.

Okay. I give up. Who the hell is Enoch?

Enoch is Dan's oversoul or that's my name _here_. My Dan-ness is only a part of Enoch, yet Enoch is me. Your oversoul is Boooo… can't get through any longer.

(But my "oversoul" could.)

No, but you (meaning me, Stephanie) get to continue on with this one (life) without having to play wet-nurse any longer. The sheer nerve! Well, now I'm mad!

Enoch and I have been "partners" for a very long time. We usually come in as friends, but this time we decided to be lovers. And I would be a girl – you. I'm not usually a girl. I'm usually a guy – that's why you like being a girl so much. You revel in your girl-ness. You always have, but that's also why when you saw there were no girls playing drums (in the Rose Parade marching bands, when I was seven) you were furious. You would show them.

That's why you drove a cab so easily. And well, I might add.

Now you need to focus on you. Let Enoch go off and lick his wounds. You loved him, helped him and would have died for him. Actually, you almost did. The nerve of him! Letting you take those drugs, knowing he didn't want that baby.

That "baby," by the way, was furious – still is, in a way. Other plans had to be made. But they didn't include you directly. Lily and Athena (my neice) are both aspects of your daughter, but that doesn't make up for not being a mother yourself.

Then I asked more questions until…

Dan the man back. Phew!!! He is mad. I don't blame him. But you, Stephanie, my sweet Stephanie, still have our love. Don't doubt it.

And then I just crashed – fell right to sleep on the couch.

When I woke up, I read over what was written. I understood what had happened, but I still needed to make rational sense of it.

Sunday, May 19, 2002

What's going on? I'm channeling Dan one minute, then my own angry oversoul the next? And it all just wipes me out!

Dan the man – believe this is so. Believe this is authentic. You're not going mad. You're just opening up. Too intense for you. I have to go.

He'd come like that – like he was "checking in" to say "Hi," before going off to do whatever else he had to do in the In Between.

Monday, May 20, 2002

Dan the man here. This weekend I was with Sam and Maggie and Chris. A lot. Not with you. We hashed out old wounds, and I got some clearance vis-à-vis my own part in that trashy drama.

The pain I repressed for all those years. What a waste! Sam had a lot of trouble with it all and it will be better for you if you don't say anything about it. He is very protective of his mom.

So I followed Dan's advice and tried not to say anything more to Sam. I'd spent far too much of my time and energy processing that drama as it was.

***

As I said, in mid-March I started working with Aliah, a grief healer. By late May, I'd seen her a few times, and when I told her about my channeling Dan, she wanted me to connect with him while she was in the room, and so I did:

Dan the man here – Aliah's talking and I hear her and I see the scope of the work set out before us all. It's a lot to do, but as a team it can be done easier than anyone can do it alone. I can do this faster on the machine.

So I sat down at Dan's computer in the living room and Aliah asked questions.

May 20, 2002

Dan the man reporting for duty – (I could just see him saluting.) **In this environment we have different agendas. I think we've already established that. Your agenda was to love me and mine was to love you. That's an example of a simple agenda. Up here, different agendas demand more energy.**

Your love for me is still so strong; it's what permits this connection to occur. Yet, as Aliah pointed out, you are easily swayed by my needs. Even now.

As I said earlier the cluster we belong to is a teaching cluster, and we are involved in getting this information out. It's coming from lots of directions, so you are not alone in its transmission. You are only a tiny cog in a giant wheel, but you are needed.

Your oversoul is named Barushe – and Enoch and Barushe will oversee this small portion of the project. Transformation is a very long, very tedious affair.

Think of water wearing away a mountain, as opposed to dynamite. Just as effective, but far less destructive. An organic change is occurring. I say this all just so that

you understand your place in the adventure. There will, at some point, be a tipping point, but that unfortunately will happen after you are finished.

Aliah to Dan...
What is your function in this project?

My function is to serve as a conduit of information.

What has been the historical role of Enoch?

Enoch plans the comings and goings of many – I hesitate to use the word "soul" because it's not a clear enough word.

Re: Aliah's take on "Enoch." It's a partial understanding, but Enoch/Dan goes and comes to earth quite often. The "Dan entity" had just so much potential that it was disturbingly disappointing to Enoch and to Dan. It was impossible to fix in transmission, impossible to fix with helpers.

The stubbornness of the Dan entity was frustrating, to say the least.

Enoch here. My work in the historical sense is to continue to try and "get through" and I do manage from century to century. I manage within the context of the centuries' prejudices and phobias. I manage. Thomas Aquinas was a channel, as was Meister Eckhart. The clearness of the message is present in poetry. The transmission...

(But Aliah cut him off.)

What's the purpose of the Enoch/Dan journey to Earth? What's the body of work that you're engaged in right now? What are you trying to accomplish?

Dan back – I don't know yet. I'm still in training, but because I was able to communicate so directly with you, we are partners in the endeavor. I will be a part of the book you are writing when you write it. It contains much of the information that will be delivered in a form that many people, who would otherwise not be attracted to the material, will read.

They will read your book, because it will have to do with sex, and getting more out of the sacred connection. That is only a beginning. But it is a beginning.

After that, there are many books to come and we are all on the project. But Stephanie's health is a problem, in that she isn't the strongest tree in the forest. The production of the books will take up much energy, but the publicity will take up more. It all has to be done.

The books await. Just make sure you arrive at the "work place" with your hard hat and lunch!

Aliah to Enoch...Enoch, please help us understand the work and the purpose of the work?

The purpose of the work is multifold. First, establishing the direct give-and-take between the two worlds is our ultimate goal. Direct, without all the garbage that "religions" foist onto it. The "creator" does not need sacrifice, worship and adoration. The give-and-take within and between the two worlds seeks to be more joyous and filled with not so much serious self-importance.

This work seems to attract a lot of self-important people who look down on those "less enlightened" souls. But sometimes those less enlightened souls are actually more enlightened because they simply have the ability to enjoy the sunrises and sunsets of this particularly exquisite planet.

Back to point: forgive me. There is nothing wrong with "materialism," and I feel you don't approve. Yet, poverty is not blessed.

(I could feel the frustration with Aliah's somewhat pious and self-righteous attitude. Then Aliah asked about the "clearing" of negative emotions.)

The overview of the work is quite simple. Don't make it fancy. Emotions don't need to be cleared. Emotions come and go. The intuitive grace that each soul down there already owns needs to be sparked. And the spark comes from many different forms. That is, a match that lights a forest fire is just as effective as a lightning bolt. The lightning bolt is more dramatic, but the match is easier to come by. Be satisfied with a match. Be satisfied with your own divine connection, and by example, your match lights a forest fire, (metaphorically speaking).

In the spirit world there must be a kind of one-upmanship, and I felt as if I'd just gotten hit with it. Aliah, like everyone else on this "exquisite planet," has her own guides, and dealing with all that energy at once left me feeling dizzy, exhausted and sucked dry. As I stood up from the computer, I wondered where I would find the energy to lead a hypnotherapy session at work. But I had no time to think, since I was already late, and I rushed off to work.

Tuesday, May 21, 2002
Yesterday I had a session with Aliah that entailed my channeling Enoch and it wiped me out. Can feel Dan around now. His "energy" is so different from Barushe's and Enoch's.

Tuesday, May 21, 2002 – 7:38 a.m.

From Dan the man. Thought you'd never sit down! That channeling yesterday was too much for your body. Don't do that again. Let Aliah serve you, don't serve her. You are paying for help, not paying to be drained.
Barushe wants to talk to you.

To be able to dance with your soul you will have to be much more careful about the way you use your time. You seem not to understand the value of the time you give away. You must not "give away" any more time. Be a miser with it.

The work you do at Positive Changes doesn't feel to you to be worthwhile, and yet it is. Those souls that you connect with, as I'm sure you noticed, showed up to hear from you directly. More souls will come to hear from you. Give them what you have to offer. It is of service.

*But your real work is still in the books. We have been trying to get through to you for many, **many** years, but you have been busy with other concerns.*

Your career as a screenwriter might have given you the opportunity to flourish, but there were other "things" which stopped that from going forward. I won't blame Enoch or Dan, but he contributed. You, however, acquiesced. I feel you miss "Dan" and yes we are always in partnership with him.

***

So I'm struggling to write *The Married Girl's Guide to Hot and Sacred Sex*, but at the same time, coming to grips with the facts that:

- I'm channeling my dead husband;
- My oversoul is mad at his oversoul; and
- I have to "keep working" or I won't survive.

No one, however, wants to hear anything at all about this. Not even Samuel. He tells me that he's having trouble processing this "alternative reality" business, and he doesn't want to hear any more about what "Dan" says to me. He wants to remember Dan the way he was in life. And I couldn't blame him one bit.

But I needed to talk to someone about what was happening, because it was so intense. I needed to see what other people thought. And I found out fast. Most people assumed I'd gone completely over the edge. So Dan would try to comfort me:

(And you're not crazy or self-delusional, despite what most people will think. You're going to have to go it alone.)

I was so lonely in my little world, even though Dan continued to encourage me to go on with the book.

Wednesday, May 22, 2002

Dan the man here. The table of contents is important to get down, not so much for me, as for you and the "helpers." And there are helpers. As I said, all writing is channeled. That's why it's important to show up at the computer at roughly the same time. The sooner you can get yourself into your habit of the work, the work will get easier. You have too much to do to waste time, but I've said that. If I knew how little time I had, I wouldn't have wasted a single minute of it in front of that damned TV! My regrets are many, but my biggest regret is not honoring our time together. But I know you "get" the love when I send it. I know you smile and feel it.

Stay focused. This is not easy. Pick up the thoughts. Go to work.

Thursday, May 23, 2002 – 5:08 p.m.
First time today I sat down at the computer.

Dan the man here –

Thanks for coming in here. The achiness is the result of the channeling and that's why it's important for you to keep up with the walking, swimming and yoga...not that I have to tell you to exercise. Your body is still in mourning; don't get frustrated with the exhaustion.

Anything else?

You need to just be patient. I'm thinking... I'm....

I'm going to go print out and see what...Ouch! (I felt a sharp jab.)

The plan for us evolves still. The love you still feel for me creates a bridge that connects us, and I am so grateful. It sustains me. The farther I get from the earth plane reality, the more difficult it is for me to understand my own behavior...but who cares now?

The only gift I can continue to give to you is my shots of love and this connection with this interesting "world."

It's a world where nothing is hidden, so because of that, it's amusing as hell. My own fear of seeming foolish made me so stiff. That's how you differ – you're right out there. You have no fear. You actually are fearless. It was my fear that permeated the house. And fear is palpable. Dogs can smell it...

(And so can human beings.)

I worked on Saturdays, so juggling his needs with my own was difficult. I lived alone, but it felt as if I still had the demanding husband I had in real life. Only now he'd wake me up in the middle of the night, wanting to chat, and I was not pleased. Notice the time below:

Saturday, May 25, 2002 – 2:44 a.m.
What?

Dan the man – I want to say how much I love you. I know you still feel it throughout the day. The reason you're awake now is I wanted to talk to you. The business of the day makes it hard to connect.

My business, as well as your own. I am still processing my "Dan" life. It is quite a trip to watch it go by so fast – and yet it was long.

The happiness we shared in the moments I allowed it to enter my awareness, stand out as if in relief.

The most remarkable thing about watching and analyzing my life from this aspect of reality is that it makes me wonder what I was always so worried about. I really had it quite easy.

I think that's why you were so angry with me so much of the time. You _knew_ how easy I'd had it and still I wouldn't enjoy life....

(He was right. I couldn't understand why he complained about almost everything. From my point of view, he had that spectacularly amazing body, good, caring parents and a son who loved him. What more did he expect?)

...you always _knew_ what I looked like – that's why when I showed up at the door that October night, you got so nervous and flighty.

I see us both so young and oh! Not now! Not now!

I started to cry because I saw exactly what he saw: us – two strangers, recognizing each other instantly on that night that led me to where I sat now – longing for a man who had betrayed me, who had betrayed us, and whom I still loved.

Look to tomorrow and _enjoy_, my sweet Stephanie. I love you. Good-bye for now. (3:24 a.m.)

Chapter Eleven

Soul Paths
or
Let Me Get This Straight

The more comfortable I became with the channeling, the braver I became about sharing my experience. For instance, as I stood in the checkout line at Trader Joe's, I'd start to chat with the person next to me and I'd ask if anyone had ever come back to them. They'd look around furtively and say, "How did you know?" Amazingly, almost everyone confessed to having a similar experience to my own.

For instance, a fellow Los Angeles County Museum of Art (LACMA) docent and Honors English teacher told me about her husband of forty years who'd come back to her. She said he sat at the foot of her bed and they chatted for hours, then he was gone. Like a lot of people, she didn't tell anyone for fear they would think she'd gone around the bend. All it took for me to hear her story and others like it, was a willingness to share my own experience and ask about theirs.

The only person who didn't want me to talk about Dan's coming back was Sam. And he certainly didn't want me to tell people that he was "hearing" from his dad, but since I didn't see him much, it didn't come up often. Now, the only time I'd hear from him would be on his morning drive to work. He'd be stuck in traffic, so he'd call to complain about his life. Then he'd be almost to Fox Studios, and he'd ask, "So what are you doing?"

"Working on my book."

"What book?"

"The Married Girl's Guide to Hot and Sacred Sex."

"Oh."

And then he'd go on about some trauma having to do with the problematic personality disorders who produce "Cops," or the smart-assed Harvard guys who write "The Simpsons." The next time he'd call, the conversation would go much the same way.

"And what are you doing?"

"Writing my book."

"What book?"

Until it finally dawned on me that he was exactly like his dad – for all his good and all his bad.

"Dan the man," however, continued to want to have dates, and kept waking me up in the middle of the night to chat. It's no wonder my journals are filled with my saying how exhausted I felt all the time.

Dan urged me to keep reading *Journey of Souls* by Michael Newton, the hypnotherapist who regresses clients to recall their In Between memories. A few clients told him about the "making of objects," (an In Between activity) and about the "hierarchy of souls" by colors. They said that "Baby Souls" are white. Then there's a progression that goes from off-white with yellow or gold flecks, on to gold. Then gold with blue flecks or streaks, to blue with yellow flecks, then to pure blue. Then the blues go on to purples in the same sort of progression.

I read over these sections and wanted to see what Dan had to say.

Sunday, May 26, 2002 – 8:30 p.m.

Dan the man here – you sweet thing. I had a busy day. The making of objects took almost all my attention – what you just read was no coincidence.

What color are you now?

White with flecks of yellow.

How about Enoch?

White with flecks of yellow. I am Enoch – Enoch _is_ me. But that's why I write "Dan the man." It's my Dan-ness you remember. It's my Dan-ness you miss.

I began to cry, and when I cried, he couldn't get through my emotion. I felt his annoyance.

Don't cry.

It's 5 months today, Dan. I still find it weird that 1) you're gone and 2) you're back. Of course, I doubt this every so often. And yet this is so real to me.

It's real to me – but not at all weird. The weird thing seems to be your life now.
(All I did was go to work, go to yoga, and come home. Period.)

But as I said, your body is still in shock and that's why you're tired. But you're in bed and that's good.

Did you listen to those "History of Philosophy" tapes?

Some. Nietzsche was/is destructive garbage. Wish I'd never read him. Glad you didn't.
The philosophers I think people on this plane think the most of are Emerson, Dostoyevsky and Blake.
Dostoyevsky especially – Prince Mishkin was always a favorite of mine and yours too. But I don't think we ever discussed *The Idiot*.

That was so odd. Because he was right – I loved Dostoyevsky – I loved *The Idiot*, yet we'd never talked about it.

Take care.

Hey! Wait. Have you seen Bea?

Just at her arrival. She's busy with Arch and Steve.

(Her husband and son.)

What color was she?

Yellow with flecks of blue. You're blue with flecks of yellow.

I could feel his energy pull back, as if his face scrunched up – just like in life when he had to admit I was right about something. I smiled.

Oh?

(Begrudgingly…)

Yes. You are more advanced than me. That's why I had such a bad time adjusting. I "came in" with a teacher – you – then refused to be taught.
We both sat with that, and silently acknowledged how much that one sentence explained the dynamics of our relationship. In our life together, I felt compelled

to share what I knew – what I had learned – but he simply refused to listen. Since there was no fixing it now, I just sighed and changed the subject.

If I've been in training for 30 years, training for what?

To do the job of opening more the door of awareness.

And I do that with my book?

Yes.

Oh, great! I filled with frustration because I was having such a tough time writing it. First off, I was a screenwriter. What did I know about writing a book? Not one thing. Second, writing a book about sacred sex and marriage was a real challenge, considering I'd only recently discovered that my own marriage had almost killed me. So I changed the subject again.

What did you do all day?

There are meetings to go to.

What kind of meetings?

The groups – clusters – get together and discuss work. Everyone is very excited that I can have such a clear access to you.

How did I get those books? (Journey of Souls and Destiny of Souls)

Complicated, but in a nutshell she (my friend, Carol) **got _blasted_ with energy to send them. You didn't go to the Bodhi Tree when you wanted.**

How many people in your cluster?

People is the wrong word. _Entity_ – soul – better and even that's a hard concept to convey.
There are eight in our cluster. You are part of one. I am part of another. We are component parts of a unit. The unit as a whole has goals and objectives. You are important now that you can communicate with me, and I can convey the information to you.

Please try not to let yourself fall into the depression of today. Your _body_ can't tolerate it.

(I thought about how lonely I was.)

How can you be lonely? I'm here with you! I really am. I'm so much more "here" now than when my body was there. I love you truly, madly, deeply. Don't worry – you'll use your talent.

I went to bed and had vivid, weird dreams. When I woke at 6 a.m., I touched base with Dan, but he urged me to use the computer.

Tuesday, May 28, 2002 – 7:41 a.m.

Jeez! It takes you forever to settle down. Been waiting here to talk to you.

As I was saying last night, the meeting had to do with this – my ability to communicate with you so directly. My only concern is your body. The feeling you get when writing (by hand) is more comforting, but this is no less authentic.

Re: the dream. As I said, dreams are not reliable forms of communication. Too much garbage in garbage out stuff. You pick up too much in the frequencies anyway, that's why your dreams are particularly weird.

I started thinking of all the years I was a part of Jungian dream analysis workshop at UCLA's Neuropsychiatric Institute (NPI) – were all those hours wasted? Dan forced me back.

To do this, you've got to learn to stay on one channel and focus. Don't go wandering around your own head looking for distractions. This isn't easy for us to do either. It's a specific talent that many groups master but it takes a confluence of occurrences. Things have to mesh just so for it to be understood. Keep reading those books – all of them.

As for us, make the Yosemite collage...

(I'd taken pictures at Yosemite to make a collage but the photos still sat in a box.)

...and move through the mourning process. You need to put it behind you. I can't apologize anymore than I have. The foolishness of my "Dan" self annoys the shit out of me.

I know you're going to go to yoga, walk, come back and work. Talk to me then. Feel my love...

Anything else you want to say? If you're still around?

Just to let me spend time with you. The whole Dan...the Enoch Dan as well. It's the least I can do.

When do you want to spend time?

Tonight. Go work now. I love you, my sweet Stephanie...read my letters. Remember our bliss.

I had gone out to dinner with my friend Robert, who owned an upscale flower shop in Bel Air. He chatted about his fabulously famous clients, but I wasn't interested.

Wednesday, May 29, 2002 – 7:40 a.m.
The alarm went off at 5:30, but I was in the middle of a dream and didn't want to get up. Got up at 6, and God knows where the time goes. Dinner last night with Robert at Chaya off Robertson was tedious. Or am I jealous of all the famous people he talks about with their glamorous, successful lives? I don't know. All I know is that I shouldn't eat bread. My hands hurt.

Dan the man here – takes you too long to get to the computer. Tomorrow just eat and get in here. You don't have time to waste. Robert's chatter annoyed you because he never talks about what's actually going on with him. But then, he can't. He's scared to death and the anxiety makes him crazy. You offered to hypnotize him and you should. Make him a tape to go to sleep on.
Now on to your work.

Are you gone?

The schedule has to be taken more seriously. I can't wait around for you to settle down. You feel my annoyance and it's not that simple. Others affected. But go to work, I meant on your book. Tonight, if you get into bed early enough – or come back to the computer – as it is, your day is jammed. But there is a lot of work to get done. So begin.
I love you, but see in you the same lack of respect for the time of your life that I had.

Now, it's one thing to get scolded by a live person, but quite another to get scolded from the "In Between." Later on that night, I checked in again.

Wednesday, May 29 – 9:50 p.m.

You said tonight and now you're tired. I can't believe how much I miss you sometimes.

What did you do today?

The plan was to begin to look at options for my next incarnation, but the guides thought that it would be better that I stay connected with you for a while longer. I have time to choose my next learning experience.

But as I channeled I could feel his energy focus itself inside my body. He wanted to have sex. So once again, I obliged my dead, horny husband.

Hope that was good for you…

Dan the man here and grateful. You felt me asking and you gave me what I wanted. You amazing thing. You are one in a million or more.
You don't realize how hard this is on your body, my sweet Stephanie. I'm so deeply in love with you.

And I fell asleep. The following morning I woke from a long, involved dream. I wrote it down then checked back in with him.

Thursday, May 30, 2002 – 6:24 a.m.
Dan? You around?

Dan the man here. The computer is so much easier to communicate through. The writing takes up so much energy to coordinate you, me, your impulses, and muscles. This way I "feed" the thought, and you just type.

I miss you…

I know and you will, and I miss you. But we're not "over." (And you're not crazy or self-delusional despite what most people will think.) You're going to have to go it alone.

You woke up a lot last night because I was up. Busy...wanted to reach you. And I forget about sleeping now. We don't sleep. No need to renew the body. No body to renew.

Anything you want to say? Tell me before I go to work.

Only that I love you. Write me in for Sunday night...in ink. And don't forget. Sit with me. I know it's "Six Feet Under," but sit with me. Here.

Are you really ready to reincarnate?

No. I'm not even done processing the last life. Although, I've made the amends I need to. I've had quite a time with Bonnie. (His sister.) **She's very obtuse, refuses to hear me. Ignores me completely. Just like life! Oh well, I tried.**

Use your energy right now on you, my sweet Stephanie. You don't have much time to finish this and you don't have spare energy. You know that. Take care.

The love you feel for me throughout the day feeds my soul so sweetly. When you touch "my nose" on the photos as you pass, it breaks my heart, but I feel the love.

Hurry...go to work. Talk to you later.

And I got another love blast from the In Between.

Friday, May 31, 2002 – 6:12 a.m.

Dan the man here – finally. Feel the time constraint of the day already. The pages need to be written, so I don't have much time to chat.

Thank you for yesterday. Love is the only thing I can give you, and as it turned out, the only thing I ever had to give you. I'm sorry I didn't let you hold me longer. But that's over. For now.

Sit with me Sunday night. On the couch. Read poetry. Love, me.

But that night was Friday, and Sam and I took my eight-year-old nephew Max to a Dodger's baseball game. A young Latino family sat directly in front of us, a tattooed dad in a tank top with his beautiful, golden-eyed wife, his mom and two cute kids – a five-year-old boy and a three-year-old girl. The plump grandmother, who was about my age, did the grandmother job of hugging the kids and buying them candy. I watched the tough biker-guy as he gazed down at his son with such love, and I filled with longing for never having had any part of that equation.

Saturday, June 1, 2002 – 6:00 a.m.

Dan the man – my perception of the game was so different from yours because mostly I was with Sam. He loves the game and you don't. The passion for anything is what creates value.

The Valentine you read yesterday and this morning filled me with such _shame_, because as I wrote them I knew they were only partly true. I knew I held out the best from you. Once again, said one thing, did another. It's how I kept you tied to me – connected.

The Valentine he refers to has a little lock on its front, and inside Dan wrote:

Dearest Stephanie
My love who has the key to my heart. Valentine's Day to be marked. Thanks for teaching me that love must be marked. That is an important way it is lived. But if it's good, it flows on almost continuously – and when momentarily lost in the mud and mists, almost immediately and always – at the moment of willing, gushes out oblivious of time. And fixes on You.
I love you because you instantly respond to my deepest challenge to myself to open my Self to You.
Happy Valentine's Day '98
Me

When I say you could have left, it's not really true. Too many mixed messages from me. But now the love I feel is far more authentic – less manipulative. My love for you was about me. If you read, it's always how you made me become more of me. Now my love is about you.

I stand in awed gratitude for the heroic run at the end of that particular "game." Even though it seemed as if we lost the game, we didn't. We won. Because now I sense your love so much more directly than I did when you just wanted to be held longer. Why I had to jump out of bed so fast after making love to you is beyond my comprehension.

Just know that those words express what I felt, even though I wasn't always as impeccable as I might have been.

Come with me now and look. See.

I can't see. Only lights. And space. I need to focus on being here now anyway. Thank you for Sam. If he weren't somewhat validating my experience of you, I would think this was all nuts.

You need to jump in this particular pool – both feet first. _You can't keep doubting_. Let others have their words, but know if you're honest, some people will respond.

Some won't be able to, but who cares? You only need to reach those who are ready to hear.

Anything else?

Just that the work you do has to come from passion – the passion of getting it done is what will sustain you.

I love you.

You don't need to tell me, but it's nice to hear. It's my own cavalierness that still upsets me. But hey, too late. Go. Love, me.

Then he would be gone and I'd be left to survey the disaster area that was now my life. In movies it's the "So, let me get this straight" moment. It's when the hero spells out precisely what we've just watched happen on-screen. For me, it was: I get the love of my life. Only he keeps me waiting twenty years. He asks me to marry him with the promise of a baby, but when I get pregnant, he doesn't want it. I choose my marriage over my career, but his love was really only about him? Excuse me?

To put it mildly, I teetered on the edge of despair and sometimes I would fall headfirst into the pit. Especially on Sundays.

Sunday, June 2, 2002
I went down with mourning…I couldn't move.

Dan here – your pain hurts so much. Let me help you make it through this tough patch. The point of power is really in the present – stay focused.

Monday, June 3, 2002
I'm extremely depressed once again and I know it's not very helpful to be miserable. But I just am. What is the truth of what is happening? I don't have a clue.…

Dan the man can't make the computer connection work. You're too sad and the energy is off. Please don't feel so alone in the world. You will only damage your body further. The time you have left is limited so make the most of the present. The future is now.

Our life together was so painful for you precisely because I focused on the future, refused to feel my own pain, and blamed you for feeling _trapped_ in the present. No way you could win. No wonder you wanted out. But your _determined optimism_ held on.

Then you just couldn't figure out what to do when you lost your health. And you did. Dr. Jerry saw that I was not going to be involved with you...

I can't even remember when this was?

You were so _determined_ that you almost died. Your kidneys were failing because of those toxic hormones. Even now the damage from that time still lingers in your body. That's why you wanted those string beans. It would help if you actually ate them.

That was a little snippy, I thought. The "string beans" comment refers to the Bieler Broth, but the thought of eating it again was too much to bear.

I know this is hard for you. But what isn't? You expected so little from me, but I gave you even less.

The only way out for you now is doing the most you can with what you have left. You can choose to be miserable today and be absolutely justified because in point of fact you did set up some pretty tough obstacles – or you can _choose to change the body chemistry_ and realize that you can fix this.

Go walk – make the toxins leave and then come back and work. Let me love you. Let me try to make this better.

Wednesday, June 5, 2002

Dan the man here – _feel_ me. You know when I'm here. Please love me. I miss you as much as you miss me – the fact that I can talk to you this way makes me stay connected.

You really should go to the computer now. Do this there.

At the computer, waiting.

Dan the man here – on the right channel with my channel – _you_, you sweet thing.

He made me laugh with his "Dan humor."

See? I miss you too. I've been busy here, which isn't exactly a place in space, but a place all the same. You've got access to this "space," and the more you practice, the greater your access will be.

What have you been doing?

Would take too much of your energy to give you the full picture of what I'm doing, but it's all fascinating and of a piece. We are of pieces…and you need to continue to work on the book. Stay focused and fight the fear factor that arises when you lose your direction.

That's what happened to you when I came into the picture. I so totally blocked, made fun of your way of being in the world that you lost your magic completely. I did it. I _undermined_ your belief in yourself so completely that now if I could, I'd wave a wand and give it back to you. But I can't. You have to give it back to yourself. And you can by hypnotizing yourself. Make yourself a tape and make it certain, solid that you will finish your book easily and effortlessly…see yourself on your book tour.

Okay…

Re: my leaving? Not so fast. I can stay, come and go. Recreate my Dan-ness.

I miss your Dan-ness…so much sometimes. I miss the essence of you…more than the reality of you. The memory of your smell still makes me swoon. I was so locked into you. I should have moved on, I guess, but I couldn't believe we couldn't work it out.

I know, my only true love. What fools these mortals be! Oh, well…
Did I hear you say date later? If you have the energy, come back tonight.

There he was, still flirting with me.

The house next door was tented for termites, and toxic fumes filled my house too. I had to sleep over at a friend's for a few days. On Saturday, I went off to the annual yoga party and a man flirted with me.

Sunday, June 9, 2002

Dan the man here. Hoping to get lucky again. You don't know how much I look forward to being with you. Last night at the party when that guy flirted with you I was insanely jealous. Insane, because I'm _dead_!

I smiled and could almost hear him laugh.

Monday, June 10, 2002
Just waiting at the computer to see if Dan shows up.

Dan the man here, finally. The transition between the handwriting and the computer typing is tricky. It's like learning to play a musical instrument. Only the instrument has a mind of it's own. So it's like shooting in and out of the shadows, trying to get myself heard. But you're on track right now. Stay focused.

Anything else you want to say before I go to work?

Just that I love you and if you wanted to watch the Lakers play, I'd watch with you. Otherwise, I'll be with Sam.

I love you, but watch them with Sam. I find it hard to believe that you still care about the Lakers.

I don't. I like the excitement, the emotion I feel when Sam watches. It's the _emotion_ that I miss. Not the game itself. It's why men watch sports. To get the rush of emotion. Women don't need sports to get in touch with their emotions.
Stay focused on the love we shared. See if you can tell the story. It will help many others trying, struggling to experience the same sort of authentic, soul-connected relationship.

June 10, 2002 – Monday night

Dan here – just wish I were here for real. The focus of today's work was soul paths. Kind of like books of lives we look at. They're quite fun – like movies, only much richer, fuller.

The soul path movies are fascinating. Wish you had access to them. They teach so much. Relationships between people is all that actually matters in the final analysis.

Your relationship with me is tough to sit through. I wish in this last go-round I'd been able to enjoy all that you offered me. It's like watching someone offer up exquisite gifts and see a pompous ass stick his nose up.

Thank you once again for trying so hard to educate me. I'm not as smart as I think I am. (Joke, here) I was too smart for my own good.

(Don't read while I do this. Confuses me. This is harder than it looks.)

Love, your love in particular, is so valuable. There is no "economy" of love, there is no set amount that gets used, it only grows like muscle mass. The more you love, the more you are able to love. The more you give of your experience, the more experience you will be able to communicate.

The time and your energy are finite, and that's what you need to pay attention to.

The soul path work goes on. Want me to look at yours? Okay, I'll look. I'll tell you tomorrow what I find.

Mine is a series of struggles not unlike the life I just had. My mother in this life was my friend in another life. He wanted to be more connected with me, but _hated_ being a woman. But was a woman so she could be close to me. And what do I do? Run as far as I can from her. She was so angry at me.

Need your permission to look at your soul path. I think it will help you with your work.

Granted. Talk to me tomorrow. Love you. Feel you.

Dan could see my soul path? All these years, I'd tried to "follow my bliss" just as Joseph Campbell suggested. I'd chosen a risky career and waited to find the love of my life, but nothing had worked out the way I'd hoped. My career had fizzled and my husband was dead. Maybe if I had access to my soul path, I could see what I did wrong, or at least know what to do next. I couldn't wait to hear.

Wednesday, June 12, 2002
Okay…waiting at computer. Hey, Dan, did you look? Are you around?

From Dan the man – your soul path …

But Barushe broke in.

Barushe needs to talk.

The sadness you feel, the loss about losing the opportunity to love deeply still influences your body. You are not alone even though it might feel that way to you with Enoch/ Dan gone.

As you know, the "Dan" part still longs for you as you long for him. From my perspective, you are too easy on him.

You don't like feeling your own power because there's a hesitancy because of past "abuse" issues. Your own. You have no choice but to embrace your own power now. You need to call in the troops, as it were, to finish the book and launch your teaching career – you are a teacher, but not in the classroom. What comes so naturally for you is like a foreign language for most others.

The body hunger you have for Dan will subside in a while. You hugged him as much as he would let you. You loved him with every fiber of your being. His lesson was to accept your love.

Re: Sam? Let him decide when and if he sees you.

Re: soul path? Save the energy now for the work at hand.

I was disappointed, but it's hard to argue with your own oversoul. One of Dan's business partners called to tell me they were dissolving Conflict Solvers.

Thursday, June 13, 2002

Spoke to John B. last night and it made me sad. Conflict Solvers seems to be losing steam. Feel Dan in my arms...

Barushe here. I know you want the comfort of Dan, but you need now to focus more on your own work and let him continue to work on his issues. The A.N.A. readings are high because your body is still in mourning and you've stopped crying.

(The A.N.A. are anti-nuclear antibodies that signaled my lupus was active. My own body was attacking me once again.)

You actually still need to cry it out of your body. The grief from the last ten years of this lifetime; losing the baby, your health, your crazy mother – watching her descend into madness, then seeing your father become an invalid and discovering that your brother was who he is – all took a toll on your own ability to function on a cellular level.

To counteract the anti-Stephanie attackers, you need to rest more and eat even more consciously than you already do. Try not taking in any chemicals for a while. I would say try Bieler, but I know it seems like utter torture and so it defeats any purpose, the healing.

Next time – all right, I won't talk next time, since you're still focused on this time.

"Dan" wants to touch base...

Okay...

Dan the man, but not so much so...

I'm sort of being absorbed into the full entity. It's a process. Since I've done a lot of work with the primary relationships of the last incarnation, I will be here to help you, but it's like turning my focus into the whole, rather than facing outward toward you. I'll be able to do it, because of the connection we share, but I'll have to "suit up" for it. My darling Stephanie, when we see each other again, I will be able to appear to you like I was for that one moment in time when you looked at my exquisite body and fell in love with the totality of my soul. Right then. You recognized me. And when I looked at you, yes, what I said was true. I felt I had died and gone to heaven. You always seemed so beautiful to me, even, or especially on that last day. That final day when I knew I'd be leaving, and was so utterly frightened. You were there for me at the end and I'm sorry I won't be there for you. But I will be, but not in a body.

Your fearlessness is the quality that you need to encourage and nurture. Have no fear and when you feel other people's fear for you, just nod and walk away.

John and Marc are not your concern. (His partners in "Conflict Solvers.") I've been trying to advise John, but he's like a scared little mouse compared to you, my tiger. Know that you have the ability to cope by just staying focused on the "now" of your existence and refusing to be swayed. You'll be fine.

You love your home, I know. You will be able to stay...make the tape you talked about for your body and see the "team" healing the green anti-Stephanie – antibodies. They're from the Eunice entity (my mother). She hated all her children. Resented what they took from her. She never had any nurturing herself, you know. She didn't know how to do it. She's still in healing sessions.

Friday, June 14, 2002

Barushe here.

The guides, our guides, are cobalt blue. It is when you imagine the color infusing life and healing into your body you will be able to rid yourself of the antibodies. Do that today.

The love you have for Enoch-Dan is reciprocated, but "Dan" – as you can feel – is still in the dog house with me. You experienced his "seductive, manipulative" side so thoroughly and bought it. I saw it for what it was. A missed opportunity for <u>both</u> of us.

Saturday, June 15, 2002 – 7:11 p.m.
I miss Dan. But it's Saturday night, and probably he'd be working at the computer…

Dan the man – Barushe is still angry at me, with good reason. You're angry too, but still, you miss me. And he is right; it was a tremendous opportunity to waste the way I did. But it's water under the bridge.

I can't tell you enough times how sad it makes me to see you so sad, so lonely. But you will adjust to being alone in a while, just like you adjusted to living with me. I hope you won't give yourself as much trouble as I gave you!

You were right; I brought 'nothing to the table' except an unbelievable appetite. You wondered about the "eating," and what the table manners were about. They were about having power over you. Annoying you. Making you continuously angry. One of the little soul-killing things I have to say I'm sorry for.

The realization that you don't ever have to be the person I turned you into must, should rather, make you very happy. That person wasn't you and you hated her. You never have to be her again.

I thought, Thank God!

Anything else anyone wants to say? I'll go read…

You are not fragile. Whatever happens, you know you can deal with it. Some people will hate you because of your fearlessness, just like some people hated you for your determined optimism. You need to embrace and cultivate that same sort of optimism again.

But remembering my long lost "determined optimism" made me so sad I went to sleep then woke to another lonely Sunday.

Sunday, June 16, 2002 – 7:24 a.m.
Mourning is back with a vengeance.

Dan here, you sweet thing – this makes me sad seeing you in this kind of pain. It will get easier. Don't give up. You've worked too hard to give up now. Go for broke and give this last push everything you've got.

Take care not to let yourself fall into the kind of depression that _robbed me of my life_. Literally. Please honor yourself by showing up for yourself.

Did you look at my soul paths?

Yes, but Barushe interceded.

Barushe interceded? Nothing like a fussy oversoul to keep you focused. I would get a glimpse of my own soul path later, but first I would make a sharp, unexpected turn on my current path – a turn I hadn't expected at all.

Chapter Twelve

Enter Cobalt Blue

In June, morning fog rolls into Los Angeles and blankets the city – we call it "June Gloom." That June, it felt as if the fog had settled in my head. I was trying to see my way out of it, but doing a terrible job. The fuss over Dan's death had completely died down, I'd divorced Valerie, one of my oldest friends and my other friend, Lynn, was in fresh mourning. In addition, I could feel Sam trying to distance himself from me, so I felt completely alone.

As I type these words, it's January of 2005. The book that I began more than two years ago, *The Married Girl's Guide to Hot and Sacred Sex*, is not the book you're reading. Because as I tried to write that book, I had to dig out the journals I kept during the first year of my marriage, and what I read there shocked me. I saw the "new wife" trying to make sense of a man who said he loved her, yet behaved as if he didn't. I read my own words desperately trying to convince myself that I could make it all work out. "I love him. I know I do."

When I realized that I had overridden my internal "fail-safe system," that I had chosen the marriage over myself, I slid down into a deep depression. Not that I was in a good mood to begin with. As I've said, when Dan died, he left me $180,000 in debt, with no savings, no retirement, no insurance, and I wasn't making enough money at Positive Changes to even pay my rent. Not the most comfortable place to find oneself at age fifty-five. If this were a screenplay, this would be the end of Act Two, where all looks lost, and the heroine wants to give up. That's when "it" has to happen – the event that propels our protagonist into the final battles, and on to victory. What "it" would be for me, or even if "it" would happen seemed doubtful just then.

My situation scared most of my friends so much that they avoided me as if I were contagious. If this could happen to me, who knows? It could happen to them, too. As dire as things seemed, Dan would try to comfort me.

Monday, June 17, 2002 – 6:10 a.m.

Dan? I can't think.

Life looks good from this perspective even though you're in pain. Take the opportunities presented to you. Say "yes" just like your card says. Say "yes" to whatever lies ahead for you. Embrace it…

Could I get in touch with my guides?

What do you think I'm doing? This is "guide" stuff. Just keep putting one foot in front of the other and you'll be fine. Stay focused on the work and show up for yourself. Things will be fine. Know that.

Please just get up earlier and get to the computer. That way you will have peace and quiet. You can't work well otherwise. Try tomorrow to get up at 4. You'll have to nap. But you can.

(The unrelenting racket of buzz saws as they ripped through the house next door made it difficult to think, let alone write.)

No one can give you what we had together. That phase of your life is over. "Sadie" is dead as far as you're concerned. And for good.

Life is to be enjoyed, loved, cherished. Just think of what we shared and remember. Then go forward and enjoy what you will have.

Monday night, June 17, 2002

Dan the man – back to see you. You are in pain and you no longer cry. You need to cry. Make the most of the time you have. You seem to be just existing. Please let me help by loving you. The computer in the morning will be easier to talk. Please don't lose hope.

Tuesday, June 18, 2002 – 5:40 a.m.

Dan here, you sweet thing.

Re: me/Enoch – expanding awareness makes it more difficult for me to narrow focus. You feel me "slipping away" and yet I'm just transforming into more of what my "authentic" energy is about. Annoyed I wasn't able to transmit it while I was with you. Just took from your store of energy. That's why you're so completely depleted right now. You must continue to fill your energy bank account. Do it slowly.

Dan, my need for you…your smell, the feel of you makes me ache. Re: my energy bank account? Damn you! Why didn't you hug me more? All I want now is to feel your arms…

As I said, nothing I can do now. What you need to do is cry more to move the anger out and then release it. You're feeling blocked because of the emotional turmoil, sorrow, unreleased rage. Cry more. Do it at night or in the car when you can scream. It's emotion that needs transforming.

Easier said than done. The next part you've read, but now you'll see it in context.

Wednesday, June 19, 2002 – 5:30 a.m.
Last night I picked up an old journal – the dream journal – I was keeping when I met Dan. Pretty scary. There was a dream on December 23, 1989 where a "fat, fleshy man" steals my "identity card" and Dan just stands back and watches. I'm frantic. Amazing what some dreams know. Don't feel Dan around. Would like to get his perspective. Dan? What was that all about? You wanted "out" almost immediately, it looks like. You were "acting out." Driving me nuts…

Dan here – all I can say is learn to trust yourself more. That dream was fear, but a sense of what lie ahead for us. If you had acted on it – called off the wedding, we both would have gone our separate ways. But you still would have missed me, and I, my darling Stephanie, would have missed you.

The fear that I lived with was so overwhelming – I was so tortured. My prospects were grim in my own mind. It's why I needed you so much. Your own ability to live on the edge is what attracted me to you, not to mention everything else.

Keep in mind the great times, which for us was just around the house; the days when we cleaned together, and loved each other. My own insanity should serve as a beacon of how to be brave, for you. When "fear" takes over, nothing else can be heard. So much sorrow and grief comes from fear.

You can read that journal through – I led you to it – but not today. Philadelphia was a turning point for both of us. I was determined to leave you and yet you held on to the marriage – and that one single act, your courage in coming up to that room, and standing up for what you wanted – made me fall so deeply in love with you. I knew you loved me. And you knew you loved me.

The only help I can give right now is to let you see how much you really know and yet discount. You can't believe you are as in touch with the magical as you are. Stay connected and just go for the ride.

Samuel came over later that night, upset about his girlfriend, Ho In, and I tried to comfort him. He wanted to see if he could get the same kind of "direct" connection with Dan that I had. I tried to lead him down into a trance state, but he couldn't relax enough. He was too upset.

The next morning, I sat down at the computer:

Thursday, June 20, 2002 – 6:30 a.m.

Dan the man.

I couldn't get anything else, so I tried left-handed writing:

> **Dan here – can't do computer today. The focus is different. Stay focused on you and your work. I'll comfort Sam. I tried to write through him, but couldn't get connected. Work now. Come back to me later. _Feel_ my love.**

Friday, June 21, 2002 – 6:32 a.m.
Nice morning. Hear the cooing doves and the busy birds, misty raining out.

> **Dan here – the love you seek can only come from you.**
> **Be brave enough to be alone. It is the only way for you to connect. The same sort of tectonic plate shift that you made when you married me, you must make again. Shift into alone-land, but you my sweet Stephanie, will not be lonely if you stay connected to your source, and to us. I say "us" because of the teamwork that _this_ – the communication – takes. There is a relay system, because coordinating my "schedule" with yours is not always possible.**
> **Your dyslexia is not a _problem_. It is what allows this process. It's like having an overly flexible muscle. The muscle here is the brain. Your brain makes connections other brains don't or aren't able to. But you can't read fast because you drink in the words and _play_ with them. As you read, your brain is busy finding connections. So it takes more energy for you to read than say it did for me, Dan.**
> **Yes, Barushe is now here. It's why I have access to this information.**

> *Barushe here now. Don't block...*
> *Re: your anti-Stephanie antibodies, make another healing tape. Focus on the Cobalt Blue healing light penetrating your body.*
> *Barushe book is done in other reality. Spend time trying to channel it. Spend time when you finish your Dan book. I've been waiting years for*

you to listen. All those "write books?" From me, who is expressed only briefly as you.

(Whenever I would doodle absentmindedly, my hand would automatically print: "Write books.")

Thank you for working so hard to reclaim you, my body. But you must focus on ridding yourself of the residue of your past – and the ANA toxins from the Eunice-Jerry entities, who by the way, are still in re-education classes.

Enoch and I have patched things up.

I saw that by choosing to give myself – you – no parents, I left you starved for his body. His beautiful, smelly, functional body. How you loved him. He's smiling now because your love still feeds him and Enoch. They owe us big time for this one!

You will get your wish. When you transition, it will be fast and elegant. So don't worry about your body.

Re: Sam and you – just let him seek you out.

From Dan the man again. Thank you for all the love. It still heals me. Barushe is right, I do owe you big time. I will, we will, be here to help you. Just stay connected. Now I know you need to work. Tonight? Sit with me…I love you…got that?

So I obliged my dead husband and sat in bed, pen in hand.

June 21, 2002 – 10:48 p.m.

Dan the man here, ready to chat. The day here was very exciting. Lots went on in terms of transitions. The way things really work is not at all mysterious.

You are just living in one giant illusion. Hegel, Schopenhauer were close to correct in their opinions. Heidegger, less so and… Oh well, neither of us can reach the name. Marcuse! Thanks for listening to those tapes. I liked that you thought of me in yoga. I'm amazed, flattered, dumbfounded by how much you loved me.

(As I channeled, my arm and hand cramped, then once again, I just passed out.)

Saturday, June 22, 2002 – 7:04 a.m.

Woke at 4:30 – feeling that Dan wanted to talk, but knew I'd be exhausted later. And I've got four clients today, so went back to sleep, slept until 6:30.

Dan the man – you keep feeling my "loss," yet I'm here, without the resentful side thrown in. I did blame you for making me earn a living, when you were right about my choices. It was my choice to burden myself with all that debt…burden our marriage with the heavy weight of law school and then Sam's college. Really don't understand who I was trying to impress. No one would have cared if…oh, it's annoying to me to process that again.

The chatting last night I realized was too much, too late. That's why you started to cramp. The information floods through you, and then gets backed-up. This way of communicating is much more efficient.

Aliah is concerned because she thinks you're holding me here. No one holds anyone. I chose to let you experience the true part of me, because you always knew "I" was in there somewhere. The "true" me is who you loved so deeply and who you fought for. God knows where, why the "shadow side" of me won. And so self-righteously, I might add.

The work on the book progresses. Don't worry about the structure, it's all there. Just keep showing up for it…what isn't important will fall away.

Stay focused. This is much harder than it looks.

Put the McKenna books away. (His law firm books filled a bookcase and every time I passed them, I'd fill with sorrow.) **Every time you look at them, you remember how awful those years were, not to mention the years before and after.**

The choices I made! And all for naught. Sam could have gone to Berkeley on scholarship if I'd stayed…who knows?

Dan? Just stay connected a while longer. Let me feel the love and sweetness of you.

I'm still here with you, connected in ways you don't grasp.

That Saturday I drove to my friend Lorelle's house – the friend who'd hosted the night with the "Married Girls" in April. Just after Dan died, when I told her that I was sleeping with Dan's ashes wrapped in his shirts, she said, "When you feel ready to give his shirts up, I'll make a quilt out of them." I was now ready, so I went with all his shirts and ties.

Saturday, June 22, 2002 – 10:50 p.m. – at Lorelle's.

Dan the man jealous of the easy friendships you have. Amazed at women! How much you share. The quilt will be beautiful and I'm stunned Lorelle would do that for me. You. Whoever.

Monday, June 24, 2002 – 5:36 a.m.

Dan the man – been waiting. All that seriousness about death and dying. I think if people could understand the joyousness of the process from this perspective, it would make it more meaningful.

So there he is, chipper as an eight-year-old, and I'm miserable. The pain hit me and I got mad.

Why did you do this? I hate you! I hate you for being so awful to me. For denying me our life. Whatever you could take from me, you took and left me all alone.

(Then I slid into a self-pitying rant. I'll leave it as I wrote it, even though in retrospect, it seems extremely self-indulgent.)

I don't know why I'm still alive. Everyone I've ever been close to seems to despise me. So deeply. Just on principle. My mother didn't want me, my father hated me, my sister despised me, and you…all you wanted to do was get even. So get even! Get even! Get even. You were always getting even with me. And now you have!

Barushe here…no one can feel your pain but you. No one can let it go but you. So it's good you finally cried some more. Too many months of not letting pain out. You've been lulled into thinking you weren't in mourning because of the closeness with the Dan-ness. But it's still an aching loss that needs letting go…

I still miss him! I'm so angry! If I died today, it would be no loss…to anyone. I don't understand all the fuss.

Dan the man – thinking…can't now. Go walk. (Your) body too achy.

I did two days of chest-pounding mourning – and then it finally lifted. The ancient Egyptians had the right idea; they hired professional mourners to do the heavy lifting for them. But it has to be done to release the anger. I had a client last week whose husband died over ten years ago, and she's still entrenched in the "Why am I still alive?" fury that I was in then. She, however, refused to even consider letting it go. It's all a choice.

Tuesday, June 25, 2002 – 10:30 p.m.

Feel Dan in my left leg.

Dan the man back – missed you the past few days, my sweet Stephanie. Had to be with Sam – he finally cried. The two of you were with your grief. I needed to help. The way it works is pretty interesting, but you're angry at me for abandoning you for the past few days.

I was, and I fell asleep.

Wednesday, June 26, 2002

Dan the man here – Go back (to the computer) **and be patient. Takes me a bit to change channels. See? I made you smile.**

Then I cried, remembering how he'd always try to make me laugh.

Dan the man – the connection on the computer is easier on you, but more difficult because of the re-routing it takes (in your body). I'm here under duress. No, that's not what I meant. Your grief is painful for you, but it is painful to me as well. Painful because of what I know now.

Onto other subjects: your soul path / my soul path intersect only a few times – I know you just thought, mercifully, but that was Barushe. He's still confused and annoyed at my refusal to follow through on our agreement. And it's quite a big deal, these "soul agreements / contracts." Once we make them with each other, then there's a ripple effect. Our ripple effect just stopped because of my intractability.

Free yourself from that energy completely. Move freely in your own space. Embrace the joy of your life without me. You chose two men who literally hamstringed your creativity. That's why you don't want another man in your life. Sexual orientation doesn't matter, but the feeling tone does.

All I can do to help you now is to check in with you. Sending you love as you remember me and send me love.

Don't allow fear to enter into the equation. I'm completely serious when I say that my fear of the future is what killed me. It robbed both of us of so much potential joy. Be present in the present and relish your time with Lily. She seeks you out because she knows who you are.

Re: the book? Keep going…put in the hours and it will be finished.

Dan? Tell me what you're doing.

I'm having fun, believe it or not. Sheer, glorious kid-like fun. More fun than the famous snowball fight of 1947.

(One of his favorite memories was the storm of 1947 that covered Brooklyn with eight feet of snow, which made it a paradise for a seven-year-old to have snowball fights.)

I'm so connected to the source of my own entity that my Dan-ness seems just a silly memory now. That's why I'm not so much "myself" with you. This feeling tone – is much more me. And it's more connected to you. And yours.

(He sent a love blast.)

Good. You felt that. I feel you want to work, and you need to. If you find time again today to get back to me, fine. I will listen for you. I was AWOL, as I said, because Sam fell into deep despair. He and I have a different connection and I am still his father. Because of that, it takes energy – lots of energy – for me to re-create that feeling. I'm just your lover now.

Thank you.

You're welcome. Feel the energy I send. Take advantage of this time of your life. This is your golden time. Enjoy each day. Live in joyfulness.

Dan? Thank you for staying with me a while longer as whoever you are now.

June 26, 2002
Barushe here briefly…work now. Come back, open this up later. Wanted my own file, a place to talk.
The Dan-ness, the sweetness of his soul, is what you always saw – experienced, when he calmed down enough to love you. You need to let yourself feed you the same nourishment from the same source…it's all from the source.

Thursday, June 27, 2002 – 7:41 a.m.
I was thinking about this channeling. It's as if I've been playing by the seaside – like a kid. Sticking my toes in the water, but running when a wave comes. Then WHAM! The tsunami grabs me, and takes me out to sea.

Dan just here to say I saw you become…a…can't get a clear channel right now – Dan humor. Please don't lose faith or concentration on the book. I will help. Barushe too! You've done well.

Friday, June 28, 2002 – 6:29 a.m.

Dan the ? I don't know what to call myself now. I'm no longer identified with "the man" part. And the "Dan" part I use only when I focus on you, because it's who you recognize. It's how it works here, like a file card pulled to access information. I want to be able to let you experience the fullness of my reality so that you will be able to grasp the fullness of your own. I lived so much off of your energy when we lived together. I plugged in to you constantly and drained you. So this is the least I can do. Give you back some of your own energy. Show you how to restore your own batteries.

I thought it was amusing how angry you were at all those batteries, cheap and defective, you thought. But they were just in backwards. Right now, your batteries are in a little backwards because of me, my death, and really my life, our life together.

(I'd had a meltdown when I couldn't get my tape recorder to work.)

The ability to just jump in and take what comes is the true freedom of life. That's why when you feel, smell fear, and you do, it repulses you. "Repulses" is a strong word, but it is the right word. You need to react quickly when you smell it and just get out of the way.

Fear for you is so toxic, because it's like a virus. You catch it.

I'm looking forward to being with you and Sam in the same place. Please schedule a hike. Paseo Miramar at night, so I can tag along. Yes, those were magical times, weren't they? You made me feel so needed when I led you down in the dark.

(I got an awful case of vertigo, caused by the fertility drugs, when we were hiking in the Santa Monica Mountains.)

You stopped my apology again for the drugs, but letting you take them was a bigger betrayal than you realize on far too many levels. They were so toxic to your system, but you were determined to get that soul to be with us and she was smart enough not to come.

The healing, visualization, you did with Soo-Young (a young client) the other day brought her into absolute connection with her baby. Your skill and leading amazes me. That baby will come to them. Greg and she will be proud parents and they will have you to thank, whether they know it or not. A good deed no one knows about. Fill your coffers.

Go work. It's late. I send love and healing from this vantage point…

(I saw myself kissing his back, smelling his skin, having that shoot down into me.)

Yes, I know how much you love me. How much you miss my smell, my bloodhound. You did live in a different world…see you later.

Saturday, June 29, 2002 – 6:39 a.m.
Went to the movies with Sam and Ho In last night at the Arc Light theaters – the old Cinerama Dome, redone. I noticed in Ho In the same kind of frustration with Sam that I had with Dan. Yesterday shopped downtown. Bought beautiful Harari's. Discount.

Dan the evolving man – the blues of those clothes very healing. Wear them as much as you can. Keep feeling this shooting energy. Oh, the Dan part kicks in enough to want to make love to you. I think I need another date…this afternoon? Come back and let me just love you. Bathe you in love.
Sit with the love some more, then go to work. You are distracted, so I can't get a clear channel.

June 29, 2002 – Saturday night, (in bed with Melanie, who's reading.)
We just got back from LACMA where we saw "Blowup."

Dan the spirit man here tonight – the movie tonight brought back so many memories. The times they are a-changing.
Did you notice how beautiful Vanessa Redgrave is? When I saw that movie I didn't think I'd ever be able to have a woman that gorgeous. But I did. I got you.
I know you're tired, but don't think the work you do at P.C. doesn't matter. It does. You help everyone you see.

Sunday, June 30, 2002 – 7:26 a.m.

Dan the Multidimensional Being…Mel's up…
The film last night, as I said, brought back so many memories of that era. That era that still feels like it pulled the reality base out from under me. It changed us all, didn't it? But what doesn't?
Thank you again for yesterday afternoon. The love you give me in spirit via the body is indeed sacred. You know this. The "sacred prostitute" that sits unread, by the way, is so important.

Turning around the "feeling tone" of sexual pleasure from "nasty" to the expression of love, the expression of the All That Is. That's what sex really is.

July 1, 2002 – 6:46 a.m.

Can't write that date without thinking of the beginning of the end. Last year on this date, Dan and I walked Lake Hollywood and he couldn't catch his breath. Thought it was all the bread and butter. If only. I was so mad at him. Furious that he had hurt that body. I remember how tired I was of all his complaining and yet he made no changes! Drove me nuts.

Sam and Ho In are leaving for Hawaii today. Waiting for Dan…but can't feel him.

Dan here in spirit, but not full energy. My work is fused now with the Enoch energy, so pulling out to come and be with you takes more concentration, but your love keeps me "fed." Yes I still want to "eat you up."

Those were magical times – sacred times – you and me loving each other so ferociously in bed. Your hunger for me is what I loved to experience. Your frantic-ness at the final moments terrified me, however, and that's when I pulled my energy back and you knew it. It angered you at this level. It was my choice not to give you "the whole deal." Only occasionally would I deign to offer up the "pure Dan" to you. And when I did, oh!, the love we had.

Thank you, my Stephanie, for being as patient with me, with your Dan, who as I said, is so thankful.

In your book, if you can communicate the beauty of animal, smelly, joyous sexual expression to only one other soul on this plane of reality, your effort will be worthwhile. But your time, once again, is limited. I don't say this to scare you. Only to make you focus on what is important to you.

Go to work now, and come back to me later on…this rivulet of energy that the entity Enoch keeps open for you is accessible. At some point it will "dry up." But as long as you continue to want to connect, "I" will be available.

Your "forgiveness" exercises have helped so many.

July 2, 2002 – 6:28 a.m.

Yesterday was the anniversary of the beginning of Dan's leukemia – and somewhere in my body I must have known about it. I'm "in mourning" again. Came home from Positive Changes with good intentions – I was going to walk or swim, but I just ate, then paid bills, and decided to watch TV. Listened to Carolyn Myss's Spiritual Madness tapes again. Like her stuff.

Dan the rivulet of energy man here to chat. Tried to chat last night, but you were indeed in mourning. You *are* in mourning. Your body knows that it sustained a blow – a big blow – and the only way out of the pain is through tears. Letting the emotion flush out. You've got to make time to cry again. Do it tonight, when the workmen leave. Cry and I'll be there.

You cry for what might have been, and I can't blame you. But once again you had _no control_ over my decision – my determined decision – that I was too good to be simply happy with you. I had to be a "great" man. And your revulsion at that phrase made me take notice only for a second. I would show you! That's what my "shadow" side, as you like to call it, would say. But it's not a "shadow" at all – it's right out in the open. I chose not to be integrated. I chose to be "one way" with you and present another side to others.

The Carolyn Myss stuff speaks to you, but it's not as good as listening to yourself. You have a direct connection here. Stay focused, stay tuned in, and take your own advice. You hear suggestions and then don't act on them.

Hugs from here I know are not as good as hugs from there, but it's all I've got. I still deeply appreciate your determination to save me. And you might have, but then what? I would have gone on being impossible, believe me. It's better this way, my sweet Stephanie.

Still, trying to balance the "awareness" of its being better that he died, next to the longing I felt for him, was difficult.

July 2, 2002 – 10:40 p.m.

Dan the spirit man – I like the introduction very much. Good job.

What are you doing now?

More soul progression work, but I've pretty much completed my overview. I'm deciding about my next course of action.

Were you with Sam today in Hawaii?

No, not today – yesterday I was because he hates to fly. He's not going to die in a plane, so I don't see – understand – the fear.

"Dan the man" is a memory for me too, now. So it's hard to recreate his feeling tone. I know that's what you miss most.

July 3, 2002 – 6:36 a.m.
The "Dan the man is a memory for me too," made me sad, but I know it's the truth.
   Don't feel him, but then got a "love blast."

Dan the Spirit man – I say that just to help you slide into this new phase with
   me. I'm here with you, but not as specifically "your Dan," which from my
   point of view is a good thing.

Vis-à-vis, your life with Dan, it left you very drained. Your feeling that someone
   always had their foot on the brakes was exactly correct. You were trying to
   drive in the fast lane, and "Dan" wouldn't let you. And it all had to do with
   fear.

Once again, right now, you need to stay as far away from "fear-based people"
   as possible. You are too fragile to fend off the energy. That's why it's far
   better for you to be alone.

The more time you spend working on the book – making it funny – and
   believe me, it can be – even though it's about the death of 'the love of your
   life' – the happier you'll be.

Thursday, July 4, 2002
The sorrow's back, mainly because it's 4th of July and it's when Dan was in the hospital
   for the first time. Breaks my heart to remember last summer.

Dan the Spirit here – don't let yourself get drawn back into that now. It's
   over. It's done and you will waste your precious energy if you wallow in the
   feeling tone of what was. *The future is now*, and if you claim it – feel it as
   yours – you will be able to finally realize your talent.

Just remember that you can always choose which direction your thoughts
   travel and you can choose what you want to experience. Let this last part
   of your life be filled with joy, and yes, even love. I know you don't want
   any men in your life now, and after what you just went through with me, I
   don't blame you. Once again, I was impossible on so many levels and I was
   strong. Physically so much stronger than you were. My making fun of your
   weakness was no joke. I simply couldn't understand how you could be so
   weak physically and still live. Ah, but the joke was on me. Your core – the
   "hard steel" that your father so viciously called you – is what made you,
   makes you so strong.

Your fearlessness is what will carry you. Meditate on it. Keep that feeling tone.
   No matter what. Just ride the waves...and once again you will feel the joy
   of your own existence.

Dan? When did you <u>know</u> which direction you were going to go? Was it in Yosemite?
The call from Gonzales?

(Gonzales, a famous, fussy, over-booked, New York oncologist who charges
$2600 for the first visit, agreed to see Dan.)

It doesn't matter. I chose to go because I was tired of fighting. The exhaustion
just got to me. I couldn't see how we could afford it, quite simply.

I started to cry. I knew that was true.

You asked.
The fear…it had infected you and we were both crazy as loons, as you liked
to say. But I wouldn't, once again, have been able to make the changes
in "Dan's" being-hood to make living any longer worthwhile. And the
economy of the exit, I think was really quite elegant. Not much fuss, and
not a lot of time, in earth time.

Friday, July 5, 2002 – 7:17 a.m.
At computer, but I've been up since 5:30…so tomorrow my goal is to get in here
earlier…dream last night about Dan, and being in a Dr.'s office with all these dying
people.

Dan the Spirit here. Before you become too tired, go work. Go to the
computer.

So I did.

Dan the spirit man just saying "hi" before you go on to chapter 3. It's there;
focus on you for a while, rather than me.
I'm so far away from my earth incarnation that focusing on that Dan-stuff
makes me uncomfortable, because it reminds me what a selfish, self-centered
being I was. All of my good deeds had to do with wanting approval, as
opposed to just doing the work.
Go to work now, just like I said, and come back later. I've got to cut the ties
with Sam soon, and he will be angry and lost for a while. There are some
rocky times that he has to endure before he can claim his own power. I
crippled us both with my obsessive need for his approval – my constant
comparing.

July 5, 2002

Barushe here, but so are the workmen. Just begin to wean yourself off your "Dan." He's been completely reabsorbed into Enoch, so it's hard for the "Dan" energy to even reform enough to talk to you.

I know he disagrees with me, I hear that, but you, my self, now expressed as flesh, need to now take the time to finish the book, kick start your life, and soar. Sam went para-sailing. Well, that's what you need to do. But without the aid of a speed boat. You've got to para-sail on your own. Keep up the naps, make more tapes, more healing tapes for yourself...

Encourage yourself constantly...hypnotize yourself to create the reality of joyfulness that was, quite literally, stolen from you. Once you comprehend how heartless his choices toward you really were, you'll get mad...then as we always do, you'll forgive him. But, I for one, am taking a break.

You – "I"– have a guide and she will be able to connect with you directly, through me, in a while...your Dan days are not over, because your mourning is not over. But just know the love he shot through you came from a source you have access to. But, my...you loved him! And he did love you, in, as he said "his fashion."

Saturday, July 6, 2002 – 6:00 a.m.

Today, I go get Athena. (My six-year-old niece.) *Right now need to go and put back all the stuff – my work from the last 20 years, which is all over my office floor.*

Dan your spirit man here to just touch base before you bounce into your busy day.

I am in a new phase of the re-education classes. My "amends" are all done – my true amends to/with you will continue for as long as you feel the pain of my refusal to experience the joy offered me – like you did this morning – I continue to feel the pain along with you. I, of course, would _prefer_ it if you wouldn't _feel_, but that was my problem to begin with.

(I know you feel my smile from here!) Yes, I can still enjoy irony!

Your soul paths are intimidating for me. It actually was the source for my _jealousy_ of you.

I know – isn't that peculiar? That "Dan" would _choose_ to let his own _entitled_ self be jealous of someone who had, for the most part operated, existed so completely alone? And done, I might add, an amazing job of it.

And that, at base, was the source of "my" love/hate relationship with you.

I did see you, Stephanie, now expressed in the flesh – and you saw _me_, but you also "saw" who I was meant to become. And you loved me for that and I _stubbornly_ refused to take a chance and become your _knight_ in shining armor.

Sweetie, don't cry. I _could_ have. But I chose not to accept our _life_ together – the baby, my daughter, the fun you offered. The _sex!_ My god, what was I thinking? Not worth the energy it takes to write these words.

Take the weekend off from the book. Send off your Christmas story.

Go feed the birds. I can "see" them through you when you watch them. (Many "people" are jealous of me for being able to connect this precisely with you...shhhh!)

I went outside and my neighbor Shirley complained about everything. The long lines at the post office, the young people. How she hated this and that!

I said, "Today is the anniversary of finding out my husband had leukemia, so nothing seems a problem after that." When I came back in, Dan said:

That woman! What a curse she is! Complain, complain, complain! Good for you for shutting her up!

Saturday, July 6, 2002 – later.

From Dan the now irritated spirit man...it took you so long to get back here and now you're going to run off for the entire day!

I had more to tell you about "me" and what "I'm" doing but once again, I see how self-centered I am. At least I didn't have to die to get it this time...I know you want to hear about all this, so maybe when Athena goes to sleep, you will come back to me and let me tell you...

So much to communicate! So little "time!" Thank you for sitting with me so long this morning. If I hadn't asked you to fill the bird feeder, you would have stayed with me. That's exactly why psychics can't foretell anything. There are just too many variables in reality. Everyone has a part. That Shirley is a negative force and you did exactly the right thing. You should have cut your losses as soon as you noticed it. It's all a learning curve. Go, walk to yoga, breath deep. Think of me. I have a big day, whatever it is. I am looking at probable futures, next adventures. I will stay connected with/to you for a while longer, much to Barushe's annoyance!

You are the feminine expression of his soul overview, and he hates that you loved me so obsessively. But his choices made that the only course of action you could take. Once he deprived you of family love, you gave me all your love. And once again, forgive me for taking it as my due. I so deeply appreciate and remember all the sweet love you showered me with. Ah, I do miss those showers...you scrubbing my back, my legs, my penis!

Monday, July 8, 2002 – 6:44 a.m.
Dan? Are you around?

Barushe here. Thank you for choosing to open this file and connect with this energy, as opposed to the "other channel" inside. The Dan energy is in session deciding about future challenges. Future, however, is a relative word.

How many "lifetimes" have we done together?

Too many, from my point of view. This is not the first time he has said one thing on this side of the veil and done a complete switcheroo. Like the jerk who keeps offering the guy the chair, saying he won't pull it out this time, then he pulls it out. Now, you tell me, who is the dummy? Yes. The person who keeps getting seduced. Me! You. (Yes, I feel you bring up the sweetness, and once again, it's like honey. But you, my darling, are a honey addict.)

Go ahead, fill your heart up with the love of him...it comforts you, but keep in mind, it was not reciprocated. Truth. Only in his fashion.

I know you don't want to hear this, but "take the hit" as you are so fond of saying. Take the hit and go on. Love him when it pleases you, but understand that your own need for that love is what almost stopped you from achieving your goals in this lifetime.

And now, you have to focus, focus hard, and focus fast. Get the book done. Get all the help you can. Stick to your schedule. Listen to yourself. Feed from the love of the "source" rather than just the "love shots" from Dan.

My/your choice of parents was perfect, yet problematic in that they offered you no comfort. You were like the little monkey and the wire dummy.

(This refers to the rhesus monkey experiments from the '60s, where researchers gave baby monkeys a choice between a wire "mother" with food, and a terry cloth "mother" with no food. The babies chose the comfort of the terry cloth mother.)

Eunice was the wire dummy. Barbed wire. As I've told you before, you will not need to encounter her again, and yet you are comfortable with that kind of person...Barbara, Valerie W. So now I see that you get as far away from them, as fast as you can.

Advice for today?

Monitor your energy level. Notice where you bleed energy. Keep away from the vampires.

Make your tapes, then listen to them. Keep yourself focused. That's crucial. And trust. Feel the fear, then just understand that you can get comfort by going inside and connecting to the source. Do not act out of fear. Don't take jobs.

I still can't believe you overrode that "buzz" I sent when you were sitting in that Elaine's office. Talk about a bad place for you.

(I heard a loud buzz go off in my ear, when Elaine, a principal at Metro Skills Center in downtown Los Angeles, offered me a job to teach English – one of the worst job-experiences of my life. Who knew?)

Tuesday, July 9, 2002 – 6:44 a.m.
Couldn't connect with Dan yesterday, but Barushe came through. It's now 7:42. No Dan.

Barushe here. Yes, I know you wanted to hear from "Dan," but as I said, you need to wean yourself off of his "honey." Connect with your own source when you want love. It's the only way to re-connect with your own work. And your own life. The life you lived with him was so uncomfortable for you, yet you forced yourself to live it since you thought you had no options. You wanted a man, a good man. And you thought you had one. You did, and yet you know you didn't. He was always only out for himself. He really never gave a thought to you. You didn't matter. You or your own trajectory didn't matter to him.

And that was his lesson. One, I might add, that he only learned after he died. A lot of good it did you.

Well, no, it did do you a lot of good. If he had not come back and made all those amends to you, you would not have healed quite as quickly. For believe it or not, your energy is back on track.

Do the "knitting" exercises I see you doing…they will continue to mend your "blown out" aura. Let Samuel contact you, let Lynn do the same. Stop the calling and micro-managing of that relationship. If she wants to see you, let her invite you. You can verbalize that to her.

The "future" is never "seeable" because it is so variable. Your legs hurting are the "process" this takes. Temporary…

The Fly Girls is a probable, but may or may not happen.

Brigitte, a friend who then worked with Michael and Mark Polish, the twin filmmakers who wrote and starred in "Twin Falls, Idaho," asked me if I could come up with a story about the WASP – Women's Air Service Pilots – the women who ferried fighter planes throughout the U.S. and England in World War II. I'd seen the documentary, "Fly Girls," but it had no story, just facts. I told Brigitte I would try to find a beginning, middle and end, and make into a movie.

Anything else?
I know I feel like a stern parental voice from within, but it's only because of the distance. "Dan's" energy danced with you on earth and he knows your coordinates. I know you miss that connection and you will be able to connect again with another of "our" friends, but I'm a little leery of the connection, as you are. You won't seek out men, but they will continue to notice you. Even at 55 you still clean up well.

Tuesday, July 9, 2002 – night.

Miss talking to Dan…

Dan the honey man – so you're an addict, so what?
About my next adventure? I haven't chosen a "life" yet, but I do have the era. I want to try out somewhere harsh physically – like "drunken horses."

"A Time for Drunken Horses," is an amazing movie about three Iranian Kurdish children struggling to survive. When Dan and I saw the movie in 2000, it seemed so bleak and startling – yet so poetic. It surprised me that he wanted a life filled with such intense survival challenges. No accounting for taste.

Tuesday, July 9, 2002 – 10:05 p.m.

Dan the spirit man here – you have so little patience for letting me come through. It's not easy, especially since you are "pretty open." So keep centered. Know what energies you listen to. We will all help on the books you are going to write. All writers get help. You heard the man in the wheel chair? He needed to be slowed down so he would listen. You don't need to be slowed down. You're slow enough. And if they had slowed you, you would have "opted out." We, I say we, because I'm the Dan rivulet, yet the Enoch spirit as well.

Barushe wants to speak. Don't let them confuse you.

(I wondered if I was simply schizophrenic.)

Re: schizophrenia? It's not that – it's people's oversoul not getting clear enough communication and the "earth entity" gets "scared out of their wits." Don't go talking to yourself. Focus.

My connection with Sam?
Intense.

I had sold Dan's car in April or May, and stuck the $4500 away – the money I would use if I had to become the homeless, shopping cart person everyone expected me to become. Then Arthur, an old boyfriend, called and asked, "How would you like to make $5000?" "Great," thinking that it was a writing job, given that he's a writer. "How about loaning me that $4500 you got for Dan's car, and I'll pay you back double." I was stunned, since he'd already borrowed $1000, with a (still unfulfilled) promise to pay it back immediately.

Wednesday, July 10, 2002 – 6:46 a.m. (From handwritten journal)

Dan the spirit – know you still miss my Dan-ness. That big, smelly wonderful body I was blessed with. I miss it too!

The men in your life! I, too, was stunned by Arthur's request. The utter selfishness simply defies the imagination.

If you loan him that money you know that there is no guarantee that you will get it back. He'll want to give it back, but he won't, for any number of good reasons, be able to part with the money once it's in his hands. He's crazy when it comes to money. He's an addict.

On a soul level, however, he literally saved your life. He offered you *hope*. He helped you get into Berkeley, and without that "piece of paper" (my diploma) you wouldn't have the confidence in your own intelligence that you do.

Don't forget that while other children had parents that cared about them, you had parents that *actively* hated you. He threw you a lifeline when you were drowning. Now he needs the lifeline. Better $4500 in his bank than in that box. You want to give it to him.

You just don't want to feel like a sucker. Well, my sweet Stephanie, too late for that one. But that's not important. Give the money with no expectation of getting it back. It's an old debt and one you're pleased to pay.

Don't tell anyone.

(I wondered if this was Barushe.)

Dan here. My perspective.

Any more?

No, my new adventure can wait. The connection is clearer today because you calmed down. Work on book and type up your Christmas story…before it's too late.

Wednesday, July 10, about 10:30 p.m.
The day was a nightmare with the jackhammering next door. I put $4500 into Arthur's bank account. What a mess of things he makes.
Barushe here now…

But then my hand drew a butterfly-like cobweb.

Dan the spirit here – Barushe can't get through – for whatever reason. I want to say how much I still miss you. I know last week was hard for you. Keep going. Don't be discouraged.

But I was discouraged – I wanted to give up, crawl into a hole and hide. Still, I forced myself to get up, and sit down at the computer to "listen." I sat there for forty minutes, and was about to give up when this happened:

Friday, July 12, 2002 – 6:51 a.m.

You think this is easier than it is… you don't have enough patience. Stay in one place long enough to listen and then you will receive.

Not Dan here, nor Barushe…you don't like the feeling of this because it, "the transmission," is one step farther away. I, we, can't send the "emotion" that "Dan" can, does send to you.

You don't want to…have an active aversion to "entities" around you who you "know" are not friends. They now swim in your environment pretty freely… just honor your own dislikes enough not to be more than courteous. Don't let yourself be drawn into "emotion" with them. Any kind of (emotional) **draw and they will drain you. That's the game. Get you angry so you will react. It's just like you told Max** (my nephew). **You can only be manipulated when you are emotional.**

You will need all of your energy to focus on the rest of the book and the treatment – which is, by the way, meant for you. It will lead to other things.

Your "Radical Changes," which you pulled out, should be re-done.

("Radical Changes," the first script I wrote in film school, was the story of a young Berkeley radical who falls in love with a twenty-two-year-old dying soldier, a Green Beret. I'd won the Women in Film Award for it.)

Do the Christmas story.

This is your connection…the physical exhaustion is from the "plates shifting" inside.

I woke you at 4:30. You could have gotten up and this would have been easier for both of us. The "Dan Enoch" entity is busy and Barushe is in consultation. Making sure he gets "time off," I think. It's all up to them. Barushe is still leery of the "Dan" energy because of the cost to you, one of his earth incarnations.

I am only a "guide." And no matter what you do from now on, you have me on your side. You can use me if you allow yourself the time to sit…you don't need "shamanic hypnotism" classes. You could teach them. You are a true channel and you will do the work you are _designed_ to do. You have the wiring for this. So does Samuel, your soul playmate.

Do not mourn Valerie W. She was never a friend…there is a meanness to her that you always overlooked and you really "took the hits" in that relationship. She will seek you out, but you did enough time. Now open the book file and finish chapter 3…

Okay. So I had a guide? I let that soak in, and went about the day. Late that night, Sam came over and I tried to help him sort out his feelings. Dan, apparently, had been trying to help him too.

Friday, July 12, 2002 – 11 p.m.
Sam just left – so upset. He and Ho In are fighting all the time – the 'What are we doing?' fights. He's in so much pain, yet doesn't want to feel it.

Dan back for Sam. I told him the same thing you did. Only you said it better and in words. Once again, "To the moon!"

See? I can still make you smile and now cry too!

Thank you for still loving me. Do what you want. Don't worry about the money. I am not so much me.

Thanks for coming.

OK.

Saturday, July 13, 2002 – 5:44 a.m.

The gifts you give so freely and generously, I might add, are not really heard. You need the time for yourself. Let other souls find their own way.

Who is this?

The guide, your guide – not Barushe. The focus on your own work is what needs to be maintained if you are to access your own energy.

Do you have a name?

Yes, but it won't make sense to you. I am the Cobalt Blue guide you seek. When you look at your glass, when you wear electric blue you are seeking my wisdom. My advice. We are in connection. I am in the planes, I am the aircraft.

Planes? Aircraft? The planes that filled my dreams? I was always in airports or on planes or spaceships in dreams.

But I had no time to think, because I had to become an expert on real planes – the fighter planes of World War II, and "The Fly Girls" who flew them – the WASP. And I had to do it fast. Maybe my life would work out after all. Maybe my "it" had happened.

Chapter Thirteen

We've Got a Movie!

Los Angeles is a company town and the company is the entertainment industry. Everyone knows someone. As I type these words, it's February of 2005 and a few days ago, when the Academy Awards were announced, I knew two of the nominees. One went to film school with me, the other goes to my yoga classes, and I'm nobody – that's how small the town is. Six degrees of separation? Not even. Feels more like three.

So because I knew someone, Brigitte, I would now get another chance to grab the brass ring if only I could come up with a compelling story. In the totem pole that is the movie business, the writer sits at the bottom. Figuratively and literally. Nothing happens, no one works, without the writer coming up with the story first.

For me to come up with a story, however, I needed to find a hook. Once found, I'd tease out a tale filled with likeable, yet flawed characters, whom I would then force to overcome insurmountable obstacles. I'd create a conflict-filled journey that would lead them to a shattering realization – a catharsis – where they would at last gain the wisdom they so desperately needed. Then, I'd finish it off with a satisfying, yet unexpected resolution. In other words, I needed a beginning, middle and an end. Welcome to screenwriting.

But where would I dig up a story about these girls? Where else? The library. Librarians are saints, and once I told Laurie, the children's librarian at the Gardner Street branch what I needed, she scoured the Los Angeles Public Library system and into my hands flew book after book.

Books on World War II fighter pilots, planes, and the WASP teetered in high piles on my office floor until at last I found the hook I needed: Jacqueline Cochran, the fiery pistol of a dame who had the balls to fight for what she wanted. No one remembers her these days, but in her own day she was a superstar. And it was Jacqueline's relentless determination that made the WASP a reality.

She, on the other hand, was a complete work of fiction – she even made up her own name – plucked it right out of a phone book. She claimed to be an orphan who clawed her way out of a dirt poor Southern mill town. Yet she managed to marry one of the richest, most powerful men in the country, and became a world class flyer in the '20s and '30s, when aviators were the country's superstars. As I researched her life, what struck me immediately was that she kept referring to what she called "her special knowing." She "just knew things." For instance, she "knew" that her good friend Amelia Earhart was down and dead. Telepathically she received the name of the Japanese ship that heard the final radio message sent from Earhart's plane. Was she psychic? Was she a channel? Did it matter?

Life goes by fast and that month flew by. I read book after book, and worked on the treatment while working on my own book. Since I had to make money, I also saw clients at Positive Changes. At the same time, Sam was making plans to take some of Dan's ashes to the top of Mount Whitney, where he and Dan had hiked just two summers before.

Even though it was beginning to dawn on me just how unhappy I had been with Dan, I still missed him. One morning I sat down at his computer in hopes that his energy would surge through me again.

July 16, 2002 – 7:11 a.m.
Just want to see if I can reach...the Dan Rivulet or whoever before going to Chapter 4.

Barushe here – Once again the "Dan" energy that you long for, is, I hate to say, long gone, but he is. He's completely been reabsorbed into Enoch's energy and is being reformed to create something else.

It's why Samuel is so depleted just now. He had no idea how much of his own sustenance he received from Dan's undying love. And yet, it is still there, accessible to you and Sam, but now through your own entities. You need to get closer to your own source and stop expecting it to come with no effort. It takes effort.

Now you are connected. Stay focused and remember <u>this</u> feeling tone. You need to write chapter 4.

Do the treatment. As I said, Jacqueline's energy is accessible to you, if you focus.

Okay, I had my orders. Yet to write Chapter 4, I had to read over my old journals. I'd see where Dan would say one thing, but his actions said the opposite, and I saw how I had just accepted it all. It frustrated me because juggling the past, as seen from my new perspective, confused me no end. What was memory? What was real? Would I be able to tell the story of our marriage for my *Married Girl's Guide*? Would it help anyone else? Would anyone believe me? My "present" presented such a challenge to me that I wanted to give up, but if I gave up, then what would I do?

That evening, Dan's cousin Judy, and her boyfriend Jerry (the two other people in the room the night Dan died), met me at the museum to see the premiere of "The Kid Stays in the Picture," a movie made by bad boy producer Bob Evans all about himself, and he was there to be interviewed afterwards.

As I watched his movie, told by the quintessential "unreliable narrator" in literary terms, I felt jumpy and uncomfortable, and I didn't know why. Evans was married briefly to the actress Ali McGraw just after her rise to stardom in the late '60s, and once again, because Hollywood is a tiny town, we know people in common, and everyone adores her. But not Evans. In his movie, he trashes her. He brags about being out of town two-hundred days a year, thus abandons her with their newly born son, but has the nerve to get upset when she complains (i.e. nags) that she wants him home more because she loves him. To solve the problem, he suggests she go back to work, and arranges that she do a movie with Steve McQueen. When she falls in love with McQueen, he's angry and shocked.

Now I ask you? Who among us would <u>not</u> leave Bob Evans for Steve McQueen?

As Peter Bogdonovich sat up onstage interviewing him, I got more antsy by the moment. I saw a man who had looks, health, talent and early, easy success. A man who lived the Hollywood high life of drugs, sex, and rock-and-roll, and now wanted sympathy. From my point of view, it seemed to be the same old story – hubris, coupled with a cocaine addiction, facilitates yet another fast fall from the heady heights of Hollywood. This was interesting?

Judy and Jerry wanted to stay to hear the whole interview, but I couldn't listen to another word. I jumped up and walked home. Maybe Dan would have perspective.

July 16, 2002 – night.
Back from Bob Evans movie.

Dan, the rivulet here – said I'd stay to comfort you.
Been thinking about your journals all day. I know now how blind I was. Hindsight – 20/20 vision.
Was with you in the movie. It's why you were so antsy. No way to do this without the discomfort.
Be courageous. Be fearless. There is nothing to fear. Stephanie is Barushe here. Barushe is angry at Enoch.

Wed. July 17, 2002 – 7:13 a.m.
I don't want to lose the "sweetness" part of Dan – the part I truly experience when I "channel" and yet no wonder Barushe is angry.

Dan, the Rivulet here. Reconfiguring myself to be with you and Sam is a job, but one I take on freely. Especially for you...for it is you I truly betrayed in not becoming the "me" you expected. You always saw the hero I was. The places we could have gone if I had not saddled us down with all those obligations. Oh, well. If I had not destroyed your self-confidence.

Get it back. Steal it back from wherever you see it. The movie last night is a good example. He (Bob Evans) didn't know more than you do. He just had a direct "plug in." Get your own "plug in." You have it. Stay in touch...

I love you, and even though Barushe is still annoyed, the fact that you still long for me, my body, my soul, keeps us connected. You could have chosen to be angry, and leave like you did in the dream. And you would have been justified. For the Riva-Dan connection nearly destroyed our marriage. What a waste of my energy! And yours! I did suck your energy like a vampire and you knew it. Just be aware when it happens.

Where are you now in "your progress?"

I am reconfiguring my energy, or rather Enoch is...the part that is "me" to you, my Dan-ness can stay connected to you...if you want. But there is, there are, other considerations.

Your guide, the one who was so angry at me, the Cobalt Blue? She wants you to focus ahead. And that, my darling Stephanie, is where you will find the courage to continue to place one foot in front of the other. When the "fear" of the future comes up, just acknowledge it, see it like a goblin and use visualizations – use your Durga self – to fight it. It is a hob-goblin. It – the fear – is the negative. The reason the world goes so awry. Fear of life.

I should know. "Fear" destroyed my body, my happiness, my joy. The fear in every cell was so palpable to you...fear of my mother. Fear of "what people thought." Who cares! People only really think about themselves anyway!

You will be sorry today that you didn't get up at 4:30...the workmen are here already. Too much noise so distracts you. But get out of the house today. Go to the bookstore or the museum and work. It's quiet there.

Dan? The Durga tee shirt in May...did you know then?

My body knew, but I didn't. I never paid any attention to warning signs. I could have turned the tide, but chose actively not to. You know that...you knew too. I read that dream over with you. That pit of your stomach roiling fear? That was me, mine. Our life was over. Thank you for loving me with everything you had.

July 18, 2002 – 7:18 a.m.
Advice for today?

Cobalt Blue– The advice for today is the same as it was. Focus on your own needs and when you get the inkling of what to do, like for instance not listen to other's woes – just don't. You've got to stand up for yourself. You don't need to help anyone right now. Take a year off. You need to focus on you. Use your energy for you, and that includes Sam too. Let him become a man, if he chooses to. Or let him decide not to. It's his choice.

Barushe and Enoch are coming to terms again, but since you are still "out," and your connection to his "Dan" energy is still so specific and "calling," I will monitor the process.

The book continues to unfold, although not along the lines you once envisioned. Your reading from your own journals was so jarring to you that you lost focus.

Read the "Sacred Prostitute" book and get grounded on your energy that you brought in to that marriage. I know you never understood how much Dan's energy sucked off you. You felt it, but as you usually do, discounted your own feelings.

You discount them, because it's learned behavior. You were taught not to believe anything you actually felt. The task for you now is to trust everything you feel, act where it is appropriate and evaluate. When you know something is going to be a problem, you can by-step it.

I would read over the channeling, feel the authenticity of what was said, but putting the advice into practice was not always easy. I was happy, however, to hear that my oversoul and his were patching things up.

Sometimes, I'd feel Dan's energy calling me, and pick up a pen:

July 18, 2002

Dan, the rivulet calls to you too. But you know our time is coming to an end. It's not as if you will ever forget me – you won't. Just remember the best…remember the love we shared. Feel the warmth that still forms in my being toward you…

You said you'd stay…

But I didn't know then what I do now. I'm already "on my way" elsewhere. Literally. New adventures. It's why Sam is spinning out of control...but I'm glad you pushed him toward yoga. It might help soothe his soul. But he needs to get un-pampered. "I"/ Dan focused way too much of my energy on him...both for negative reasons and positive.

At night, I'd crawl into bed, exhausted and see if he'd be there...

Thursday, July 18, 2002 – 9:49 p.m.

Barushe, not Dan.
I am a class IV entity. Barushe is a name I took from one life I particularly enjoyed. The life was a time before written language...long before. Then our mind trained us to remember.

Is this a past life of mine?

Yes and no. Feel the connection. It is authentic. You are such a <u>woman</u>. I feel you still <u>longing</u> for Dan. He's off having a ball. You refuse to acknowledge the damage he did to you and me. He loved you, though, and because I chose no love for you, you got hooked.

Friday, July 19, 2002 – 6:20 a.m.
Advice?

Dan, the spirit – sneaking back in to say "hi." Yes, I can do this so much more easily because I do know your soul so well – this soul – it's not that Barushe doesn't, it's just that there is room.
Re: me? He's right. I'm having a ball before I "go back." Won't elaborate.

"Won't elaborate?" What did that mean? My feeling was that my "horn dog dead husband" was off expressing his energy elsewhere.

Sunday, July 21, 2002
Mourning back. Tired. Feel awful.

Barushe back now. I don't have the same intimacy with your body that Dan has, which seems odd since you manifest part of me. But because Dan knew your body so well, he could recreate the "love" feeling you miss so much.
The mourning is not through. You will continue to miss him, although not the man you got, only the one you wanted.

Wednesday, July 24, 2002 – 6:40 a.m.
Mourning hit again.

Dan, the rivulet of energy, just reformed enough to say hi. I miss you too, and yet am still so relieved that I didn't have to play out "that hand."

I would have continued to destroy you – literally. When you feel happy that you don't have to put up with all my miserable takes on the universe in general, it is authentic. Your first initial response to my looking over that beauty you tried to share with me and finding fault was an alarm you simply ignored.

I'm here via special permission.

I miss the love.

But it came at too high a price. Never pay that again.

Barushe here. Just allowed the "Dan energy" access because you still mourn. You need to allow yourself the crying time again.

I felt like crying all the time because fear that I wouldn't be able to come up with an exciting, well structured story for the "pitch" was beginning to over-shadow almost everything else in my life. At work, I had an impossible client – a nasty, condescending Beverly Hills woman who really upset me. So I asked for help.

July 24, 2002
What is it that Barushe needs to learn from this incarnation?

From Cobalt Blue– the focus of this experience is to overcome a sense of "inferiority" left from a victim-hood of...a bitter victim-hood. In this experience, the "valor" with which you handle each challenge is what you will remember. It is what makes you repulsive to cowards and fear-based people. The woman you reacted to yesterday, her smugness, and self-satisfied containment comes from deep fear. She needs to control all situations and your task, which you accomplished, was not to hook into her negativity.

The energy waiting for you now, the energy calling to you, will seek you out. Just continue to trust your impulses and listen to your/my guidance. Trust that the good of Dan's energy stays with you as protection. For he does still long for you in much the same way you long for him.

The only thing that can weaken you is fear. It is contagious. Only think of what you want to do. Your desire is what you need to embrace. Don't allow

your thoughts to travel down paths that are non-productive. It is your thoughts that determine your life. And you can indeed control them. It is all that you can control – but it is everything.

Brigitte called to tell me that we had a meeting scheduled for July 31ˢᵗ with Jason Reed, a vice president at Touchstone/Disney – the place I'd worked ten years before. Now I completely panicked, and Dan tried to comfort me.

July 25, 2002

Dan, the disembodied spirit here, to cheer you on. I know when the meeting is and I will be with you.
You deserved my support when I was alive and I couldn't give it. But now I can. Call it penance or just so much love. I will be hiking with Sam this weekend, but if on Sunday you wanted to reconstruct me and let me feel the intensity of your "connection," that would make me remember your love.
I'm ready to head out again. The "turnaround time" is pretty fast.
There is no failure. Only information.

(My Qigong teacher, Chris Fernie, sent me a flyer for his workshop in Mendocino. Qigong is a Chinese form of energy movement, now popularized by "Crouching Tiger, Hidden Dragon," "Hero," and "House of Flying Daggers." I'd done Qigong for four or five years, and I wanted to go.)

Dan the man feels so sad that I didn't ever want to do anything. I never wanted to just have fun. Go and have fun.

Friday, July 26, 2002
Everyone who called yesterday dumped a load of grief on my doorstep. All long conversations. I don't need to offer any advice to anyone, one, because what do I know about what anyone else should do? And two, because no one listens anyway. It's just a huge waste of my energy. Which I don't have too much of.

Barushe here – you finally sat down. You need to focus on your work and forget the rest.
Find the access to your energy again. Let the fear leave your body. There is nothing to fear. Stand up to whatever presents itself. Once you don't fear death, what's the problem? Just remember that you don't fear death.
Then take that awareness and let it inform, activate and empower you. You don't fear death. You don't fear death. You don't fear death. And because of

*that, you can't let yourself be influenced by everyone around you who fears
life. Life is what people fear.*

Take the energy class. Take your car. You like your car. It's a good car.

*Jackie's "spirit" can be reached – not her precisely, but the essence of the spirit.
And you can connect with her during the pitch and just channel...*

Easy for him to say. Turning a mountain of information into a riveting, sexy
story still eluded me, and now I panicked. What does a girl do when she panics?
What else? Shop! The California Mart's showrooms sell off designer samples and
overruns on the last Friday of each month, so I headed downtown.

Saturday, July 27, 2002

*I woke up at 2:30 a.m. and couldn't get back to sleep. My fear of failure – failing to
deliver the goods – is so strong. My body is fried from all the tension. My circuits feel
as if they're blown out.*

**The beauty of body pleases you so much that sometimes you make the wrong
decision. You were deprived so completely as a child that it's impossible to
make up for it. You love looking beautiful and that is why your need to go
shopping overrides other needs. Yesterday the need to focus on the work
would have been a better choice.**

**The nervous energy got trapped in your body and instead of standing up and
releasing it, which you know how to do, it careened around and did blow
your circuits.**

How do I get "me" back? I need my energy back.

**Go outside now and just walk as fast as you can, do the exercises...connect
with the Jackie of your soul... and you do have connections. All your
"flying" dreams are of a piece.**

**Don't think about the work today...tomorrow you will wake up early and work.
It will be ready by Sunday night. Know that you can do it because you can.
You have the talent, you have the skill. And you have the confidence...you
just have to plug into your own courage and keep encouraging yourself...**

Sam called me from Mount Whitney to tell me that Dan was chatting to
him almost non-stop. So much so that Sam said, "I had to tell him to shut up!" I
laughed out loud. My own head was so filled with World War Two pilots, fighter
planes, and Fly Girls, that I had no time for my dead husband.

Sunday, July 28, 2002 – 6:27 a.m.
Still don't have the thrust of the story.

Dan, the man back to say goodbye, my sweet Stephanie. It is a fast turn-around. I will miss your sweet soul. I will miss your love. I will miss you.

Stay connected. Both Barushe and Enoch will help. I still stand in awe of the miracle of love we got to experience together. You took it as "expected" because I had promised. But as Barushe keeps reminding both of us, I broke the promise. If you have an inclination to be with me tonight, I'll come back and really say goodbye.

But once Sam plants my ashes on Whitney, I go to the "take off" platform. And you're not even through mourning.

Barushe here –
Your love for Dan was so filled with sorrow because he refused to accept it. It depleted you. It almost took you out and the damage still lingers. Hug him to your heart, forgive him – but now move on.
He needs to live a loveless life to understand – just like you have.

Monday, July 29, 2002
Was that Dan yesterday?
Yes. He still longs for your warmth just as much as you long for his body. Once he understood how much of "you" he had trampled over, ignored, rejected, dismissed, made fun of, not appreciated, held back – yes, I am still annoyed at him – he felt bad. But once again, the damage he did to you still lingers. It's why your life took a nose dive downward after you got married.
You expected it – the marriage – to lead you into discovering more aspects of who you were. But it only made you experience the side you don't much like anyway. But you were angry at him. He cheated you, dear, and you had every right to be mad. Once again though, you were in a no-win situation. For your own reasons you could not leave him. Your health was so damaged from the drugs he let you take, despite the fact he didn't want the baby. You thought you had no choice but to stick it out until you were stronger. Only you never got stronger.
The last 10, 12 years have been difficult…your two sisters, mother, father and brother…all dead to you…
Your brother needs to be kept at long arm's length. He doesn't wish you well. He only seeks revenge, because you rejected him and wouldn't play his game.
Thank you…

You should not fear anything. Just look. When you feel your body go into fear mode, know deeply that you are fine. You don't need anything...you will be fine.

Wednesday, July 31st arrived, and I drove onto the Disney lot once again. Butterflies filled my stomach as I walked through the wide doorway below the towering statues of Snow White's Seven Dwarfs. Upstairs at Touchstone, Mark and Michael Polish, their tall, young assistant and Brigitte waited. Everyone was dressed in black, as usual. As we were led into a big sun-drenched office, I met the boyishly handsome Jason Reed, with his tussled chestnut hair and deep blue eyes that almost matched his crisp blue shirt. When he and the twins finished with the usual pleasantries, I began to talk. I told Jackie's story and the amazing tale of these heroic women pilots. I talked uninterrupted for almost a full hour. When I finished, Jason just nodded, turned to Michael Polish and asked about his schedule, and then we all walked out and into the elevator.

As soon as the elevator doors closed, the twins high-fived each other, and said, "We've got a movie!"

"What?" I said, "How do you know?"

"He asked about when we'd be available," Michael said.

Could this be true? They both seemed so sure, and who was I to argue? The following day, Brigitte called and told me the deal was being hammered out. I would be paid $75,000 to write the first draft, and Michael and Mark would do the second. Fine. We were represented by the same agency, so I told my agent to talk to theirs. I was so excited – my new life was about to take flight. I would get to write the movie.

At the same time Dan, too, was moving into a new phase:

August 1, 2002

Barushe here – the Dan that was your Dan is no more. He is heading for a new adventure. He is about to be conceived. The time is here.

Just as Dan said, it was a fast turnaround. Since he was heading "out," I thought about heading up to Mendocino to do the energy workshop.

August 2, 2002
The trip North?
Go if you want to. The drive will be good.

Then Dan broke in:

I've been conceived! I've been conceived!

Where?

Africa!!

Africa?

He'd said he wanted something harsh, but Africa? Africa now consumed in famine, war and an AIDS epidemic? That Africa? Was he nuts? All I could think was, Good luck!

Chapter Fourteen

Travelin' Man

In August, everyone in the entertainment industry takes their vacations, so like Paris and New York, Los Angeles closes down. Since inking the final deal among agents, lawyers, studio heads, the financial departments and the Polish brothers was going to take time – and hearing the details filled me with anxiety – I decided to head up to Mendocino.

Brigitte called to tell me that the boys, who were in pre-production on a Miramax movie, had a huge run-in with Harvey Weinstein. "Don't worry," she said, "they'll patch things up." Harvey Weinstein, who ran Miramax, is famous for his temper and willingness to seek revenge when crossed, so naturally, I worried. I woke up with my stomach clinched in fear that all my work would be for nothing.

I tried to concentrate, but the drilling from next door made it impossible to work.

August 7, 2002 – 8:43 a.m.

Barushe – too much clatter for you to do this. Come back later. You're too blown out with the swirling of negativity that now is trying to pull what is yours away.

We are fighting the fight for you. That is all that I will say. Go off to Mendocino, and when you come back, all will be settled. One way or another. Don't worry about it. It's out of your control. All you can control is your reaction to it. Keep working on the project and keep focused on what your job is. To write. The boys have other problems. Big problems.

So off I went. As I sped north along the straight-shot freeway that slices through the flat farmlands of central California, I listened to The Teaching Company's, "The History of the Jewish People," and "The Philosophy and History of Judaism."

Chris Fernie, my Qigong teacher, taught the workshop high up in the mountains above Mendocino, at a YMCA camp – the rustic Camp Gualala. For five days, under tall pine trees in a beautiful meadow, we "ran our energy." I could feel precisely where my energy was blocked – around my heart – and I worked hard to open it up, and clear it out. At the week's end, we cranked up the stereo and "Qigong" danced. Music blared while all the girls danced together and focused energy flew around the room. The dancing filled my body with such sheer, joyous fun that for the first time since Dan had died, I felt alive again.

The next day, I decided to take the coastal route back to Berkeley, which is much longer, but unbelievably gorgeous. As I drove down the mountain toward the Pacific, the sun streamed through moss-covered pine trees onto the shimmering lime green ferns that lined the roadway, and I marveled at the profound beauty of it all. I could feel Dan's energy seeing through my eyes, and I could hear him talking to me. Mendocino was his old stomping ground, but wasn't he in Africa? Wasn't he supposed to be gone?

I stayed overnight in Berkeley to see old friends, and my friend Laura gave me a tape for the drive back home. I listened to a sultry rendition of "One Fine Day," which made me cry as I sped past the smelly cattle herds at Harris Ranch. Then, as the BMWs and Mercedes whizzed by me going a hundred, Bob Dylan's scratchy voice sang "It Ain't Me, Babe." That song, and his young, entitled attitude, made me so angry, I turned it off. Right then, I could hear Dan chatting again. As I've mentioned, if I didn't have a pen in my hand, I couldn't remember what he said, but when I got home, even though I was tired, I found out:

Thursday, August 15, 2002 – 11 p.m.

Dan, the spirit man here. Was with you in the car. That was me marveling at the beauty of that land. The coastline is so magnificent.

And yes, it was me apologizing for our "trip" stuff. I always got so angry at you on vacations. You had a good time – a better time without me.

Then he sent a "love blast," which made me long for him again, so much against orders, the next day, I opened the "Dan file."

Friday, August 16, 2002

Dan, the spirit man here now…not fully present, since I'm monitoring my "new" self constantly. I'm all over the place. Seems so long ago that I was so intractably depressed. What a waste! Don't ever let yourself not experience the magnificence of the world as it is now. Not how we think we'd like it. It's fine just as it is. I don't know why I was so critical of every little thing. I was so jealous of the way you looked at your life…no expectations.

Just accepting what happened and dealing with it. That is what makes you strong.

I was with you all the way home and felt the anger when Bob Dylan came on with all that rot about "it's not me, Babe." And you were right, that was my stance entirely throughout our marriage. I didn't care about you, in truth. I wanted you dependent, but then once you became dependent, I despised you for it.

The amazing thing to me is that you continued to love me. You just loved how I smelled and felt. You are the little beastie thing. Yet your intellect understood how cheated you were.

This is all postmortem, literally. They – my guides and the "elders" – made me see all this.

Our relationship is the clearest, most honest of this last incarnation. And it's clear only because you insisted on clarity. If it had been left to me, I would have made it fuzzy and inauthentic. And I knew this deeply. That's why I kept thanking you for all your work. Thank the stars that I did that. It's what made me see how off base my own petty jealousy of you was. My "Enoch" part was trying to get me on track, because he knew what had been promised to you. But I refused to let go.

The "Jewish" tapes resonated with you because of your "background." You actually were more Jewish than I was. We both knew that, but I know it for certain. You were killed in the Holocaust, but not as a child, as you think. I know the specifics, but I don't want to see them and filter them through. They are not pretty. But the people who you lived with in New York were all friends. Your building? All survived what "you" did not.

(I always joked with Dan about my being more Jewish than he was. When I lived in Manhattan, I lived in a building owned by an Auschwitz survivor, and filled with people who had tattooed numbers on their inner arms – all survivors, bless them.)

And does it matter? You were a doctor in your last life. That's why you thought you'd be a doctor again. A Jewish doctor in Berlin. Enough. The child you see being killed was yours. She is back in your life.

None of this is necessary for you to embrace what is left of this life.

What is necessary is for you to take the opportunities presented and just work as hard as you can. Your own energy is now back to "normal." Normal for you, which isn't "normal." Ordinary. You still have to take care and not run yourself into the ground. Which you did, and that's why all this happened in the first place.

In real life, Brigitte kept me current on the movie deal as the agents and law-yers hammered it out. Throughout the day, however, I would feel the familiar tug of Dan trying to reach me.

Saturday, August 17, 2002 – 8:14 a.m.
Was that Dan's energy? Or what?
Barushe here.

> *"Your Dan" is a strong character. And when you went to Mendocino, he finagled "permission" to revisit it with you. To try to heal your "driving" karma – the car karma – he was so awful to you when you drove! How you stood his complaining is more than I want to deal with right now.*
> *Just keep connected to assuage your own doubts and keep working. Everyday. No matter how you feel. You are strong, yet delicate and it's such an odd mix for you to manage. You are fierce and your temper is not your best feature. So when you feel yourself "losing" it, just pull yourself together. The anger that fills your body doesn't serve you.*

(The anger concerned my new neighbors, Mike and Pedro, who had bought the house next-door to re-do, then sell, or "flip." They screamed at each other constantly and called each other mother-fucking-cock-suckers, which seemed quite amusing since after all, they were gay.)

> *How to deal with these neighbors? Just send out good vibrations – literally – and they will come around. They are actually very sweet people. You just both got on each others nerves.*
> *Enough? Go walk, since your body is still stiff from that drive, which you actually liked. You loved that drive up north. And yes, your Dan stayed with you and he's actually still around. That's why you "miss" him so suddenly again.*

Sunday, August 18, 2002 – 8:09 a.m.
> **Barushe here.** *Dan's energy is still here because you flirted with him and said you'd have a date. And it's unusual that a sexual connection is still so alive in both of you. So say goodbye to him today. He needs to focus on his "new" life in this young girl.*
> *But an old soul...and an old love of your Dan's. Enoch's really. Your Dan was yours...very specific to the time and place. But he reassembles himself quite easily, which is obvious to you because you feel him. That's why you're so "mourning-filled" this morning. It's not good for your body. So get on and over it. You need to move on. You need to let him go. Finish with all of it.*

I wish I had been able to "finish with all of it," but the process of letting go is difficult, to say the least. If you've read, *The Dead*, by James Joyce, that feeling of "the dead" never really leaving us is shared by so many. And now I understood why. The "dearly departed" hang around the living to experience the love energy we feel for them. And at that time, I felt nothing but love for Dan, so he hovered near me, much against orders. I began to worry about "him/her," off in the wilds of Africa.

Wednesday, August 21, 2002 – 7:39 a.m.
The famine part of Africa? Is that where Dan is?

Cobalt Blue– Don't worry about Dan. You have enough to worry about in worrying about you right now. You have to stay focused on you. You are important. You make a difference. You can't keep hiding your own light. It's a big light and you should begin to share it. It's taken a lot of effort to keep you alive. Effort on your own part, but effort on many entities who need you for "communication" purposes.

The book, and the information contained in the book, will help many, many other souls who are in the same kind of pain. It will lead them to make the journey to connect with their lost loves, children, parents – and then connect with their own source.

And that, my dear, is your true mission. You are part, a small part, of the working whole that is set in place. But you have to commit to do the work. If you don't do the work, it won't get done. No one up here can type!

You wanted to "channel" because you were a channel. Silk purse, sow's ear? You wanted to write because you are a writer. Remember? You need to write stories of heroism, because you are a hero. These girls. The fly girls are women heroes.

Advice for today?

Sit with the love that now streams into your body from the "source." Feel it. Yes…let it make you smile.

Anything else?

You need to keep your life little now. Keep your energy focused on your work and don't get side-tracked. You blow away energy on Sam, but you love him so much that it's what you want to do.

Thursday, August 22, 2002 – 8:06 a.m.

Cobalt Blue connected to circuits you can't see, but you feel now. It's uncomfortable, but breathe, push and your body will settle down in a few minutes. Just breathe through the discomfort. Believe you can reclaim your life not as it was lived, but how you dreamed it could be lived, and you will be able to claim what was stolen by that younger spirit you loved. You tried to fix him, but what a waste of your energy.

Stop trying to fix Sam. He needs to fix himself or suffer the consequences. It's the name of the game. For you to not work on your book is what makes you antsy.

Don't block energy flowing through you, even if it's the mourning being released. It's got to get out of there. And don't worry about next door... mixed feelings are all there ever are. Scales just tip one way or another. "No expectations?" I beg to differ. You always had big expectations, only you never let yourself realize them.

(I used to say that if I ever wrote an autobiography, I'd call it "No Expectations.")

You could not have been a doctor because of your recent past – the victimhood – was just that. A good, pious Jewish doctor who believed that his good works would save him. But he didn't realize that he was in a larger drama that had little to do with his own "needs." He did the "right thing," but he still wasn't happy about his own performance.

You need to "perform" in a way you'll be happy with.

Great. Now I worried about my own "performance." I still wasn't working on the book – it was simply too painful. The next day was Sam's birthday, and he was angry at me. He was breaking up with his girlfriend, and he'd call me for comfort, but I was depleted and had nothing more to give him.

I'd been reading Michael Newton's books, *Journey of Souls,* and *Destiny of Souls,* where his clients talk about "resting energy" available in the In Between. And so I thought I'd ask for some:

Saturday, August 24, 2002
I want to take some energy out of my "resting" account – if that's possible. I'm tired of running my life on such "marginal energy."

Cobalt Blue here – your marginal energy is more than most peoples'. If you took anymore you would really blow your own circuits. Your body is just in mourning and you took that damned disease...

The work you do on the earth plane is not the only work you do. Your dreams are so weird to you because you have memory of places you go.

You are our project right now, and it's not a done deal. Everything changes constantly. It changes with the, rather, like the winds...only the winds are your thoughts. So if you can discipline your thoughts to work for you, rather than against you – which because of your/Barushe's choice in placing you with those "younger" souls – you learned. You thought that that way of being toward your body was the best way to be. It's very Christian. And even though at three we told you how silly those beliefs were, you couldn't listen to us over those huge people – actually that sweet person – who taught you. Your reaction to "Jesus in your heart" still makes us smile.

(When I was three, a sweet neighbor lady held a Bible class where she told me that I had to get "Jesus into my heart." At the time, I thought, "But he's so big! How could he get inside me?" She also explained that all the Chinese people would go to hell because they weren't Christian, and even at three, I knew that couldn't be so.)

It was hard; it is always hard – for an old soul to be in a baby's body. Re: your book – as we said, all books are channeled in a way. Your book needs to be finished before "Fly Girls" hits. We are working to make sure you get the opportunity to do the first draft. After that, it won't matter. You will prove you can do the job for the boys and they will appreciate you.

Re: the WWII incarnation Dan told you about? Yes, you were more Jewish than he was...are more Jewish, but that life as a pious Jew taught you much about organized religion...well, not that you needed – you've had many lifetimes in organized religions of one kind or another. Ultimately, they all fall short because they become infused with power-driven people.

Thank you. Anything else for today?

Let us fill you with love. You still long for "your Dan." We fear you might get hooked again by one of those wily men. You've been one too many times, yourself. Just keep with the girls for a while. Focus on your books. Get your kids story out.

Sam is back and he will want a pep talk this morning. Turn off your phone. He needs to schedule time that works for you, rather than calling you as a "fix" when it suits him. Don't let him feed from you like Dan did.

Your relationship with him is important to both of you and you do him no service to let him take your time for granted. Call him tonight when it is convenient for you. Start weaning him off your "mother tit" energy. Begin to claim the "friend energy" that is appropriate for "friends." Because Dan passed up the opportunity to parent Sam together, fully, Sam is attached to Maggie as a mother. He doesn't see you in that light. And that's a good thing, really.

As we said, the relationship is "intense," but it's been only one way. Totally non-reciprocal. So pull back. Let him begin to initiate. Let everyone begin to initiate.

But you must not lose your gentleness towards him. You love him so much, just as you loved his dad. He appreciates it more.

The song keeps going through your head because you are worried about "your Dan."

(The song was Julia Fordham's "Missing Man.")

He is in for an "adventure." And in his dreams he will probably try to get back to the comfort of your arms, while you still long for him.

Advice? Love the man that might have been, but never was. That was the man you waited for. That was the man he refused to become.

You must become the "Stephanie" you wanted to become. The reason you only thought about being an "artist" is because you are an artist. How much proof do you need? Just work now. As Dan tried to tell you, you only have a limited amount of time to accomplish some pretty stiff "goals."

(Become the Stephanie I wanted to become? Who had the energy? Not me. Not then.)

On to the "Fly Girls." Disney lies about everything; it's how they do business. So it's hard to keep them focused on getting things done. The boys are busy elsewhere. You have forces on your side that are more effective than an agent right now. Stay humble in your expectations and just do the work. The work is what's important to you.

Thank you.

You're welcome. You can access this information when you need it. Continue to take good care of your body...you are still feeling the effects of Dan's death and the mourning. But less so.

The "Disney lies about everything," will come as no shock to anyone who pays attention to the business pages and reads about the war between Michael Eisner and Michael Ovitz. But right then, I was hoping that "Fly Girls" would still take off.

In the meantime, Sam and I planned a trip back to Yosemite to put some of Dan's ashes in a few places he loved – Sentinel Dome and the Panoramic Trail, which overlooks Glacier Point. Sam agreed to go, somewhat reluctantly, so I booked the cabin and paid for it, while Dan continued to bombard me with his focused energy.

Thursday, August 29, 2002 – 7:28 a.m.
Advice for today?

Cobalt Blue here…that was Dan back.

Can I talk to him?

If you want.

> Not Dan anymore at all, but still miss you. Take what remains of my earth body and throw it to the winds in Yosemite. Even what's in the jar. Especially what's in the jar. Save some for France if you want, but there's no need to keep me around the house. It pulls me back. And I need to move on. I'll need all my energy to adjust to this new environment.
>
> I've been coming and being with you, somewhat against orders. But we really can do what we want.
>
> And I always did, much to my chagrin, with you. The "letting me go" will help you with your final move out of the mourning.
>
> I miss what you wanted us to have together and what I accepted all too briefly from you. I saw it so clearly from your eyes…"they" – your guides and Barushe – still don't like that I want to comfort you and me in the process, but I know how much you miss my hugs. And I know how much I miss yours.
>
> Re: Sam? He's fine. I'm sorry I crippled him so much. He does need to toughen up.
>
> How you can still cry over me is beyond my comprehension, but what wasn't? Such a determined oaf! And yet the sweetness of your love still makes it… enjoyable is not the right word, but it's dreamy, delicious to go back and feel the warmth of your body.
>
> I am startled by this new reality I'm just getting used to. It's very noisy! People scream at one another constantly. The young girl doesn't have AIDS, as someone said. She doesn't even know she's pregnant yet.

Say goodbye to Sam for me. I could go and talk to him, but I'm a little uncomfortable with his "interior" monologues. They are so self-obsessed to the point of reminding me of my Dan-ness, which only cared about my Dan-ness.

Just remember when you think of me, that when all was said and done, I appreciated you for doing the "wife" job. I know you appreciated me and I thank you for wanting me to become a man. I hadn't bothered to before.

Your love for me still makes me happy, even here. I think they're giving me the hook, my love. Let me be on that trail (Panoramic). That way I'll be able to find my way back there. I'll recognize the DNA. Literally. Love you from Africa!

Cobalt Blue here again after your "visit." Barushe may be angry with him, but you still need to feel the love you have for him – he is in your house. In your body as well.

Today? You're achy, so go off for a walk and come back and work. You've mostly got to read the book over and make changes. Stop by the Bodhi Tree and see what publishers might be good.

Friday, August 30, 2002 – 7:29 a.m.
Yesterday feels shot to hell. Both Sam and Lynn were in meltdown mode. I couldn't focus on work. I woke this morning at 4:30, but didn't want to get up, because I didn't want to be exhausted all day.
Advice for today?

Cobalt Blue here – you need to be nicer to yourself. Just because we can't recreate emotion as easily as "your Dan" does not mean there is not love. The love for you is intense from here. And yet you feel so totally abandoned now. You feel so totally alone in the world. It's what's making you so deeply sad. Give yourself the weekend off. Just do things that please you. Go hear the music at the museum tonight, if you want.

Go to the movies. Go to the beach in the morning. Spend the time alone, but enjoy your aloneness. When you spend time with Sam, it's all about him.

Just keep your "channels" open. Do the Qigong.

If and when you want a "channeled book," all you need to do is sit and ask for it. I can't tell you what it will be about. Read the James book (William James, the philosopher) and you will have a grounding so it (the channeling) won't seem so odd to you. But it doesn't feel odd to you anyway. You have been doing this quite a long time. Now it's much more efficient. The

**luxury of not having to transcribe it, or deliver it out loud as in the case
of Rupert and Joseph.** (Jane Roberts and Robert Butts, who channeled the
"Seth Books.")

I need more energy.

**Then stop squandering it where it's not appreciated. Keep to yourself this
weekend. Putter around your house. Clean the rugs if you want, but don't
get on the phone with the blood suckers. You don't have the energy to offer
up. You make the choice. You, we might add, are still in mourning. But no
one seems to remember that. So you have to remember that.**

**Your Dan...what a mix. I hoped he would come through for you. He didn't.
Next, as you would say.**

Saying "Next" was easier said than done. September was almost here, and Dan
continued to burst into my system and then drain my energy. He'd apologize for
what couldn't be fixed, and fill me with his "love bursts." It felt so good, because
it filled my brain with much needed oxytocin, the love chemical. I was now an
addict – a love addict – and breaking any addiction is tough. I had to let him go,
but how? Maybe the trip to Yosemite would do the trick.

Chapter Fifteen

"Porcelain"
or
We Have a Song?

In September, Yosemite is tinder-dry. The Merced River flows at half its springtime fullness, the grand Yosemite Falls become nothing but a trickle, and the warm winds smell of dried pine needles – the park feels almost deserted, so to me, it's sheer heaven. Once again, I rented cabin 42, the same cabin we'd had in April when we first spread Dan's ashes. Now I wanted to say more than "Good-bye," I wanted to say, "Be gone! Move on."

I tried to follow the "advice" I got daily, but my own emotions made it difficult. My working on *The Married Girl's Guide* came to a halt, because telling the story of a marriage that had ultimately been so destructive seemed senseless. How could my story help anyone else? Would anyone even believe me? I didn't think so, right then.

The only thing I wanted to do was watch TV. If I'd "coded" myself out, using the DSM III model from my research days at UCLA, I would have popped right into the column marked "acute depression." I got a stern talking to:

Sunday, September 15, 2002 – 10:30 p.m. (after watching The Sopranos)
Barushe here – to tell you that the focus of your life is expressed in the way you live it. If you continue to not write your book, you will not survive. You must write query letters tomorrow. Go get the Writer's Market and send them out. Believe there is a need for your work. It is simply why you were born. You weren't born to have babies – even though you wanted them. You were born to write your books. So do it. How much encouragement can we offer? Go to sleep. Get up and work. Forget all else.

I wouldn't survive? At that moment, that felt just fine with me. I felt like one of Samuel Beckett's trash can characters who laments, "I can't go on. I can't go on." He sits in silence, considers his options, and then says, "I guess I'll go on." What else is there?

Wednesday, September 18, 2002 – 7:25 a.m.

Last night, I watched a show about African Jews – the lost tribe of Israel. Their DNA matched the DNA of the Priest line in Israel. Advice for today?

Cobalt Blue here – keep reading your new book. It will reinforce the work you are doing and inform the next phase of your life. You will find much information that will help to integrate what you are doing on the conscious level with what you do on other levels of consciousness. You will notice that I didn't say unconscious. Nothing you do can be unconscious now, except the running of your marvelous 'machine,' which you do pretty well. Yesterday's response to the pain in your body was impressive.

Today your need to walk will present itself again and follow it, then you must come back and work. Even if it's just editing the book and re-reading your "Dan" stuff. You need to begin to get it out there.

It will find its place. Keep focused on you. There is no way to see advance events because of all the variables. Deal with "what is" in your reality now and know that you change the course of your reality just by how you respond. So continue to respond in the knowledge that you will be able to handle all that comes your way, as you told yourself on your tape.

Continue to connect with your mission in your mind and continue to bless your life – enjoy the day and then we have more work for you to do.

There is another book waiting to be delivered once you send off your own book. But you need to re-read the *Sacred Prostitute* to understand the majesty of the sexual connection. It's in not honoring it that people get confused. Sam will come to his own awareness of his magical self, but you can be there when he asks. He is one of the loves of your life, as you are his. You just don't need to express it sexually and that is, in fact, very liberating for you both. For the two of you tend to be somewhat obsessive sexually, no matter what form you take.

Anything else?

That's enough for today, unless you want to chat with your Dan, who is here, "reformed" in more ways than one. That was "his" joke.

Of course, I want to talk to my Dan.

Dan, the ? Here from…

I am not wanted in my new life. How different a feeling tone. My "young girl" knows she's pregnant now and is terrified at her parents' reactions. She knows, but no one else does yet. But it's only a matter of time before I will grow so big that she will not be able to hide me from the world.

What's interesting to me is that, of course, you must have had the same experience with your parents. Your example will help me to get used to this new reality.

You watched that show last night because you wanted to "see" Africa at a distance. I see it up close and it is indeed different. I am not, unfortunately, in that lost tribe. Their life is very structured and organized. I am somewhere else where the beliefs are "askew" is the only word for it.

I want to be with you on the drive up (to Yosemite) because I like the tapes you listen to, and I like just hanging around you. They don't really want me to, so I need your permission. I want to be there when you eat the steak and have fun with "our" son. Mine, really, he's your friend. That's why I was always jealous. I knew you had a direct connection that had nothing to do with obligation.

Yes, take me to Sentinel Dome and to Panoramic Trail…it will comfort me in this life to come to be able to find my "old white male" DNA. I am going to live a long life, I think.

Feel me on the drive. Let me love you like I could have, should have when I lived with you. And then I will let you go, so you can begin to find the courage to love someone who will reciprocate your sweetness. But when I loved you, my darling, it was the best I could do, and you know that.

I miss making love to you and will miss your kisses for a very long time. They need me to leave, and I must behave or I won't be allowed to visit. Bye.

When I read the channeling over, "There is another book waiting to be delivered," caught my eye. What did that mean? And Sam was an "old lover?" An old friend? In this life, I was not even his stepmother anymore, and whether or not he wanted to be friends remained to be seen.

Thursday, September 19, 2002 – 7:48 a.m.
Today, I drive up to Yosemite. I need to move on, and yet I want to hold on to what I feel for him.
Advice for today?

Cobalt Blue here – yes, you're right about having "two tracks" within you right now. "Your Dan" wants to talk because you "invited" him so specifically. And he, as usual, will focus on his own plight. But it is your trajectory that I am more concerned with just now. You will make a conscious effort to just cut the cords that bind you so tightly to him. He is not even a him anymore. Your "memories" of his Dan-ness are really all that will exist for a while, because from my point of view – and he, too, has guides who would like him not _to use_ you as much as he does – he needs to learn to be alone. It doesn't help him for you to continue to need him. And of course, it doesn't help you to move on with your own life.

I wanted to say truncated life, but it's not. You set yourself up with some pretty stiff challenges and you've done a good job. You can help the process along, and be very pleased with yourself if, when you come home, you will devote all your energy to finishing your book. No matter what happens with your script work. Your book will make you stronger. Your book and the work that follows is what you are "contractually" obligated to fulfill.

You cannot allow Sam to infect you with his own "worry." You must be firm with him. It's not helpful to him for you to listen to him complain. He needs to become a man. You were, I might add, a good man, so you know what it means.

Yes, the image of your daughter in the last life and the connection with Lynn is authentic. But you two are more than just that lifetime together. That's why she's so exasperating to you at times and why she needs your approval so intensely. Give it to her without hesitation. You love her deeply.

Just bring your written journals to connect with your core...and with your Dan...for what we would like to think is the last time, but he does do exactly as he pleases, your Dan. Enoch's actually not pleased.

Here he is...

Dan, the? Now in and out of realities like a sprite. Ah, yes, you and my son. What a team. I love you both so much. Thank you for taking all this time to honor me. And it is _honoring_ me for you to take this kind of ceremonial time. _Ceremony_, as you so rightly insisted upon both from the outset of our marriage and in the living of our life together, is so fundamentally important to "being" and so totally devoid from most of how everyone lives their lives that, again, thank you for insisting.

I can feel you wanting to get up and shower and get on the road. But I just want to sit here and chat with you all day long. Because a part of me, and a very large part, knows that I will be asked not to return for awhile. And please don't cry now, because it will stop the process. The emotion that comes up wipes up (away) my ability to communicate.

Just once again, my sweet and wonderful wife that was, thank you for everything you gave to both of us. If you can give any of your wisdom and

my fucked up experience to anyone else – *even one couple* – it is a mitzvah.
(A good deed.) **And you should know from mitzvahs! You devout Jew, you!**

**Forgive me for denying my true self from both of us. I missed me more than
you did. Nothing is preordained and everything's in flux constantly and
that is the magic and wonder of the universe.**

**I will be with you on the drive, but then you will not remember anything I say
to you. You're right about it – the information bypasses memory centers.
You hear it, but can't quite capture it. Just like you hear this, but can't
capture it until you read it over.**

**That's how it works. We wouldn't be able to do it otherwise. The ability that
you've developed now will be useful to you, and I'm glad that I was a part
of the process. As I said, your magic is my reality.**

**You are right about my "settling" down within my "old love." She will
recognize me when I pop out and I hope will be smart enough to love me
then. If not, then I will have to deal with it, just like you did. My love, my
teacher who I refused to study with. Oh well, as Mr. Benny would say.**

Thank you for your love.

You deserved so much more. Okay, go shower and get on the road.

As I drove up to Yosemite, I could feel his energy with me. After I got settled,
I sat out on the porch that overlooks the river, and listened to the crickets, the
sound of wind, and the rush of the river. A full moon shined down through the
pines onto the river, and I could feel him appreciating it all, so I called to him.

Sept. 19, 2002 – (The Redwoods in Yosemite)
Dan?

**Dan, the ? – I can only stay a while tonight – it's day in Africa and I need to
monitor my new situation. Very bizarre, having this kind of "being" be me.
But I guess it seemed odd to you too – to go from what you had – to where
you wound up.**

You're going to be a little African girl? All I can think to say is, "Good luck!"

Yes! me too!

Any last words? Tomorrow I'll take you to Sentinel Dome, and Saturday to Glacier Point.

Be forgiving when you see me. I only wish I could hug you with my big, strong arms. Thank you for loving my body so much.

September 20, 2002
Dreams – with people in acting classes.

Cobalt Blue – the dream represents all aspects of probable realities that were open to you. The child you saw represents the child that might have been.
Take time to acknowledge what the choice you made cost you. Don't blame anyone else, even your Dan.
You acquiesced by giving up your power when he asked you to. You had only recently gotten it, so we were stunned when you gave it away so cavalierly. Your task is now to let him go with love. All the love you have for him – send him on his way. He needs to be free to participate fully in his next adventure. Sam needs to let him go, too, but you have no control over Sam.

How best to do it?

Exactly as planned. Take him today with you and tomorrow with Sam. Cast him to the wind and watch – see him fly away. It is _your love_ and longing that keeps his soul connected here. A bad habit that needs to be broken. For both of you.
You can only reclaim your life and your full energy by focusing on the present, and not allowing the past to constantly flood your consciousness.
You were so unrelentingly unhappy with him so much of the time – you need to step into the joy of your own life. Do that, as you would say, one moment at a time, one choice at a time. Know that you will be fine.

So I hiked up to the top of Sentinel Dome. I stood, looking out over the awe-inspiring view of Yosemite Valley, and thought of a time when Dan and I had been up there in the fog. An ancient, gnarled tree – a dead tree – grows out of the rock, so I sprinkled some of Dan around the tree, then sat down, leaned against it, pen in hand. A chilly breeze made me shiver, and I could feel him shower me with love.

September 20, 2001 – 12 noon – at Sentinel Dome

Dan – yes! Here – and thank you my sweet soul-connection for putting me on this _sacred_ ground. I will be able to connect with you from here – at least I "think" so – I see now through your "eyes," and feel that crisp, hard breeze

as it rustles your shirt and makes your skin shiver. Oh, how exquisite to be
alive! And yet it's fine not being alive. Don't long to "go" – you'll be out of
your life far longer than you are in. Let me go with love; let me go with the
generosity of spirit that you honored me with in life.
I remember the day in the fog up here – it was so magical. I will wait for Sam
to say a final goodbye.

Then I drove back to the cabin and went to the river, with Seth's *The Way
Toward Health*, the book I'd brought with me.

Later I sat by the river, pen in hand:

You wanted to come here to the river side – do you want me to put "you" around here?

You can if you want. I can experience it more directly through your body.
At least I can now. This is a huge gift, another one you've given me. This
weekend. Very few people or souls get this much devoted attention. I know
it's for you as well as me, but thank you, my sweet Stephanie.
Who knew how much I loved you? I had <u>no</u> idea. Yes, I wish I'd acted like it
while I was expressed in flesh.
Again, my sweet Stephanie, I feel I owe you an apology. You recognized the "validity"
in the Seth books and all I did was well, the three D's – dismiss, demean, destroy.
(A narcissist's method of dealing with reality.) **Anyway, keep reading.**

Later that night I read over all the Dan channeling. I could feel him want to
comment:

September 20, 2002 – 11 p.m.

Dan here – yes, reading that over in one shot is fascinating to you. The ache in
your legs is because this does stress your "currents." Tomorrow when you
dump what's left of "me" on the trail and over the ridge, sing our song.

We have a song? What is it?

Porcelain.

Julia Fordham's "Porcelain." A beautiful song that I'd play on our date nights.
"And you treat my skin like porcelain," is one of the lyrics, but for the life of me I
couldn't remember the rest of them, so I changed the subject.

What's happening in Africa?

Don't ask. It's a mess. The girl, who is 16, is very frightened about telling anyone – she wants to abort me.

Then what happens?

Back to square...not 1. (Maybe) 5 or 6? But she's going to see a wise old woman who will tell her how much I will help her.

Sam arrived very late that night, stressed with work, and obsessed with the San Francisco Giants' shot at the World Series. The next day, after a Giants' playoff game, we drove up to Glacier Point, threw Dan to the winds, then hiked down Panoramic Trail to sprinkle more of Dan's ashes there, as we watched a family of deer nibble on leaves. Sam asked me about Dan's relationship with his own father. Later I could feel Dan want to chat.

Saturday, September 21, 2002 – 6 p.m.

Dan here, barely. You put me exactly where I would have put myself. The question Sam asked about my father was too non-specific to really answer. We just didn't have much "connection" on earth or in other realms. Bonnie's (his sister's) connection much more intense, but I know you don't want to talk about that. I'll be with you tonight, my sweet Stephanie, and then they want me _gone_. At least for awhile. You will marry again, believe it or not. I will be filled with joy when it happens. All, the beauty of all this, my love.

The next day, Sam left early to rush back to Los Angeles to go to the Emmys. I stayed in Yosemite as long as I could, just to sit under the sequoias and listen to the river.

When I got back home and walked inside the house, it felt different. I assumed that I'd finally let Dan go. His clothes still filled his closet, and his desk still sat in the front room, unused, a reminder of all those frustrating, sorrow-filled years.

Monday, September 23, 2002 – 7:28 a.m.
It felt very strange walking into the house last night – seemed different. Didn't feel the same longing for him. I will type all the Yosemite stuff later. But Yosemite was great, the time with Sam, easy. Although he passed up an opportunity to swim in the Merced to listen to a baseball game, but it was his loss, from my point of view.

My body's stiff from the drive, I'll go walk, then come back and work.
Advice for today?

Cobalt Blue here – to help you minimize the impact of finally letting "your Dan" go. He has been with you in one form or another for almost 13 years, and now he is indeed gone. Your cells know it and your body knows it, even if your "intellect" wants to move on. You will, but be easy on yourself today. The heaviness you feel now is the emptiness that will miss him for a while longer. Just fill yourself with joy – playful joy, if you can take your memory to joyful places rather than down paths that won't help you heal. The healing must happen before you can fully embrace your new life. You must honor yourself as much as you honored your husband.

The love you shared was authentic and if he had not been able to come back to you and reassure you that he truly did love you – all appearances to the reverse, all actions as well, remember. So it is in remembering the best of him that you will continue to heal from the trauma of those 13 years. And they were traumatic for you. You lost yourself so completely.

But now is the time to reclaim yourself and your full energy and go out into the world with it. Even though you are lonely and still a sexual being and long for another male – don't do it yet. Give yourself the full year. It will prove better in the long run. You're not ready for another male anyway. They will only want to see what they can get from you, and you have nothing to offer right now. Remember that.

The machinery will continue to turn slowly, vis-à-vis your "project" ("Fly Girls"). We have only so much influence, but continue to remind the boys (Michael and Mark Polish) that it is your project. They will have the feeling that it will be jinxed if they cut you out, even though everyone else wants them to.

Re-read the "Dan material" and compose a query to editors who might be interested.

A kind and generous friend, who had trained with a shaman, Alberto Villoldo, Ph.D., and did "soul retrievals," offered to do a session for me. My problem, she said, was that my "dreaming Stephanie," my inner, uppity self, had left and refused to "come home" until I gave up the man who'd tried to murder her. I asked Cobalt Blue for perspective, and got pages and pages. I've edited them down, but left what I thought might be helpful.

Friday, September 27, 2002 – 6:44 a.m.

Woke up to a gonging in my ear.

Yesterday, I did an "illumination" with Rahmie. She kept asking what "spirit" was going to show up. She said it was a part of "Stephanie" that had been trying to get in for years. The "artist" side? Question to Cobalt Blue or Barushe: What really happened? And advice for today?

Cobalt Blue here – re: the illumination? The piece of your missing self needs to be encouraged. Do your Qigong with filling the pieces of your body energy...

Keep away from men for a while longer. You don't need one in your life for a long time yet. They almost have managed to kill you on many occasions. Remember your "father" taking you to the hospital and caring nothing at all for you. Only caring about his book. Remember that Paul thing (the man I lived with in New York) **offering you a baby, then reneging. Just like your Dan did. Refuse to give any more energy away to men.**

You need all your energy for yourself. That is the only way you will be able to fulfill your destiny.

Re: destiny? No one's destiny is assured. It is a moment by moment choice. Your strength is considerable. You just need to honor the force of your personality and not hide it away from whomever you come across. Read the books you bought. Take time to visit the people you love.

Saturday, September 28, 2002 – 7:39 a.m.

Dream: In an apartment, where I find a broken cell phone. Smashed in frustration, but destroyed. Know that Dan's done it, and now I'm annoyed. Angry. Everything he's done drives me nuts, so I finally walk across the hall to where he lives and tell him I want a divorce. He says, "Fine. I'll just leave." Then, I'm really angry because he won't fight for the relationship.

But I woke up happy that I don't have to be angry at him anymore. I realized that I was angry at him, low level anger, for 12 years. I knew he'd cheated me, but I just took it. My own choice. My own decision not to stand up for myself.

Advice for the day? Help?

Cobalt Blue waiting – transmission delayed.

Set the alarm from now on. Even on Sunday. Don't override your need to stay on schedule. The comfort you seek in the television is not comfort, but numbing of pain. Just feel the pain and move on. You can take it. Feel it like you did yesterday and then release the hurt and anger and move on. You can't fill yourself with you when you are filled with rage. You've been

filled with rage for a while, so release it. There will finally be a relief. The relief you felt when you woke to never needing to be angry all the time? Authentic.

Keeping people angry all the time is a technique. A technique we talked about yesterday. A technique your Dan also had down pat. He kept you annoyed on purpose. It was soul-killing, but a way he could hook your energy. And then waste it.

Draw yourself to yourself – the piece of you that left, left when you refused to honor your own creativity. Visualize your future and yet stay focused in the joy of the present.

Sunday, September 29, 2002 – 6:39 a.m.
Okay. I got up @ 5:30 without an alarm.

Cobalt Blue here – you see? The information is there. The "missing part" of you still hovers, not fully focused into you, but you need to encourage her more. To encourage your creative side, you must make the place in your life for her. And to do that you must clean up your office and make it neat. Get the "sorrow" papers out of there. Put them in the plastic bin and move them to the garage. You'll know where they are.

Encourage yourself the way you encourage other people. You are the only one who cares about you right now. You are the only one who cares whether you complete the work you set out for yourself, so if you don't make yourself a priority, no one else will. Just know that taking time to be alone is the only way to do it.

Anything else?

The mourning is not over, even though you want it to be. If it comes up today, let it go. Your Dan does want to talk to you, but he's no longer "your Dan" at all. He's losing the memories and it's making him nervous. He's learning a new language. That's why he wants to have the comfort of your memories. You can choose, but we suggest you choose in favor of your own needs which send him love from afar. Send him love. You couldn't have given him more.

Make the choices that feed your own life now. You need all your energy now.

I opened up a *New Yorker* and saw a cartoon of two people walking on the beach at sunset. She has a sly smile, but his bespectacled face scowls as he says, "All right, Stephanie, you win! It is great to be alive." I laughed out loud. Stephanie? Was that just a coincidence? Or was Dan chatting with cartoonists?

A week went by without my hearing from Dan, and then I felt a sharp pain in my neck and the familiar tug.

Sunday, September 29, 2002 – 8 a.m.

Dan, the ? here –

Thank you for opening up this file for me. The pain in your neck was me. I was such a pain in your neck. Your whole body. I'm a pain in someone else's body right now. I'm not me, or your "Dan" at all, but something so weirdly different it's amazing and the fact that I can still get through to you softens the blow of seeing all this "dryness" here.

That was a funny cartoon. I will try to enjoy "life" more this time around. I will still long for you, just like they said, but I will try to do it in a way that won't deplete your finite resources. You really already did give me enough of your time and energy. The reason I'm back is to add my voice to the voices of your own guides. My connection is more direct because I know your body so well.

When I thanked you for Yosemite, I don't think I thanked you enough. The ability to ground myself down on those sites you chose for me, the river rocks, the waterfall, the sequoias, the Panoramic trail, the Glacier Point, and around that old tree, which is, actually not dead. Just seems to be. Like I seem to be dead. I'm not dead. Only my stubborn, egotistically, unappreciative idiot part of me that never fully loved you while I lived with you. The idiot that refused to honor all you gave me. The idiot that still would give the world, were it mine to give, to crawl back into bed with you and hold you with those fabulous arms I got to inhabit for almost 62 years. What a gift. A gift I didn't fully appreciate. But you were my greatest gift. So when you wish you'd never met me, I understand. Just know that I will do my damnedest to make sure you get your "Fly Girls." And even though "I'm" in Africa, Enoch, who is me, still owes you and he is focused, along with Barushe, who is still a little standoffish.

That's my girl. Feel my love – let me welcome your other parts. Don't take my desk apart yet. I won't be born for seven months yet. I can still come and go. Let me stay and help when I can.

I wish we could go dancing. Damn, you tried so hard to put joy in our life. And I wouldn't let you. Now, let me not just think about myself, which they rightly think, is all I care about.

Monday, September 30, 2002 – 6:27 a.m.

I don't want to be disappointed with myself when I die. I want to figure out what the "task" is and just do it. I feel as if I can't quite ever do a good enough job of anything. I just read over two pages in my journal from the first few months of being married, and what a nightmare! Why didn't I pay attention to what was happening to me? I was being worn down. No wonder I was crazy.

Advice for today?

Cobalt Blue – The advice you seek you already know. You could easily give it to yourself. The glitch in taking it is a black slab of resistance and fear. If today, you can just begin to override the mechanics of it, begin to override the fear, override the "sabotage" of it, you will do it. But doing the work of the day is the only way around it. Not letting yourself fall into your own morose feeling tone that drags down your energy. If you need to, walk, and then work. Be more flexible, yet stay structured.

The last two months have been a waste of time you couldn't afford to waste. You accomplished not one new page of writing on your book.

When Dan saw the book disappear, he was right. It disappeared. Just like that. You need to encourage the book back.

Send out a query letter today. Make that a priority. Other writers have faith. You need faith.

I did need faith, but choosing faith over fear is easy to hear, but so much harder to do. September came to an end, and my life seemed to be on hold. I wouldn't work on the book, nor give up my dead husband, and because I refused to let him go, my "dreaming Stephanie" stayed clear. I still hoped that "Fly Girls" would take off, but it looked grounded.

Sam, on the other hand, was flying sky-high. The San Francisco Giants had won the National League Pennant, and he'd managed to get tickets for the World Series. And Dan would tag along with him. It was beginning to feel just like old times.

Chapter Sixteen

It's How You Play the Game

October is still summertime in Los Angeles, and the Boys of Summer were playing on our turf. The San Francisco Giants vs. Los Angeles Angels. (They were the Anaheim Angels then, but it was still San Francisco vs. L.A.) At one of the games, Sam caught a fly ball, and he was positive that Dan had sent it his way. Sam said he could feel his dad with him at the games. Dan was there, all right, but he was beginning to have a different perspective:

October 1, 2002

> **Dan, the sliver of positive energy expressed in joy for you to hook onto today. I will only be a moment, but your feeling that I was with you last night was authentic.**

(I'd had a dinner party, and I could feel him there.)

> **You know when I'm with you. You know when I'm not. But you can always feel me when you do the dishes, because I wish I could do them for you.**
> **If I could only give you back the energy I stole from you. I see it now. Don't let Sam steal from you. He doesn't appreciate you at all. Pull back for a while. Let him go it alone. Only focus your energy where it is reciprocated.**
> **Read over the "red book." Let your own creativity structure the pages. You'll figure it out, but get help.**

The red book contained the proposal and chapters for *The Married Girl's Guide to Hot and Sacred* Sex. To continue writing, however, I had to keep reading through my old journals, and I would sit there, stunned. Why had I allowed myself to be treated so badly? Was I that needy?

Even though I'd been advised not to encourage Dan, he chatted to me constantly. Sometimes, I'd be in bed, and I could feel his presence lying there next to me. I was doing a terrible job of letting him go, and I got a stern talking to.

October 6, 2002

Before you can do it, you have to want to do it. And you will want to do it, if you read over how much you suffered. If that's what it takes, go into your own journals and then ask yourself how much suffering do you need to withstand until you stand up for yourself?

In a last life (my German Jewish doctor life) you didn't stand up for yourself, because you assumed a great god would intercede for you. You expect the same kind of god to intercede here. And yet the kernel of god-ness is contained within you to access.

Don't think your suffering adds to the joy of the world. It doesn't. Your ability to experience the joy of your own existence is what will make you more joyful. Your ability to find the fun of the day no matter what's going on in "the world" is what will continue to make you strong.

(President George Bush, the younger, was leading the country into the war against Iraq just then, and Yellow Alerts filled the airwaves.)

It's all a game. The stakes seem to be rising to a very high pitch. But the game of cat and mouse that Mr. Bush, Jr. and Mr. Hussein play is just a settling of old scores. It's personal enmity.

Your Dan wants to say "Hi."

Dan, the sliver of awareness just now. Aware enough to know once again how much of your energy I stole and frittered away on sports, games and just unconscious bullshit. All I can do is to keep encouraging you to just show up and become the glorious personification of generosity you showed to me. Only don't waste it on another scoundrel who seduces you with "I love you's."

You were so easily captured. I flitted into the party last night and realized how much of a drag on you I was, even at the parties. Especially at the parties. You worked so hard, and I showed up at the end to light the candles. And I gave myself so much credit for that. I had no idea how much work you'd done.

You still long for the "authentic" me, the authentic Dan, who didn't bother to "come to the table," except to eat! What a man. Yet how you loved me, him.

I'll let you take apart my desk in due time. Not yet, though. I will try not to drag your energy down. I will try to just send you love. When I am in your "vicinity," as I was all day yesterday, it's why you feel so unhappy. You miss me, yet are so glad I'm gone. And I don't blame you one bit. I literally ruined our lives.

What's happening in Africa?

That's my girl. Let me talk about me, my favorite subject. But no, they don't want me to. I'm only here on a "pass." The transmission of that energy would take you out for the whole day, so I'm doing what's best for you.

Your circuits need to be strengthened to receive more energy. Think of cable lines under the ocean. Laying the cable lines took a great deal of effort. The connections were not very clear. Then they sent up satellites and wave lengths of information could travel faster and more easily.

Well, your cable lines are in place. But it's the satellite transmission that needs to be encouraged so you can receive information without too much energy depletion.

Re: Julia Fordham?

(She gave a free concert at the Getty Museum, and I waited in line for an hour, but didn't get in.)

They didn't want you to go. We're over as a couple. I do set you free, my darling Stephanie. I set you free to move into your life with the same vigor that you tried unsuccessfully to move me into mine. Move into your own. The fifties are for freedom. Free at last! Free at last! Thank God Almighty, you're free at last! And you didn't have to die to do it! Lucky girl. But we are both so lucky to have had this amazing opportunity to experience the true love we shared together. The love you made us experience when you insisted upon the dinners, the dates, the romance. And my darling, my sweet, if you can help any other knuckleheaded "husband" understand that the goddess in his bed is a gift from the cosmos, well, you have done a great good deed.

Read your books, write your books. Love your life. Think of me with love, even when you read your journals. I had no idea how miserable I made you. I can't stand it when you read them. My god, how you put up with me!

You shouldn't have. But once again, too late to change that. Go for a walk and let me tag along. It's a slow day in Africa, and I get bored. I don't have much to do with my body that's being formed. The miracle of life is incredible!! I love watching it happen!!

Love everything you see, just like your Cobalt Blue says. She's not my guide, but she's the best.

My day-to-day life continued as I tried to work on the book. I would continue to feel the familiar "nudges," so I'd put a pen in my left hand:

Talk to me.

Who is this? About what?

Dan, the tiny sliver of awareness. About the shifting of the focus of your work. The book is being…

I felt the huge energy drain that channeling by hand takes, then…

Barushe here – don't encourage him to take more of your energy. Do this in the morning at the computer.

Tuesday, October 8, 2002 – 7:19 a.m.
Okay, so what happened? Dan wanted to talk to me? Barushe interceded? What's shifting? Did it shift because I agreed to go on this job today?

(I'd taken a part-time job with a company that facilitated continuing education for doctors, and I got to travel to Oregon, Utah and Nevada to host teaching-dinners.)

Dan, the sliver of awareness – been waiting all night to talk to you. Forget how much sleep bodies need to function. It was me who woke you at 2 a.m.
I feel you miss the Dan-ness that I was supposed to be much more than you miss the Dan that I was. My concern is that you get back the Stephanie I married and then tried to destroy. So cavalierly, I might add. It's the gift I can give you. That vibrant, funny, opinionated thing who just thought everything was fun. How you did that wedding on no money is beyond me. You planned and executed it in hours. I just showed up to your wedding, just like we always said. I didn't even bother to invite people I cared about. Of course, the people I did invite didn't bother to come.
The shifting of your work doesn't have to do with the job. It does have to do with the book. Catch it before it goes. You can by working as hard as you can on it this week. Get the proposal all done. Get the chapters ready to send out. Go to the library and actually look for an agent. Follow through, my love. I took, stole your drive from you. I made fun of your determined optimism until I wore you down. I didn't appreciate you at all. Nor does my son, I might add.
I won't be able to talk to you at all in a month or so. I'll have to be with the body most of the time. But since I can do this, however much it annoys your Barushe, I feel I owe it to you. I need to encourage you enough to make up for all the times I just simply hated you for being you.

It's why you had to smoke dope to make love to me. You had to get down to your core, where you knew so deeply how much you loved me. Forgive me for not loving you back. I only cared about me and my preposterous goals of saving the world. I have no idea what made me think that was my job.

Your "dreaming Stephanie" is furious at me. She knows what I did to you. She's the missing piece of you that is still missing. AWOL.

The direct connection I have with you feels different from both Barushe and Cobalt Blue because I know the physical "lay of the land." They don't want me to give you "advance" information, so I won't, but please, my darling, sweet Stéphanie who worked like a dog to love me, don't let the rest of your life slip away from you just because I let our life just drift by me in some idiotic, sports-watching, computer-sitting fog. Not poetic, but who cares! I'm just so serious about the way I stole your 13 years from you and wasted them.

When you said that Paul (the man I lived with in New York) *and you were different sides of a coin, what did you mean?*

We had similar backgrounds and soul trajectories. He was given an education that he squandered, much the same way I squandered my time with you. He never loved you either. He only cared about "the great man" sickness. And you were attracted to it because of the unfortunate choice of your father.

Anything else? Should I bother to contact Judy (his cousin)?

No one cared about you for you. Spend your time with your own friends. Don't waste time with people who connect you to me, it doesn't do you any good. Move out into the world with your fearlessness intact. Let me give you back the courage that I ate away. I literally ate your energy up. You tried to move a mountain, a stubborn intractable mountain of conflicting desires. That's why you're still in healing.

Do the things you wanted me to do. Go dancing. Go to the beach by yourself, or with Mel. I didn't even want you to have a home. I resented the fact that you wanted to be middle-class. I think I will miss "middle-class" very soon.

If in the grand scheme of things when we meet again, and we will, if in this brief time you have left you can re-connect with the Stephanie I fell in love with, the Stephanie you had worked so hard to become, you will have an easier time forgiving me completely. Yes, it's about me again. But it's about you too. I long for your kisses, like you long for my arms.

On the anniversary of our first date, take some of my ashes and put them up at the Bel-Air hotel. Who knows? Maybe the African girl I'm to become can go there at night when she dreams. I don't know how that works yet. I only know I'm hanging on for dear life around here.

Anything else from anyone else?

Cobalt Blue – your love for your Dan is what keeps him connected to you. Barushe is frustrated that you refuse to let him go, but you can't let go of your love. Not yet, at least.

Your Dan seeks to warn you about shifts that can occur by inaction. But the juggling of a body as temperamental as yours is, along with your own stubbornness in giving up your none too helpful beliefs, is what is wearing you down.

Continue to read the Seth book and see what you can use. Make yourself new healing tapes. Do the gratitude exercise. Pull away from Sam, until he wants to include you in his life.

Go walk now. Create the feeling-tone of love of your life when you walk. It will heal you more than the Contac. (I had a bad cold.)

I'm very fond of your Dan, too, even though he was impossible. It's my choice that he is still able to connect with you. The more seriously you take your life right now, the better off you will be.

Tuesday, October 15, 2002 – 6:20 a.m.
Woke up to the alarm at 4:40, but turned it off without jumping out of bed.

Cobalt Blue here. Find a way to get up earlier – easier for us to get through even one hour earlier. See if you can get to the computer by 5 or 5:30. Keep up the effort. Sometimes your body needs to sleep and we are not such stern taskmasters, no matter how it seems to you, that we don't acknowledge your body's needs first. It's your own ability to get yourself into bed by 9 or 9:30 that will determine your success in the world. Funny that such a small "adjustment" will make it so. But there are always circumstances of "living" that intrude. We just ask that you make the best effort you can. Do your best, as the little book *(The Four Agreements)* says. Channeled, of course.

If you want to begin on "another" book then open another file and sit with the emptiness in front of you. Your time is not unlimited – a concept that seems to elude you constantly. You actually don't have a sense of "rushing," because your core knows full well that if you don't complete a task this lifetime, you'll have another lifetime. But I want to encourage you to not be so lackadaisical. You need to jump-start your engines now. Your energy is on the rise. You will be surprised at how good your "tests" will be once they come back. There will be no anti-DNA activity. I don't think I'm wrong there. You've done a remarkable job of ridding your body of your anti-DNA antibodies. (That was right!)

Continue to do the work, so that we can do our work. We are all so interconnected. Even this channeling that soothes and sometimes annoys you needs to be "limited" time-wise. Set up schedules that are specific to function just like you did this morning. Then you'll know exactly what you must do, when. You like that structure. You are good at this, very good.

That is your Dan in your body, and he wants to visit, but not just yet. Make a big effort to, no, use some time today to focus on "Fly Girls." It is coming closer and we are doing everything we can to make the boys understand that it is yours. You actually have legal rights on the project and they will call the Guild and understand that simple point. They will figure they will have to pay you anyway – might just as well make you work. And you will work hard. So put the books on the table and begin to read them.

Advice for today?

For today, follow your schedule. Follow our advice in general. Work on your book.

Your Dan wants to chat. Give him a couple of minutes, then I'll need to fix your circuits. He still drains you.

Dan, the ! here – it's how I feel after that baseball game with Sam! What delirium! Sheer joy! Wish you could have gone, been there too. But it doesn't mean the same thing to you. The sorrow we both felt last night when you turned on the end scene of "Moulin Rouge" was wrenching. But what you must remember is that he told the story – their love story. Tell ours. Ours was a love story that is far more common than you might imagine. Don't lose your courage.

Anything else? Where are you in the world, precisely? Can you tell me?

I'm on the Ivory Coast, I can't tell you the town because of the mechanics involved with language. I can't speak their language, yet I know what everyone says. I feel their energy coming at me. The girl is still very frightened because she is not married. When I "am with her" I can't reform "Dan" energy at all. So I can't be in both places or come and go quite as freely. There will probably be a time when I get locked down, as it were. But it's not now. So while I can visit with you and Sam, I visit. I've let everyone else go, as you should. None of my family likes you. Let them go. Sorry to have made you do all those waste of time dinners, but you once again were so hungry for family that you just went along.

I feel you a lot of the time, and I do hear you. I just have my stuff to do. And who knows, maybe today we'll have a date. I won't tease you, even though I loved to tease you. We could have had so much more fun, oh well. Too late. I miss your big, beautiful back. Your wonderful strong legs. Your butt. All ashes now.

Good-bye, my love. They want me to leave.

Bye.

Cobalt Blue here to vacuum his energy out of you. Don't flirt with him. You're such a vixen. My, how you loved that belly dancing. That was fun for everyone! Keep it up. Now work. Do the book, the walk, the reading, the managing of your body, and you will create the coordinates that will lead you to the outcome you have worked so long and hard to achieve. Do the Qigong; your body is now stiff from taking in Dan's energy. Eat.

Thank you. Namaste. (Sanskrit for "I bow to the Gods within you.")

Wednesday, October 16, 2002 – 5:34 a.m.
Yesterday's a blur. All I did was walk, go to Venice for a Rolfing session, Trader Joe's, dinner and bed. Dan was with me last night – channeled a little, but it was too draining by hand, so I stopped.
Advice for today? How do I get "Stephanie" back? Need her to be present.

Cobalt Blue here – to remind you that you are still in mourning. You are the only one who remembers, but if you don't take time to cry, which you don't seem to do, your body holds onto the sorrow of losing your husband. So take time today. Turn on the music and cry. Do it later. After you work.
The sorrow that was unleashed in your shoulder last night could have been pushed out. Go do Qigong this morning after yoga. Then take a bath, soak in Epson salts to release it. Cry in the bathtub. No one will care.
Your "Stephanie" won't return to you until you've given up your Dan. Your Dan hated her. He married her, and then went after her to destroy her. Rather than

let him do that, she ran for the hills. Took planes all over. You were always at an airport in your dreams, trying to catch her comings and goings.

It's your "Tup" self (Tup, for Tuppence, my inner three-year-old) who yearns for him. Let him go. Let him join you for a drink on Monday and then say goodbye. He needs to focus on his new life. And your ability to connect with him is making it hard for him to let go of this plane of reality. Have a date on Sunday if you two want. Put what's left of "him" into the Chinese vase. Get him out of your bedroom. It gives him too much access to your sleeping self. If you want your Stephanie back, get rid of "your Dan." He did her no favors. Keep in mind he wouldn't even make love to her, Oh fierce goddess that she is. To reclaim her you've got to let him go once and for all. Make a ceremony of it on Monday. Take your belly dancing class then take yourself up to the Bel Air. Take some of Dan with you and toss him there. What a contrast for him/her. Keep in mind that he is no longer even a man – he is a she, just forming. And his "consciousness" will be pulled in a matter of weeks to allow him to fully integrate with his new body.

Thank you for coming and holding my hand. I just feel so totally alone. Anything else for today?

We wonder how you can feel alone when you have a cheering section behind you. Because we can connect so directly with you, it makes it easy for us to give "nudgings" in the world. Just pay attention. Know that your "uneasiness" needs to not be overridden. Do not override your instincts. They will save you.

I feel Dan wants to talk to me.

He does. You didn't talk to him last night. I will let him come through, but will need to clean up afterward. He still steals your vitality. Say goodbye to him.

Dan, the sad spirit here today. Seeing the world from your point of view is heartbreaking to me, because I so avoided you, your real self, so utterly, while I lived. I was so afraid that you wouldn't love the real me, when that is the person you really loved.

Don't cry now. I can't get through if you do. Don't be mad. You see? I don't change. But my love, my favorite wife so far, let me be with you this weekend, and then I will say good-bye.

Your ability to hear me, even when I don't channel through you, makes it difficult to leave and go be with people who ignore me. They're very busy in Africa. Lots of dramas. Very small drama, but drama all the same. People steal from each other, just like I stole from you.

I can't help with your "Stephanie." She keeps away from me, as well she should. When she comes back you will feel anger toward me, and my behavior toward you, that is truly justified. Then forgive me with every ounce of your generous heart. Please? When you see me lying next to you in the bed? I'm really there. I can't reform me, but I'm there. They want me to go. I love you from here. Bye.

Cobalt Blue back. If you don't understand how much of your energy he takes now, you're not paying attention. Pay attention. Say good-bye. Cut him off.

And now even Dan seemed to understand that he needed to leave:

October 16, 2002

Dan, the Going Guy – I know we both need to move on. I need to be present in my new life and you need to move on. The beauty of this time with you – this time after my time of life – was in some ways better for both of us. I got to see you clearly, authentically and love you so deeply because of it. And you, my precious love – you got to experience me – the me you so truly loved.

Don't go until I can channel you on the computer to talk faster. My legs hurt doing it this way.

I know, but I'm here without a "pass." They want me to stay put in Africa and I will soon. But not until Monday night. It's the World Series, after all! See? I can still make you laugh!

Thursday, October 17, 2002

Dan, the fragmented energy today. It's why this is so uncomfortable. You invited me to come say good-bye. But now I know that you made the choice for me, I want you to make the choice for you.

As I said yesterday, this time we've been able to spend together after my death has in some ways been so much more fun for both of us than the time we were actually married.

Did we agree about your death before our incarnation? Or just after you refused to live our life?

There are so many variables, but our "love story" continues. I am going on my way soon. I have to connect this week with the fetus and begin to focus on the new world – what a difference a life makes!

I will have no memory, of course. How could they stuff a 61-year-old Brooklyn born boy into the body of a little African girl? They'll wipe my slate clean – but before they do, if there is any way that I could make up to you what my refusal to live up to my "agreements" cost you, I would do it. The best thing I can do is to try to leave you with as much hope and acknowledgement that your pure love, the love you showered me with daily, is now truly appreciated. If I can nudge you in the direction of your own bliss – the bliss you looked for in my arms – then that is what I need to leave you with.

The Monday night date will probably be the last I can connect. And that is not a done deal. Just go up there alone. Sit in our spot, listen to the piano player and have your glass of champagne. I will be there if I can at all finagle it.

The love we had was true love. When your "Stephanie" returns, and she will, remember only the best about us. Forget the rest. It won't help either of us.

You are my goddess, now and forever. Just like I said. Your life was a gift for me.

I hear you wanting information about Africa, but it's intense without being particularly interesting to me right now. As I said, I seem to be with a great deal of yelling people.

I got up, and walked through the Museum Park, Park LaBrea and The Grove, our local mall. That night seemed magical, because I heard Russian, Korean, Chinese, Spanish voices, and who knows what other languages being spoken, and everyone was laughing, and having a good time. When I got home, I could feel him wanting to chat.

Friday, October 18, 2002
Hey...

Hey back. It's still hard on you no matter how I come through. But the walk tonight was amazing. To just see the world through your eyes. What a gift. Solid love? (refers to another Julia Fordham song.) Oh, what love! I feel it so intensely and yet know you need to let me go. I...

Just then, Jenny, a sweet friend from yoga, knocked on the door, and we walked to a local Indian restaurant. Over dinner, she told me about her lawyer turned wanna-be-actor husband. How they'd married young, and how he was never ready for children. When she found out he'd been unfaithful, she divorced him. That was four years ago, but she still seemed so sad. She was almost forty, and feared she'd lost her chance of ever having children. As I told her about Dan and our marriage, I could feel Dan with me, listening. When I got home, I put the pen in my hand again:

> Sad about the way you talk about me. It's the truth, and yet it makes me sad. I wish…it doesn't matter what I wish now. I only need to let you go. Finally. You're too tired to do this, and I'm sorry that Jenny didn't get her family. What do men want?

Good question – I only wish he'd answered it. That weekend I was going to see a friend in Thousand Oaks. We planned to spend Saturday in Santa Barbara, so I could put more of Dan's ashes in places he loved.

Saturday, October 19, 2002 – 5:15 a.m.
Advice for today?

> Cobalt Blue, here later than we'd like. Channel first, eat afterwards. When we get you up, just go straight to the computer after your coffee. Watching you bounce around the apartment makes us nervous, because it makes you nervous. We don't know whether you'll sit down "in time." We do have schedules to keep. Get your walk in up in Santa Barbara. Go to the waterfall – love your life today. Experience the joy of your own life, reclaimed. Visit all the Dan places and continue to love and leave him behind. He needs to release you and you need to release him. So you waited 20 years for him. You won't get those years back.
>
> "Attention must be paid." Pay attention to your life-affirming thoughts and follow them. You choose, moment by moment, the trajectory of your life and we think it is finally sinking into your consciousness. Pay attention to where you let your mind hang out. And stay connected with your joy. Give yourself the "affirmation" that your work flows easily and effortlessly into your consciousness.
>
> Write up the following affirmations and stick them on your mirrors and bulletin board:
>
> I am a being of pure light and joy and it is my job to express my joy to the world.
>
> I always follow my best impulses and they lead in the direction of my bliss.
>
> I follow my bliss moment by moment.
>
> I gratefully embrace the goodness that flows effortlessly into my life.

That's enough for now. Let's just see if you can get those "hard-wired" into your brain.

The hesitancy you feel in "believing" that you are able to "hear" so clearly is fine. You continue to show up and channel. That's what's important. Do not denigrate what you are doing. When you feel resistance, however, do not blow out your energy. Lead others to discover their own "guides," for indeed every soul has one. It is somewhat like a huge corporation, although we do not operate without scruples the way Enron did. Our "profit margins" come from the "awareness" we are able to communicate.

It is why our connection with you is extremely important to us now. Your skill, talent, and now ease of communication, makes our job much simpler. When you finally get your book out in the marketplace, and then continue to work on a daily basis (it's been slow, oh so slow, in coming!) We will be able to produce quite a lot together.

Continue with your circuit-healing exercise. Tomorrow, bring your notebook. That is Dan in your legs. He wants to talk. But just for a minute. You should work on the book.

Dan, the chastened thing. Your directness with Jenny so upset me because her Josh did to her exactly what I did to you. Promised one thing, and then did another. But at least I wasn't unfaithful. Yes, you are so right about infidelity being "soul killing." It kills both souls. It kills the love.

Come with me today to the waterfall, the tree and the temple and begin to let me go. We both need to move on. I love you, but I need to reclaim my life. Reclaim my joy. The joy, I might add, that you resented.

I'm staying for our first date, and the World Series. Then I go. Lock down for me, I guess. Don't think I'll be very long in that next lifetime.

Namaste.

Cobalt Blue back to clean up your circuits. He drains you in ways you don't realize – and he knows how to do it. He'll spill your energy out with the ballgame today, and you'll be left empty for no reason. It's how he works.

Your sense that he was a vampire to you was authentic. "Attention must be paid." Pay attention.

Monday, October 21, 2002 – 5:29 a.m.

Was away the weekend – didn't channel at all. Too tired on Sunday.

Talked to Sam last night until 11 p.m. He's crazed with the World Series and has the "feeling" that Dan will have some effect on its outcome. I told him that I thought his experience with Dan was the important thing, but that didn't seem to comfort him. I had no idea why I was so exhausted yesterday, and then I read over the last entry, and saw "Dan will spill your energy at the ballgame and you'll be left empty for no reason."

I woke up at 4:40 a.m. with a dream. I'm being pursued by a lover whom I finally say good-bye to. He's driving a bus away, but then he comes after me. It's a dark road and he aims a gun, and shoots me in the head. I seem to know it's only a .22, and as I fall, I think, Maybe I didn't die. But then I seem to be the "lover." Confusing. So who killed whom?

Advice for today?

Cobalt Blue waiting – the dream was a wake-up call in many aspects. It's an old memory and a reminder of what anger can do. Your Dan is angry at you for choosing yourself, finally. And Sam will be angry at you too for choosing not to let yourself be sucked dry. But you can't keep showering "the men" in your life with your energy and get nothing in return. And you don't get anything back – not a thing. So show up for yourself. Let Sam and Dan dance this last week out together. Let him see if he can suck from Sam rather than from you. You've given enough to him, energy-wise. He doesn't intend to live off your energy, but in life he didn't "intend" to do it, and yet he left you sucked dry. Just like the vision you kept seeing – the worm sucked dry. That was you, my dear. You were constantly left empty by your big slug of a man, who only showed up hungry and brought nothing to the table except an appetite. As he admitted. Read over his "amends." Love him, forgive him and next Monday, let him go. You have too much work to do to let your energy be depleted by ungrateful entities.

Even if Sam wants to dump on you, show up for yourself instead. Don't let him. Put the toilet seat down. That's what those images were trying to tell you. You were taking in everyone else's refuse. Simple enough? How more direct an image did you need? But you didn't or wouldn't understand.

Read over this information when you're 'conscious' – we know you can't hear it now. But you "hear" us clearly right now. Your channel is open.

Your Dan wants to talk to you and we suggest you let him. He is a determined soul and he will continue to bombard you with messages if you don't give him access now. But know it will come at a cost to you. So only do it until you need to stand up and eat. Then let me come back and clear up the energy.

Okay. Hey, my Dan. Were you at Lorelle's? At the Temple with me? On the drive? Or were you just at the game? When I look at the Yosemite pictures, all I remember is your irritation. Your distance. There was no way to connect to you. You kept yourself to yourself, sweetie. Now you get to go on.

Dan, the dream image. I am no longer "your Dan" except when you see me, and when you see the negative parts of your experience with me, it reminds me how difficult your life with me was. Love me anyway. Focus on the positive of the relationship. My hands that worshiped your body. My heart that opened to yours, my penis that wanted you.

Let Sam do his own mourning. You don't need to go along for his ride. He won't appreciate it. He can only think of himself right now and really doesn't give your sorrow a single ounce of thought. So why connect with his? He hears me just fine, only he won't "hear" me. It's what it is.

For the week, I will try to gather up anything I need to say and I will "pack my bags" and go. You will be fine. Actually, you will begin to have full access to your energy once I'm out of your house, your life. I'll be there, here, with you until then. When you smell my t-shirts, I feel how much you love me. Your Stephanie will return when I'm gone – she and Barushe are not happy with me at all, and I can't blame them. I betrayed you, my darling. I betrayed us by my refusal to embrace the life I wanted.

I can't cry over this anymore. My legs hurt with you in them, so you need to pull out. I need my energy for my own life now. Pull from Sam's energy. Let his energy be expended at the ballgame.

I deserve your anger. Don't look at the Yosemite picture. You see too clearly the "face" you recognized finally back, and you remember my horridness toward you. Put it away. All I see is the love you offered and I rejected. I'm sorry, my sweet Stephanie. Bye for now.

Cobalt Blue, back to vacuum out his residue for today. Let him stay with Sam for the week. He'll be back on Monday. He does pretty much what he wants, as we all do. But what you want most is to finally focus on your work to the exclusion of all else.

Tuesday, October 22, 2002 – 8:27 a.m.
Can't concentrate. Read over last few entries, and I'm amazed at what I don't remember. It's as if I'm just reading it for the first time. Felt Dan with me last night when Sam was here. Barushe doesn't want me to connect to him, and yet I want to talk

to him while I can. Double-edged sword, though. Know it will drain me. I got my "Lopsided Little Christmas Tree" story back in the mail. I'll just keep sending it out. I want to talk to Dan, but don't want to give up my energy.

Dan, the Sliver of Awareness that you called back. But my focus is mixed with regret and the sorrow at the emptiness you feel this morning.

You see how "your Dan" destroyed your happiness. Oh yes, I was there last night at Lena's. All that abundance of life. Those sweet people. Those babies. And I wouldn't give you one. Not one.

That is the truth of our marriage. I offered you a home and a family and then I refused to give you either. And I see all too clearly the position I've left you in. It's why people are so afraid of connecting with you.

Live today in expectation. Shake off your anger. Go walk and come back and work. There is _no way_ that I can make any of this up. I'm really "off." I'm barely here. This is a strand of Enoch's energy that allows me to even talk. I will be there with you on Monday, but that will be it. Final lock down for me.

The World Series is between Sam and me, and that relationship is separate from the relationship I had with you. You are the love of my life, but he is my continuation. He does hold my DNA.

Good-bye for today. I'll talk to you next Monday, unless you have more to say.

Only that the only way you are going to want to continue along this path is to work harder than you think is possible now. Work is really all you want to do, and that is fine. You don't want to expend any energy elsewhere.

Thank you. I'm going for a walk. Then I'll come home and work.

Thank you for bypassing the instructions not to connect. You heard me trying to talk to you. This is easier and more efficient. I do have easy entry, as it were. I need to remind you that I kiss you with my spirit when you sleep. Today, I will try not to disturb your energy. I try not to rob you, but it happens. I'll hang with Sam, he is so much stronger than you are, but you hear me so much more clearly. He's just like me in his self-obsession.

I went over to my friend Rahmie's house and she said she could "expunge" Dan. I said, "Not yet."

Wednesday, October 23, 2002 7:27 a.m.

Yes, you heard me. Thank you for not wanting those people to expunge me last night. That would have been too harsh. I'll leave when I said. I know what I'm doing far more than they do, trust me on that one.

You've offered Samuel everything you have, and still it's not enough for him. I tell him the same things, but his fear is so enormous. And yet he won't admit that it is fear of his own future, destiny. He'll calm down. But don't let him drag you down with him.

Work on the book, no matter how uncomfortable it is to tell the truth of our relationship. It might help other people understand the connection and the choices that they make. It will speak to those it speaks to.

I'm trying not to drain you, but it's hard not to. I'm in your body. It's the only way you can do this fast.

Dan? I sometimes see that moment in the magical grove behind the Roosevelt estate so intensely, so real. What happened that day?

I had made the drive miserable for both of us, as I usually, no, always did. I made every trip a nightmare for both of us. I didn't think I deserved a vacation and I didn't want you to enjoy yourself. And I knew that by withholding my precious self from you, by manipulating myself, just like I always did, I could punish you for all that I felt you had done to me. I was always "getting even."

But in that moment, when your delight, your joy just burst out, I had to stop and enjoy the day too. I smiled at you and you smiled at me. How you tolerated me, however, throughout those years is so far beyond what anyone could have asked of you.

Go walk and come back and see what you can do with sending off queries. I know it's hard to work on this book about "hot and sacred sex" when you hated having sex with me a lot of the time. I withheld constantly, and you knew it. But my god, my darling Stephanie, when I loved you and you loved me, we were magic. And we knew it. Just lying together on the couch, or hugging you in bed. Maybe I did gobble up your energy like they said, maybe I did waste it all with my crazy Jewish brooding. But I appreciate you now. And you need to take comfort in that.

I had gone to see Dr. Bae, and he said my real problem was the baby-loss sorrow trapped in my womb. He placed needles all over my stomach to release it. Now my anger bubbled to the surface, and exploded:

October 24, 2002
I miss you! I hate you! You cheated me out of so much! You cheated us!

Dan, the sorry soul, feels your pain so directly. I find it impossible to see you suffer so much, but there's nothing else to do. Your core opened up and spilled out the baby damage. The baby damage is flooding into your body. It's what woke you up – all the rage at men. And you deserved better from me.

What will I do when you really leave me? Finally.

You'll cry some more. But I can't stay, and you want me to go. Go sleep.

Sunday, October 27, 2002 – 5:15 a.m.
Went to my belly dancing class and bought a jingle belt.
Advice for today?

Cobalt Blue here – re: your own dreams? You need to make them a priority and so far you haven't gotten back into that mind-set. We are going to be with you tomorrow night to say a final adieu to your Dan, who is not Dan at all. He's just having a difficult time accepting his assignment. What else is new?

Start on your new life filled with expectations. Expect the best. When you feel yourself sliding into old "patterns," acknowledge it, then flip the switch in your body. You have to locate it. But you are skillful enough to find it.

You and Sam are an old team. He still needs you and you are still 27 years older than he is, so give him what you can of your hard earned experience and he will choose to "listen" or ignore. His father ignored you completely and so maliciously that it almost destroyed your belief in your own power.

It was your "power" that attracted him to you, and your "power" he needed to kill. Once again, he almost killed you. You almost died, but you chose not to. You chose. So stop with the "exit" strategies. You will be fine if you just accept your life so completely and trust that when you listen to your own best instincts, you will be supported. "Follow your bliss" is not just a message tacked on your bulletin board. It's got to be the way you live your life.

If you don't, you will be disappointed when we meet face to face. Yes, fuzzy entity to fuzzy entity in your present "world view," but face to face no matter how you experience it. Your own ability is growing now by leaps and bounds.

Just give yourself every opportunity to hone your skills. Yes, we woke you up early because of the time change, but you call the shots when it comes to your body and you do a good job of that. You knew that your body still needed sleep. Or you thought it did. You're doing *quite well*, with the naps and the sleep. You really can get along on just a five-hour sleep cycle with an hour's nap thrown it. You'll notice that even when you don't sleep, you manage to restore your body.

Good. Reading that over helps us both. It cements it into your cognitive brain. The channel in you is just that – like a pipe that flows through you. If you don't actually read over what you get it does no good, because even though you think you hear, you don't really "hear" until you read. Then read it again.

Read everything you have time for. But you are the juggler of all the information. And you are the juggler of your emotion. If you choose to let other people's need throw off your balance, you can't keep your balls in the air. And you are your only responsibility right now. No one else in your present circle, except maybe Lynn, if she calms down, "gets" it, and sees you for who and what you are. Let everyone else go, for the time being.

Encourage your own passion everyday. Yes, you chose to be involved with men who hated you on some level. Stay away from men for a while longer. You have too much work to do to waste your time.

Anything else?

A part of your Dan, the sneaky part, wants to say good-bye, and if you don't invite him, he will crash the party. So I suggest you hear what he wants to say, and then let me come and clean up. He tears through you, like the bull in the china shop that he was in life. He was the bull, and you were porcelain.

(I could feel his energy climbing up my legs.)

Dan, the slithering energy up your leg. Wish I could be there in real life. But I know tomorrow is my deadline. I always resented deadlines and I still do. But you love deadlines, don't you? My final good-bye after the game and the glass of champagne, I will make quickly. Yes, wear the red skirt. I'll see it, I'll see you. I may have wanted to kill you, but you wanted to kill me too, my darling. For good reason, however. What a scoundrel I was. If I had really "acted out" you would have left me immediately, so I knew I couldn't do it. I just did it subterraneously. And please forgive me.

Don't let go of the book idea. You will figure it out and get it out. Just keep persevering. My connection with Sam right now is so much fun because of the game, and it was great to be there last night, even if the Giants lost. It doesn't matter who wins or loses. It's how you play the game. Who knew how true that was?

I want to scream at you how much I love you, and I want to let you know how sorry I am you are so alone. And how sorry I am I left you in such jeopardy, but there's nothing I can do about it here, or where I really need to stay.

Africa. I do need to be bolted down; otherwise I will "bolt." I can feel my own reluctance to accept what I "accepted."

It is my lesson. Use me as an example for your own life. You accepted a life of "no security." You have none. Not even Social Security. But you will be fine.

I would ask to let me linger in your body, but I know that's not allowed. And it's too draining on you. I just got used to sucking from you. I see that now. I will let you let me go tomorrow and I will thank you from the core of my being for giving me this time with you to make the amends. No one, or at least no one we know, has been able to communicate this clearly with a friend. And ultimately that is what we are, my darling favorite wife so far. Friends. I wish I had understood that in life. You tried to be my friend, but I wanted a mother, a slave, a whore. And you gave me what I wanted. All you wanted was a lover and a father for your baby, and I refused. What a jerk!

Smile along with me when I see the good times we had. Almost always in the house you made so pretty, and the bedroom you insisted be painted gold. Gold and cobalt blue. Just like you, my love, my teacher, my friend. Now go off for your walk and see the world sparkling new.

Let me tag along for the day, I won't drag your circuits too much. Well, I guess I can't. They won't let me. I love you my darling. I'll be back tomorrow.

Cobalt Blue back. Now, feel the energy he sucked. Let him come tomorrow and then you'll have to be on guard. You do him no favors by encouraging him. Take off your rings after tomorrow. At least your wedding rings. Let me clear your circuits…sit.

Thank you. Namaste.

Do the Qigong. He's still around you. What a stubborn entity! Love your life. It's the only way you will want to continue on.

That day, on my way home from walking around Lake Hollywood, I listened to "The Savvy Traveler" on NPR, and I heard about a great deal to Paris – $298 round trip from Los Angeles. Paris for only $298? If I could swing it, I was going! The traveling job I'd taken gave me some spare cash, so there was a chance I might be able to afford it. I called Sam, told him my plan, but he didn't seem interested in going along.

Cobalt Blue began to "dictate" a book, *The Seeker-Soul's Guide to the Authentic Self*. I would just sit, close my eyes, and type. It made me nervous.

Monday, October 28, 2002 – 5:18 a.m.

The Giants lost to the Angels last night. Seems almost poetic. Sam will be totally nuts, however. I'll deal with him later. Advice for the day? Re: the best action toward Sam today? The best action toward Lynn? The best action toward me and Dan?

Cobalt Blue – the order is wrong there. You must begin to start with yourself. It is your base of power – you can't help anyone if you give up your power. It didn't help Lynn for you to listen to her ranting. Out of control ranting. But for you to even listen to that was the mistake. You just didn't want to hang up on her, although you should have.

Isolate yourself today from everyone's energy. Take yourself to that movie. That was a good idea, but only if you feel you have time. If you spend your energy worrying about other people's drama, you won't have the energy for your own. And it is your own drama that interests you most, and for good reason. You are shedding the skin of your old life right now and that is why the relationships are flying off you like so many rats from a sinking ship. And it is only by letting yourself sink into the quiet of your own life that you will find the courage you will need to face your new life.

You need to just live empty for a while. Empty and with great expectation. Do the work. You are fine for 10 months. That is a given. Just take one 15-second increment at a time. Let everything else fade into background noise. You don't have the time to focus on it. You are in a fight for your creativity. You have to call it back to you and to do that you will need to streamline your life. Even more.

No one cares about you. It is the truth of your life. And if you don't care about you, you will choose to leave your life. And that will disappoint you – you're not through.

Continue to show up for your work. Show up for yourself. Let everyone do what they want to. Don't let anyone treat you badly. Be clear. Be honest. Be present.

Re: tonight? Just hold Dan's energy with love and see him leave your body. Then over the next two months, begin to pack up his things.

Tomorrow will take care of itself if you take care of today. Just keep yourself in a good mood. Do like your little calendar says…replace the sorrow with action. Take action. Work on your book. Work on your creativity. Call your Stephanie home. She's still out. She's just as stubborn as your Dan. I don't know why I always get the most stubborn of spirits, but it's what I'm good at.

The book that I started will be accessible to you after today. You're too scattered with anticipating the pain of letting him go once again. But you will be fine by tomorrow. Just don't let Sam's mood swings infect you. He pays for a "therapist" that he believes in. He doesn't believe that your advice matters because you don't make him pay for it. And you won't. You love him. You love Lynn.

Anything else?

Not for today. We have other dimensions that need to be explored and communicated. And now that we have you "on schedule," you will be able to work. Just be happy today. Let go of your Dan with joy and gratitude.

Yes, he wants to talk to you, and we suggest you only let him for a moment.

Dan, the tiny sliver of love that fills your body. That was me nibbling in your nether regions. You felt it. Oh, how I loved you. The taste of you. The smell of you. I do have to go tonight and I will. But sit with me and drink champagne with me. And love me with your heart. Don't let anyone spoil today. Don't return phone calls.

When you saw Ewan McGregor's face...

(I'd turned on "Moulin Rouge" on TV.)

...the sorrow of losing me came so sharply back. You were my courtesan. And what a good courtesan you were. I'm sorry I wasn't your "lover." Once again, I thought it was my due to have you so devoted to me.

Don't worry about your future. There is no destiny that you didn't agree to beforehand. Just know that whatever challenge you face, you will be up for it. I stand in total awe of your strength. I stand in total awe of your passion. Just now, focus it on your life. I give you back your life, tonight. I give you back the joy I stole from you. I give you back the energy that I wasted. I wish I could give you back the 13 years. I can't. But I can give you the awareness that "we" are not through. Barushe and Enoch are speaking again, and both you and I are only slivers of their awareness.

You want to go to Paris? Go. Go over Christmas. Give yourself that present for Christmas. No one else will. See Paris before you die.

There are no more words that I can give to sooth your pain. There are no more poems I can write to you. Only finish my book. I feel it is my book. Finish it and send it out. Let Janet's example of courage be a guide.

(Janet Fitch wrote, "White Oleander." She's my neighbor Ken's cousin, so I'd heard first hand what it took.)

I will be with you all day, if I can. But I just heard that I can't. I have to go. This isn't good for you, and once again, my selfishness is apparent.

Cobalt Blue...yes, that pain in your body is the damage he causes. Tomorrow I will pull all his connections to you out, and you will be empty. But tomorrow you have much work to finish. Finish it up and on Wednesday morning, begin your new life. Like a warrior.

Thank you. Namaste.

And to you.

So that night, on the anniversary of our first date, I went up to the Bel Air Hotel by myself, had a glass of champagne, and said yet another good-bye. I came home, took off my wedding rings to make it clear to both of us that we were over as a couple. I believed that Dan was finally gone. But once again, I was wrong. The last piece of the puzzle would have to fall into place before I discovered exactly why I had married him, and what I would have to do to put this relationship to rest.

Chapter Seventeen

"The Nun's Story"

November marks the beginning of the holiday season: Thanksgiving and Chanukah/Christmas/Kwanzaa, (which is the way it's celebrated in Los Angeles), and then for me, the anniversary of Dan's death, December 26th, his 'Yarzeit' in the Jewish tradition. Luckily, I've never had good holidays, so this year would be no different. All I wanted was to get through them and find a way to go to Paris. And it looked as if my new job would be the ticket.

Off I flew to Salt Lake City to host a "continuing education" dinner for doctors, then I flew back home. While I waited for planes or flew through the sky, I read through all of Dan's channeling. I'd feel the sweetness of his soul, and then I'd long for what might have been. Back home, I tried to reignite my enthusiasm to write my *Married Girl's Guide,* while Cobalt Blue began to dictate a book. The "advice" I got every day began to take up pages and pages, and I wish I could have followed more of it. Alas, I'm only human. I've edited it down to what might be of value for you.

Friday, November 1, 2002 – 5:09 a.m.
At the airport and on the plane, I read over a lot of my "Dan Channeling" file. The love and sweetness of him after death is so intense and healing. Sam called and wanted to talk about Maggie and Chris, but I couldn't hear it.

Cobalt Blue, here. Ready.
To reclaim your life, listen. Listen to your thoughts and pay attention to your impulses.
I could continue on "my book," if you want to take the time today. But it would be better to physically schedule it in your day diary. Give me an hour a day. Then take two hours for your book. My book will kick-start your own work.
When you read over your "Dan channeling," yes, you got his core of goodness, which you always knew was there. Too bad he couldn't have showered you with more of it while he lived with you. But his nasty "blame" side kept you

both in a state of perpetual panic. You got sucked in within the first year of your marriage to him. You felt him suck at you every chance he got. He did suck your energy, especially during sex. (Dan used to joke that he loved giving head so much, he should have been a lesbian.) No need to elaborate on that one. You saw exactly what I mean. Wish him well. He's in lock down. He will be flitting in and out of your environment, just because he can, but don't encourage him. It's not good for him.

Re: you, Sam, Maggie and Chris. Keep as far away from that disaster as you can. It's already caused you to lose so much of your own life, because you had to first analyze what really happened for Dan, then you had to experience the anger before he would even acknowledge that anything was wrong. It wasn't your stuff and yet you swam in the muck of what was a painful and destructive learning situation. But it wasn't your lesson. It was Dan's. He just refused to learn.

Let Sam decide what he wants to do there. Tell him you love him, but on this single issue, your help will not be useful. Just let him know he has a therapist to hash this out with. And his "therapist" is not you.

You are his friend, but he must learn to become your friend, too. He hasn't yet. He still has no concern for you. He either will grow up or he won't. He was crippled far more than he realizes by Dan's obsessive love.

Re: your work, which I feel you have lost direct connection to, you need to honor your time of working. Do whatever it takes. Do your two hours everyday. Four pages, just like Miss See says. (I'd read Carolyn See's wonderful book, *Creating a Literary Life*.)

The more you can show up for your work, the more the work will show up for you. Simple as that. Your fear of failure – which you inherited from your father – which you were actually taught (the only thing you were taught) is what inhibits your progress.

Forgive the meanness of that Jerry thing (my father) that was expressed in flesh. He is not out of reprogramming, as is your mother. See them both as the fragile children they once were.

My time with you is up for today. Advice? Just enjoy your life today as much as you do. You love your house. Plant your plants.

Saturday, November 2, 2002 – 7:09 a.m.

Slept until 6 today. Feels so late! Perspective is weird. Yesterday, I went into "Mourning Ville" once again, but don't know if that was just from sheer exhaustion or what.

I got the house cleaned by a sweet Guatemalan woman. Wanted to give her all of Dan's clothes, but I called Sam, and he wants to go through them first. I need to get Dan out of the house. Advice for today?

Cobalt Blue, but not fully. Advice for today is simple. Get yourself organized and excited about your work. Do what we've already advised. Get yourself up earlier. It's easier for us to communicate when the whole street isn't awake. You can't do it late at night because your body is too tired then.

Just be happy today. Give yourself a day off from worry of any kind. Keep to your 15-second time frame and just enjoy. That's what will give you back your life. Then you really will be able to reclaim your life.

You are indeed in mourning. Why you won't let yourself mourn fully is, well, not beyond us, because you are tough on yourself. Just spend today and play with your clothes. Organize your clothes. You worked hard to shop for them, now enjoy them on your body. Not just in the closet.

Tomorrow, if you get into the room earlier, you can access deep information, if you want it. The contract with your writing still remains unfulfilled, and you need to encourage yourself.

Anything else?

Yes. Separate your "channeling work" from your book work. That makes it more specific and you will know what you are doing then.

Cultivate the love you have for yourself. That is your contract with yourself. You don't need to bend over backwards to make people like you. Those people who love you, love you. Those who don't, don't. It's always been that way for you and why should you need it to be different now?

The tangible results from the work you do with your body shows up in the physical world. The tangible results from the book work you do will also show up. There's just an enormous "glitch" in your circuits, and it comes from such cavalier abuse. But the positive thing about all the abuse that you took is that you didn't really think much of it. You never felt like a victim, principally because on a cellular level you remembered your direct past life. And the monsters you lived with were only baby monsters compared with the monsters you encountered in your direct past life. (The German Jewish doctor.)

But it is this life, this incarnation, that you must focus on. Re-read Dan's channeling along with ours, and get the thrust for your book. Get it in your head. You could do it tonight, if you want, but you should schedule it in the afternoons. Your afternoons seem to be some sort of energy vortex for you. You just collapse and waste that time. Once again, you don't have time to waste. Not a minute.

The comfort you seek from the TV set, the numbness, needs to be replaced with reading. When you feel you have no energy to do much else but "veg," then sleep.

So tomorrow, if you want, we can come to chat again, or you can take a day off. It's good, however, to keep the channels open. It's much easier for us to "hook" in everyday, because this is far more difficult than it seems to you. You have no idea how talented you are at this or almost everything else. Because things seem so simple for you, you assume that they are simple for everyone. They are not.

Anything else? Can I do anything about "Fly Girls?"

The "Fly Girls" project is not yours right now. Just go forward and remember that you have first claim on the project. It's yours at the Writer's Guild. Stop by and ask about legalities.

Thank you. I do feel vulnerable and sad without Dan.

Dan didn't help you one bit. When you actually grasp how much of your life – the only life you have right now – he wasted with his intractability, his refusal to even acknowledge any of the hundred things you did everyday to make his life better, you will feel relief that he is gone from your life. And when the relief that you don't need to take care of his completely selfish, self-centered needs sets in, you will be able to forgive him and move into your own life fully. Then you will thrive.

The only caveat emptor is the _fear_. Do not let other people's fear for you infect, or influence anything you do. If you want to go to Paris, go. It's your choice. What do you want to do? We just want you not to let fear or lack of anything affect your decision.

Thank you. Namaste.

I called Sam, and he said he would come over on Sunday to go through Dan's clothes so I could give them away. He seemed annoyed with me when I refused to hear about the strife between Maggie and Chris.

Sunday, November 3, 2002 – 5:38 a.m.
Advice for today?

Cobalt Blue, here – the anger that comes up in your body when you think of Maggie and Chris is not your anger. It's dumped anger that your Dan refused to deal with. You still carry it, and it's best if you let it go completely.

212 • Love From Both Sides

It has absolutely nothing to do with you. Not one thing. Their connection to each other is intense and a little out of whack. Chris should have left many, many years ago, but his refusal to become a man is what stopped him. Do you see a theme developing? Men who refuse their own man-ness are extremely toxic creatures. You have no respect for them, because you became a man when you were a man and you became a "man" when you were a woman.

Send love toward Sam and have no expectations. Call him this morning and tell him to sleep in. Otherwise he will resent coming over. Clean out your closet – which is no longer Dan's.

Try again tonight with the TV – although you like your Sunday night program. (The "Sopranos," my guilty pleasure.)

You lose confidence too easily. Fill your coffers with your affirmations. Let the affirmations speak into your brain when you're tired. Don't allow any negativity to float in. It's all just words – but the intent differs greatly.

One isn't the loneliest number. You were more alone when you lived with Dan, because you lived with someone who actively fought against you. You have no concept of how much of your energy you wasted trying to budge a solid concrete wall. It was the concrete of his mind, in his body that destroyed him and almost destroyed you. So don't mourn his loss too much longer. Just experience the joy of the love you two shared when he let you. But he insisted on the control. He withdrew into his own petty despot, emotional world.

Anything else?

Thank you for putting my book on the schedule, but I will not begin it today. Tomorrow put me down again, but make your own book the priority. Your Dan book. Today, read over all the blue books. Highlight the Dan channeling in them and complete the circle of his life. His life with you, anyway.

If you see Sam today (for if you feel any reluctance from him, just reschedule), let his negative energy be dissipated somewhere else besides your house. But if you do see him, be careful not to hook into his energy. You can only offer assistance to him if you let his energy be his and not infect yours. He's "out of control" because he's facing life without either his mommy or his daddy. But it is time for him to become a man. He will either do it or he won't.

It's time for you to reclaim you life. You will either do it or you won't. And the only way you can reclaim your life is to stand up for it. You don't "need" anyone's approval. Just put one foot in front of the other and try to be as generous with your love as you can. You love Sam, but it doesn't help him or you for you to be a doormat.

Go walk. Enjoy the morning. Love the day. Love your house. Clean out that closet. That's the project.

Thank you. Namaste.

Feel the love from your own source. Feel the sweetness of your own soul. Feel the connection with us and know that we love you and send you good wishes for the day. That's all you need.

There is not much deeper thought than that.

Thank you. Namaste.

That night, Sam came over and we went through Dan's clothes, then he took the things he wanted to keep. He seemed distant and standoffish, but I followed the "advice," and just loved him as he was.

Monday, November 4, 2002 – 5:55 a.m.

The end of a dream: I'm in a house where my family's rented out a part to an older, nasty-mouthed couple. The man criticizes everything all the time. I get angry and go inside and kick his head back – it's encased in a space-suited ball. I kick it again and again, until he yells, "Stop!" and I see I've really hurt him. I woke up worried, concerned, about my own anger.

Advice for today?

Cobalt Blue – your anger is beginning to surface and the dream just served as a kind of letting off steam. You could help yourself along if you punched a pillow today, took yourself and screamed your head off in your car. Let go of the anger at losing 13 years of your very valuable life to deception. For the deception you felt was a manipulation of emotions done by both you and Dan. Dan first, and then you followed. You "fell in" hook, line and sinker – fell into the reservoir of love. The deception of Dan's constant inauthentic emotions caused such havoc in your own emotional life, that you couldn't make heads or tails of anything. He said he loved you, yet you knew he really didn't care anything at all about your future, what happened to you. He didn't "provide" for you. You might just have been a single woman.

You would have been much better off, quite frankly, if you hadn't married him. But then, he really was what was planned for you – so it's not as if you had very many options. Barushe and Enoch didn't give you any other directions to move in. Not good planning on their part. But they had no idea that "Dan" would refuse to take part in your drama. That he was only concerned about his own.

Do I have "dramas" I've refused to take part in?

Let me finish with Dan's refusal to embrace your life's work. You were so "gas lighted," as you like to say, by his ability to focus his intense emotion on you one minute and then turn completely and utterly away the next, that you just accepted it. You thought you had no choice but to try to make the marriage work.

That marriage almost killed you. Now that he is gone from your environment – and he is for a while – you need to acknowledge for yourself, at least, how toxic his "manipulation" of his emotions was. He discovered his "ability" very young – his ducky moment – and then continued to live his life from the perspective of a six-month-old.

The only thing that you can do to right yourself, get yourself back on track, is to continue to do exactly what you are doing. That anger expressed last night in your dream needs just to be "let out." Scream in the car. Go to Lake Hollywood today, walk, and do healings.

You can't reclaim your own life until you fully process – and take responsibility for – your not leaving him when you could have. But, in retrospect, even I don't see when that might have been. You wanted to be married – you wanted that family. Well, there is no family for you. You only have this moment in time. Don't think about a future for you – there really isn't a future. There is only the present.

Just continue to live in the continuous present. You are surrounded by people who planned all their life for retirement – now they're retired. And now what? Keep away from them.

Live your life now. Enjoy each second to the fullest. Don't allow other people's anxiety to infect you.

Is there anything I can do to get "Fly Girls"?

The deceptions involved in that project are too underhanded, and quite frankly, mean-spirited, to waste any more of your time on. Just focus on work that will provide you with a sense of accomplishment. Stop at the Writer's Guild and chat with them if you want. You'll have options later perhaps, but not now.

Thank you. Namaste.

Tuesday, November 5, 2002
Last night, went to the Academy to see "On the Waterfront." I had never seen it all the way through, which is pretty amazing to me. Going to do another "illumination" with Rahmie today. Want to call my "dreaming" Stephanie home.
Advice for today?

Cobalt Blue, here – the "dreaming" Stephanie is reluctant to come back if you refuse to complete the contract. The contract with her, with you, still involves your writing and your work. You can call her back today, but if you don't really get excited about your book, really encourage the "fun" in your writing – take delight again in what you do – she won't stay.

Do your time at the computer today and call her back yourself. Then, when you work with Rahmie, see her being integrated into you. She is an idea construct to you, but very real to herself. And she is afraid you will make fear-based choices. You would have never married Dan, however, if you hadn't been forced into it. And even though it didn't turn out for the "best," there was no way for you to side-step that experience.

And when you get through processing the pain of it all, the love of it all is what will remain. For it is the love that you two shared that was the gift for you to carry into the next phase of your life. His refusal to accept what you offered made it impossible for you to continue together, but that wasn't your choice. That was his choice. You had no control over him. No one had any control over him, quite frankly. Enoch, his oversoul entity, had no control either, so don't feel bad. What a stubborn, sweet soul.

To rid the house completely of his "negativity," and it still remains, clean out his closet and pack what you don't want in the garage. Let it stay with his Mendocino things. Let Sam handle them, though – you don't need to touch those clothes. They carry energy that you don't need to interact with.

Sam is angry at you right now for pulling your energy back from him. But let him stay in his anger. Don't fix it. If he cares about you, it will change to, transform into, concern for you, finally. But he's having a hard time growing up.

Anything else for today?

Cultivate your own garden of new relationships. The last part of your life is drawing to a close. Get ready for the next and final phase of your life. Let it be filled with excitement about the present. Let go of the past so completely that you only feel love and compassion for all that has gone before. Don't "own" your wounds – see them for what they were, learning tools that enabled you to develop the gifts you have. There is no other way to reach down to certain truths about reality. You needed to suffer to understand fully your own exquisite sensitivity, your clear-sighted talent. You just need to now use your talent to help other "like-minded" souls discover their own "core" of goodness. For you do indeed see the cores of those you interact with. You see them, yet you don't know it on a conscious level.

The sadness in your body today can be walked out and talked out physically. When you walk, continue to encourage yourself. Create fun.

Thank you. Namaste.

Then I felt Dan bombarding me with energy, wanting me to connect.

Yes, that is him. Even now. Don't encourage him.

Wednesday, November 6, 2002 – 5:44 a.m.

Woke at 4:50 – just here now.
Advice for today? Comments on my "Stephanie" retrieval?
It's my mother's birthday today, and my "inner juke box" just started singing "Ding-Dong, the Witch is Dead," just like it did when she died. Jesus!

Cobalt Blue, here – to discuss yesterday.

Your "dreaming" Stephanie, which is actually your most focused Stephanie, is indeed grounded once again. And she will only stay put if you begin to take her seriously. Honor your work. Make your work your first priority or rather, your first priority after your body. For your body still needs monitoring.

Anything else vis-à-vis the work with Rahmie?

Now that your "Stephanie" is back, you have access to many other levels of the work. Just continue to "show up."

For today, just work hard not to feel the fear we see trying to gain a hold on you. No matter what happens, just let yourself acknowledge the fear and then like a movie monster, like Boris Karloff as Frankenstein – smile at it and send it on its way. Know it just needs to be comforted. Frankenstein just needed a friend and that tamed the monster. Know that you can, and will, handle whatever comes your way. And in that lies the excitement of your life. Connect with the true adventure now. Think of yourself as an urban-adventurer. You don't need to climb Mount Everest – you faced challenges just as great in your personal life.

The "ding dong" song you just heard was because your mother's energy is back from reclamation and she looked in on you, and left when she realized what kind of reception you'd give her. Your inner-self needs to let go of any residual anger. I know you feel that the abuse she heaped on your little body was unnecessary, and it was, but once again, if you hadn't been so completely "abandoned" as a small child, you would never have made it this far. You would have crumbled long before now.

Keep in mind that there are still people in your own sphere of influence who are shocked that you didn't just crawl up into a ball and die along with Dan. And the fact that you walk and talk serves as a reminder to them what cowards they are. And so it is for that reason that they hate you. But you can only wish them well. Just wish them well, bless them, and move on your way.

Vis-à-vis your work on your books. Don't throw out your chapters. Just reorganize them. And make it a "novel" if you want, but it is still non-fiction, as all good novels are. Because the better the fiction, the more truth it contains.

Anything else for today?

You can enjoy the beauty of the day. Get your garden planted. Don't waste time with people who don't appreciate you.

Thank you.

Thursday, November 7, 2002 – 5:52 a.m.

Stopped at Kaiser to get sunscreen, and on a whim, got a flu shot. Then felt like hell the rest of the day.

Yesterday morning, I "pulled up" the whole physical memory of Dan's dying – I tried to write it down for the book. I talked to Sam, and he said, "I don't know why, but I saw – or kept thinking about the day Dad died." Are we connected, or what?

Advice for today?

Cobalt Blue, here later than we'd like. The schedule needs to be taken seriously. Set the alarm tomorrow. Get up earlier. If 4:30 seems too punishing, at least set the alarm for 5:00. That way, you can get to the computer before six. Once again, because you live on such an early-rising street, it makes it difficult to do this. Or at least it actually takes more of your energy, and that is what we are trying to conserve.

The work will continue to unfold if you can quell your inner-critic enough to let it. It is not even your own inner-critic; it's the constant disapproval you met with as a child. Your parents and your sister actively hated you. You were with enemies. You grew up with enemies, and that's why you actually have no problem dealing with them. Just continue to smile and walk away. They have power only if you react. Your power lies in your own determined optimism. It is no joke. Your own determined optimism is what enabled you to take the leap of faith that landed you back in Berkeley, then at UCLA, where you thrived until you fell in love with your Dan, and gave away your power. You had no choice. His way or the highway, and you knew it.

Re: Sam's ability to pick up the vibrations you sent out? You recreated it so strongly, you conjured that day up and yes, he "got" the transmission, but it's because of other connections between you two. And they are too complicated to convey right now. Also unnecessary. You are doing well with the hands-off approach toward him and that is the right action.

Advice for today? Get as much of your work done as you can. The flu shot was, in fact, a good idea. Your feeling that you couldn't be sick and alone is absolutely valid. You will be traveling and exposed to the "flu" this year and if your body thinks it's been inoculated against it, it will not make friends with the virus. It won't allow it to connect. Sometimes the body likes challenges that we have no control over. The body has as much "say" in what goes on as we do, that's why we always defer to your "knowingness" re: the amount of sleep you need. We just ask that you make an effort to go to sleep when you're tired. And yesterday, you did quite well, all things considered. You napped and you fell asleep right after your "West Wing." Get your passport in order so that if you want to go to Paris, you can. Don't let lack of money stand in your way.

Thank you. Namaste.

And to you. Don't let fear get at you. Remember to breathe.

Friday, November 8, 2002 – 5:35

Been awake since 4 – got up @ 4:30. Dan flitted into yoga last night. Dan the African, he called himself. He said, "Hi," and left.
Advice for today?

Cobalt Blue – we woke you at 4 to get you up. The machine is easier on your body and it's easier for us to communicate. There are other voices you can hear.

Do you want to do your book today?

Let's begin on Monday. The weather is turbulent today and you need to calm yourself down.

Anything else?

Listening to the correct, authentic voice is difficult. There are many levels of transmissions. For you, especially, keep tuned to the deepest frequency. Do the visualization first before attempting connection. That way you can be assured it's just not mischief-makers coming to confuse you.
Blast through the rest of the outline and see the book finished. Go to the bookstore and pick out more publishers.

I don't feel a good connection today. Thank you.

The connection is fine. You are just used to your Dan connection which is more direct, more intimate, since he has physical knowledge of your circuits. He has a physical memory of the "lay of the land." Your land, your body. That's why he was able to tickle you the last time he was in your body. Yes, that was him sneaking back to say "Hi" in yoga. It's still uncomfortable in Africa for him, but soon he'll lose his Dan memory and won't be able to find the way back to you. Now eat, and then work.

Namaste. Thank you.

And to you.

Saturday, November 9, 2002 – 5:25 a.m.
Last night, went to LACMA to see "The Name of the Rose" – I went by myself, and didn't like it really. Don't like feeling that alone at the movies at night. Cold. Best course of action for today? I feel nuts…help?

Cobalt Blue, here, to calm you down – it doesn't help your body for you to plan exit strategies. When you see yourself taking an easy out, just stop it. You short circuit your belief that everything will turn out for the best. It will turn out for the best. And your falling into a vortex of sorrow, like you did in your direct past life, will only annoy you when you get back home. So just think of yourself as a shining warrior goddess. Don't tell anyone that you think of yourself as a shining warrior goddess, but keep it just under the surface. Then when things hit you, you can defend yourself. You feel very vulnerable…your car in a ditch? How vulnerable do you think that is. Your real car needs gas, and your imaginary car needs tending to. Don't think beyond today. It doesn't serve you, because you don't have enough information. And the information you do have is not accurate.

It is the fear that permeates your environment that is, once again, like a virus. You inoculated yourself against the flu, now inoculate yourself against _fear_. The fear that whips around and hits you broadside is what fells you like a falling tree. And you go down. So inoculate yourself against it.

Listen carefully to your inner monologue and when it turns into dark corners that aren't in your best interest, control your thoughts. You can control your thoughts. It's the only thing you can control. You are participating in another mass events project, but on such a minor level that your best course of action is to ignore it. It doesn't concern you at all.

When the medieval world changed it wasn't because of the leaders: the kings and the princes and the knights. It was because the "little people" just continued to live their lives, putting one foot in front of the other. Just like you will continue to do until it's time to come home. But you still have a lot of work to do.

Now that you have your health, and you do have your health, continue to take care of your body. Both those soups you ate yesterday had little food value. Don't be so lazy. Make your own soup. Begin to cook again. Just because there's no Dan to eat the leftovers, doesn't mean you shouldn't cook for yourself.

Dan destroyed your last 13 years so cavalierly, with his absolute intractability, that you cannot let that ruin what time you have left. And the only way not to let it ruin what time you have left is to grab the present by the horns and have fun. Create joy in your life, moment by moment. Create love in your life by loving deeply. Start with yourself and it will branch out from there.

If you don't like going to the movies by yourself, don't go. You could have gone to yoga and lit the fire and read Emily Dickenson. Appreciate the house you love while you can. This is the best time of your life, so far. Enjoy it.

Being alone is so much better than being with that man who, on so many levels, hated you. He hated your courage. He hated your optimism. He was jealous of your relationships. And you still loved him. And you still miss him, which is simply insane. Think of all the time of your lives together he watched TV, played chess, roamed the internet, and watched game after game, instead of "living." His choice, not yours. You had no control over him, but you have control over you. So take control. Take the controls of your own plane, car, vehicle. Don't let yourself fall into the drink.

You're the only one who cares about you. You're the only one who cares honestly. Everyone else cares about themselves and that's how it should be. No problem with that at all. It's when you expect other people to care about you and your plight that you get into trouble.

Is that all clear enough? Print this out and read it over every day. We got through easily this morning. You have no idea how much anxiety there is on your street. Makes it like cutting a swath through the jungle with huge sabers. So much energy traffic!

Tomorrow, get up early and come back. I can start my book tomorrow. Or continue it and you can work.

Thank you. Namaste.

We salute the warrior goddess in you and want you to connect to her energy. Consciously. Directly, every day. Don't let the cowards in your life drag you down. They can't help it, but they will. It's like a frantic drowning child can take an adult down. And that's who seeks you out.

On the way home from work that day, I saw my neighbor, Julie driving her husband to the hospital. His kidney was failing, and Ken wound up in the ICU at Cedars-Sinai Hospital, which is within walking distance. I knew I couldn't go see Ken – I'd seen too much of hospitals – but I felt guilty about it. That night, I went to a dinner party and met a very angry, self-righteous couple, and had an awful time.

Sunday, November 10, 2002 – 6:18 a.m.
I know it's late, but my body wouldn't get up. It's blustery, and rainy outside.

Cobalt Blue, here – yesterday was pretty much a disaster day energy-wise. You chose not to participate in Ken's dramas, and that was okay. You've had your own hospital dramas too recently to want to be in a hospital...

What are you saying?

That moment by moment, you change the course of your life with the choices you make. Both those obligations could have been cancelled and you would have felt better about it. Your body didn't want to step into an ICU and that's why you refused the call. But you must acknowledge it. But Art and Fritzi, (Ken's parents), would have wanted to take Lily anyway. You would have felt better about yourself if you had offered.

The lesson is to evaluate the choices you make on a moment by moment basis. You don't need to fulfill your obligations, your "social" obligations, at the expense of your soul obligations.

Thank you. Namaste.

Don't let yourself get off track. Just keep living moment by moment. Don't argue with people. You don't need to express your views quite so forcefully and other people don't like it. No one changes anyone's mind. Don't expend your energy. Keep it to yourself. Sam's technique of never offering up an opinion feels cowardly to you, and yet it's very smart. It lets him be a chameleon and chameleons change colors with their environment just to survive. You change into peacock regalia and will get shot.

Monday, November 11, 2002 – 5:53 a.m.

Feel awful today. Think Dan, the African wanted to "talk" to me last night. I opened his file, but was too tired to sit long enough to "get" much.

Ken's being in the ICU brings up too much pain for me. If I could just crawl up into a ball today and cry all day, that would be my choice. I feel so alone. I see why Dan was always so afraid of losing Sam's love. There's a pulled-in quality that's unnerving, disapproving. Every time I talk to him, as soon as the conversation isn't directly about him, he says, "I gotta jump in the shower, get on the road, sort my socks." It's rejecting in a backhanded way – so what with Lynn and Sam, my only two friends gone, I feel so completely alone in the world. They both reject any kind of "getting together" plans. They'll talk on the phone when it's convenient, but no one wants to do anything. Not even just go to the movies.

I feel I'm not doing a good job of my life at all. Feel I don't want to continue to live. Tired of beating my head against intractable walls – people, work, me? There's something so deeply embedded – so destructive – there must be a way of getting it out of me.

Okay, I think that's enough self-pity for the day. I'll get the book that Terrence talked about. What's it called? Creating Optimistic Thinking?

Advice for today? Was that Dan last night, or just my loneliness kicking in?

Cobalt Blue, here, but it's late. Read over all the advice from the last months and actually take it. If you won't move to the next level, we can't help you. Your feelings of helplessness come from your own inability to quell your own fears. If you let your fear take over your life, you will find yourself falling into the pit of despair where you let yourself slip into this morning. There is glue down there that keeps you stuck. The best thing to do is not let yourself slide.

Ken's being in the ICU brings up body sensations that took you down yesterday. You've got to counteract them. Don't talk to anyone today who will drain you. If you see Julie, you will need all the strength you have to hold yourself above the fear line.

Plan your Paris trip as best you can. Plan fun. Don't expect other people to participate.

You asked for our help and then you get uncomfortable. You have to listen to the advice and then read it over. And then follow through. There is a follow through glitch in your life that is the reason your projects die. Reprogram your brain. Go read that book today. Just sit there and read that book. Try that. We don't seem to offer you enough help to get you out of your own sorrow and self-pity. Sorrow and self-pity will lead you nowhere. You won't be happy with yourself when you get back here, if once again you let yourself slide down into the pit of inaction. You cannot afford to do that. Not even briefly. Go to Paris. Take the rest of Dan's ashes. Put him in Chartres.

Now it feels as if everyone's mad at me, even me.

You are a magnet for hatred; other people just dump hatred onto you. What do you think all those toilet dreams were about? Everyone's hatred – demeaning, destroying. People don't care whether you live or die, but that's okay – as long as you do. But when you allow yourself to absorb the feeling tones, then you wind up depleted.

You just got zapped by a lot of negative energy – first that nasty piece of business at the dinner party then Janet (a woman at yoga) twice in one day.

She actively wishes you harm. When you see her, wish her well. Think, "I wish you well," and it acts like a shield. Don't let her aggravate you. That's what her refusal to sign in was – a way to hook your energy. It's the narcissists' ploy. I use that word, narcissist, because you understand it. But that's not what those entities are. They are vampires. And it's how they feed themselves.

Thank you. Namaste.

And to you, our warrior goddess. Remember, that's what you wanted to be – now you just have to embody it. The only way you can become a warrior goddess is to give yourself challenges. You've chosen these challenges. You're like Dan in that respect. He chose his African life and now he's unhappy that he can't come back and continue on with his comfy soul-connection – you. But you're not his anymore. You belong entirely to you. And in that, there is strength. You can't think of your loneliness as a negative. It's a positive. Is this enough for today? Go. Walk out the sadness, walk out the Dan residue. You let him in and I wasn't there to clean up afterward. He does damage to your circuits. Damage that is hard to undo.

Tuesday, November 12, 2002 – 6:15 a.m.
Gheri-Llynn's birthday today. She would be 44, if she didn't decide to leave. Okay. I will get in touch with my warrior goddess today, invite the muse and not eat so much chocolate. Advice for today?

Cobalt Blue here later than we'd like.

No further advice, except to read over all the "advice" and begin to integrate the concrete suggestions into your everyday existence. If you need "scientific" proof, go get Jeff Schwartz's book. (*The Mind and the Brain: Neuroplasticity and the Power of Mental Force.*)

Anything else?

Create the "love" for your own life. Manufacture the emotion if you have to. Manufacture the emotion by thinking loving thoughts toward your house, your career and your body. Think the thoughts that "spoiled" children think. You were not "spoiled" – you were tortured as a child.

Namaste. Thank you.

That day, I felt Dan with me in yoga, chatting away, but I couldn't remember any of it. At home, I felt bombarded by his insistent energy until finally, much against orders, I sat down, pen in my left hand again:

Tuesday, November 12, 2002 – 10:05 p.m.

Dan, the African, waiting to chat – yes, I was with you in yoga – you felt me – I think yesterday was the anniversary of the marriage proposal. How happy that made *me* – not you. You just wanted a family, and I looked okay. We both knew you'd love me, and when you did, you did it big time. Forgive my hubris.

I know you've been buzzing in and out. I thought you were supposed to stay with the baby.

The baby is fine on her own. If she only knew that she was once a Jewish lawyer from Brooklyn. What a trip!

And before that, what were you?

I think I had a really boring life. Nine to five sort of thing. It's the challenges that make it (life) special.

Then I felt the huge energy drain, my hand cramped and I couldn't go on.

Wednesday, November 13, 2002 – 5:39 a.m.
Dream about Dan – only he'd shrunk – was very short, but it was him. He looked like Robert Reich – a full-grown, tiny man.
Yesterday, I felt him with me, especially in yoga. Last night, I felt him wanting to connect, so I got out one of the channeling books and put the pen in my left hand – and there he was, Dan the African. Funny.
Any advice for today?

Cobalt Blue, here – your incredible shrinking Dan-man is exactly what is *finally* occurring. He's such a tenacious soul! If he'd been as present in his alive self as he is present in his old life as a dead person, you two might have been able to accomplish what you intended.

Your love for him now comforts you, but it also calls to him. We don't say not to love your Dan, because you are still trying to let him go, trying to work on a book that is about him and his relationship to you, and the marriage you tried to create with no help from him, I might add.

So it's all a juggling act and it's hard for you to resist him. But I can't tell you strongly enough, you just don't understand the extent, the degree, the unthinking damage that his in-life behavior caused your body. And now that he's dead, he does the same thing. He's using your body to soothe his soul. You are no longer connected to him.

I can hear you don't want to let him go, but in truth, you won't be able to move on until you do. Live empty without him. You managed to live before you met him, you'll live a while after he's gone.

Yes, you knew he was "out there" for you. And he was. But the frustration that his entity caused many coordinates can't be undone.

You still have the opportunity to achieve the goal of your work. Your other life goals – the big ones – however, had you partnered with your favorite friend, well Barushes ex-favorite friend. And you trusted him to do the right thing by you. He didn't. He betrayed you on such a deep level that you don't need to offer up what little energy you have to comfort him now.

He needs to be "locked down." He thinks that if he lets that body tend to herself, he'll skate free of her. He's in for another surprise. He'll just be more disoriented when he does come in.

You know what newborns look like. The fierce wisdom they have – then it goes. It's there for a nanosecond. It's a realization that okay, I made it out here again. Now what? You saw it in Max's eyes – what a fierce soul he is! Yes, all boy.

But the subject is your Dan, who you refuse to give up. And it's hard to give him up when you still long for his body, his touch. If there were a magic wand to pull his coordinates out of you, we'd say use them. When you work with Rahmie, you could ask for a realignment that would fully set you back on the right track, energy-wise.

You three will have fun on Friday. (Rahmie, the shaman student, and another woman from her class were going to practice new techniques on me.)

You can offer them validation by being able to describe the process. Then they will come to understand that it isn't magic so much as a discovery of what really _is_. The archeological dig that's going on in Mexico isn't discovering something new; it's uncovering something old that's just been buried under years of other cultures. The scientists are so excited because it's new to them.

The three of you will be "discovering" something _new_ to you, but it is just because you will be able to see – grasp – what is buried beneath the layers of cultural-bigotry is the word that pops into your mind. But that is a charged word. It is a prejudice of "seeing" and it's an agreed-upon world view. It is the illusion of life. And everyone needs some sort of "agreement" just to operate. But it's when the person can connect with the entity that real progress gets to be made.

Poets connect easily, but no one pays attention to poets except other poets. And they are a rarefied group, somewhat smug, if you ask me. They are another group of "communicators." Our work, which you are a part of, is trying to mainline this kind of work, this kind of knowingness.

You are a good channel. And because you've learned to do this kind of channeling as easily as you do now, without absolutely injuring your own circuits, we think that you'll be able to at _last_ (underlined three times), produce the work that you need to produce to fulfill your "mission."

Thank you for getting here as directed this morning. Thank you for getting to bed last night.

Continue to show up in the morning and I will continue on my book.

When you walk today, just drink in the city. Love everything you can – see it like Paris. You want to go to Paris and you might, but now it looks as if you missed the opportunity. Keep trying. Melanie's energy will be fun there, if you two can go. But don't spend too much time today on it.

Anything else?

Just this weekend, if you can begin to pack up Dan's closet and be ready for the New Year. It's going to be easier than you expect. Expect the best! Take your own good advice. No matter what.

Thank you. Namaste.

And to you. Connect with Miss Warrior Goddess, Stephanie. She's on the job.

Thursday, November 14, 2002 – 5:48 a.m.

Cobalt Blue, here – we woke you at 3:30 for a reason. Too much commotion in the environment. Lots of hysteria and it makes it difficult to connect.

I feel Dan in the house with me. Trying to connect. Chatting. Is he? Or is that just me missing him?

His big energy lingers in your house because his clothes and smell still linger in the house. When you connected with him in his journal – and that was his journal – you encouraged him. It's not good for you and it's not good for him to think he's got such an easy audience. His intent toward you is good. When he says he's sorry for all the "hubris" of his incarnation, his absolute taking your love, your care, your energy and giving you absolutely nothing in return, it's genuine. But the reality of his life with you is so shockingly selfish that we think he needs to be aware that once you live so completely self-absorbed, there's no growth. And he had an opportunity to grow. He just refused to avail himself of lots of "tutoring." He couldn't have gotten a more patient "tutor" than you. Pull away from the energy that was his and you will regain your own footing in the world.

The only thing you can do to encourage your warrior Stephanie to stick around and become integrated is to honor your own work, your own schedule and your own talent. If you wake up again at 3:30, try to get up for a while. Your street is very noisy, energetically. There's an energy jam of sorts with all the screaming that goes on.

Your ability to live fearlessly in the world is what you will remember. Keep a guard up for your own bad habits, your blame bad habits. Stick to your schedule as best as possible and go dancing tonight if you want. But just go alone.

Keep your "advice" to yourself today. Let other souls manage on their own. You only annoy them.

Thank you. Namaste.

And to you. After you eat, come back and open my book, and then work on your own.

Friday, November 15, 2002 – 5:31 a.m.
Advice for today?
Should I go to Paris? Now feel more than a little concerned about money situation.

Cobalt Blue, here – you can only go to Paris if you won't feel any constraints about the money. And since you've earned it in these last two trips, we think you should just do it. As you are well aware, the events of the world turn on a dime and no one knows which way they will go from moment to moment.

Your Dan would tag along to Chartres, of course. It is the place that most resonates for you two as a couple. You were an older nun and he was a novice. (Ah, so there it was! My life as the ugly, old nun that I saw in the past-life regression thirty years ago.) He loved you so much and wanted so much to be a man so he could make love to you. So he became a man, and what does he do? Tortures you. You've had other lovers who were kinder to you than he was, but you've never gotten "hooked" quite as badly, physically. You simply couldn't leave him. There was just no way out for you, except the one that he took. The "will you love me if" question that he tested you with? The answer was yes! But still, it wasn't enough.

I know it sounds as if this is Barushe speaking, but it's just the reality of the situation. Your own progress as a soul was hindered. You needed to explore and expand your ability to love in this life and he made it almost impossible for you. He tortured you sexually, by all his withholding, pulling back. And because you'd had such intense experiences with recent loves – Francisco, for instance – was a direct past-life love. (It's why you thought you'd died and gone to heaven when he made love to you – you did!) But by comparison, Dan withheld and you knew it. It made you sad, and it made you angry. There was no way out, once you had committed to him.

But you couldn't have avoided that particular train wreck. It was your train wreck to deal with. We only wish you'd gotten him to head in the direction you were going, and then there would have been no "train wreck." Do you see? If he could have been guided to do what was best for you both as a couple, as opposed to "Jonesing" for everyone else's approval, you would have had more options open to you both. The baby would have helped you a great deal. Oh well, as you would say.

Just be fearless in the world. Take all that comes and smile at it. It is your true strength.

Vis-à-vis Sam? You have no idea how tightly you two are bound. As Dan said, the three of you manage to "show up" quite often together. But your relationship with Sam this time provides a good mix of give and take. The respect you have for him as an entity serves to strengthen him, and his abilities. But the bad habits he inherited from Dan may make it impossible for him to realize his potential in this lifetime. His fear simply takes him over. You can't even write that without connecting to it on an energetic level, see?

It's not your fear. It's the old bug-a-boo of "how great am I?" Fear. The tyranny of having to impress other people. Other people mostly want you not to do as well as they are doing. So it's a no-win situation.

Anything else?

No, just print out and read this over. You literally cannot remember any of this because of the way it's delivered.

Thank you. Namaste.

And to you, our shining warrior goddess. When you walk today, just for fun, see yourself as your shining warrior goddess and it will make you smile. No one else has to know.

I don't remember if I followed that advice, but sometimes I hypnotize my clients into seeing themselves as shining warrior goddesses or gods. Try it; it might make you smile, too.

November 15, 2002

Give us a minute. Dan is blocking the circuits because he can. He wants to say "hi" from Africa. We suggest you say "hi" and then let me clean up your circuits.

Dan, the African here for a chat. The reason I'm being so selfish again, for the very last time, I fear, is that I want to encourage you to make every effort to go to France. Just take [the rest of] my ashes and put me in that place. You will connect with the two souls who loved each other so dearly. Who longed for each other so much. And what we had as a couple – as Dan and Stephanie – was pure love, when I let it be. Don't lose track of that. Yes, I was selfish. Yes, I was deluded about my importance in and to the world. Yes, I ignored you too much of the time. But, please understand how deeply appreciative I am now, straddling two worlds. Understanding how much of your own life you let me devour and waste. And your ability to continue to forgive me is what I take with me into this next "challenge."
And believe me, it will be a challenge. They won't let me "show" you the chaos, because it's not your life, and not your challenge. Cobalt Blue is annoyed with me, but I have all this energy that's connected to you, and I can block them. Which I did until she let me through. Still a brat? You bet.
I love that I can feel you smile. Please go to France for us. You were right; Sam didn't need to be there. It really is about you and me. I need to leave. They tell me I take too much of your core energy when I do this, and they know best. But I "know" the way in to you. I love you from Africa and will continue to check in with you until they bolt me down, like earthquake-proofing a foundation.
I wish they'd done that in my last life. I was always "off." That's why I was never really present. And I can never make it up to you. Can't change the past. Feel my love, for that I can and do send you, even when you just pass my picture in the hall. Yesterday when you stopped and put your hand over each and every picture, didn't you feel me loving you? I did. I screamed at you to feel my love flood you. And I know you felt it. If I get to be joined to you again, I promise I'll do a better job.
Barushe just said, "He said that last time." Just forgive me and go on. Clean up the circuits.

Cobalt Blue, here. You can clean up the circuits by pushing out. (Pushing out the energy, using Qigong exercises.)

That night, Sam and I went to my friend Robert's holiday party at his Bel Air flower shop at the top of Beverly Glen. Sam was fussy and irritated, and I could tell he'd rather not be going. On the drive up the canyon, he said that he wasn't even sure that his dad had ever communicated with him. He said it was probably only his imagination, and he asked me to not talk about it to him anymore. Okay, I thought. Fine.

Tuesday, November 26, 2002 – 6:41 a.m.
What a bad day yesterday was! Tired, cranky and I feel stupid. Advice for the day? And did you get me up or was that just my anxiety?

Dan sneaks in…

But Cobalt Blue pushed him out of the way:

Cobalt Blue, here – no, it wasn't us who woke you. It was your own anxiety. The anxiety over your money situation rises up and takes your circuits out. Don't let that happen. When you buy something, like those shoes, either say I need them or I don't. Those shoes are a good deal, and you like good deals. You don't own a single pair of shoes that make you feel like a "girl," and those work. End of story. They were a good deal. Pay the traffic ticket. Take care of the niggling little things that annoy you. That's what woke you up. Too many loose ends. Your brain, which is different from your mind, stores all those things, and then can't do a "delete" on them because they're not finished. So take time today to work out all the financial stuff for the trip and put it in a file, and then forget it.
You have a cold, and you're fussy. Your Dan wants to communicate with you – he's trying to burst into your "security" system. It's up to you if you want to allow him in. You're not feeling great because of the cold, the level of anxiety. But he's found a hole in your system and you feel it. So I suggest you let him say what he wants and then let me process the "damage." It taxes your circuits because his energy is so strong and focused. And you are still so battered by his choices in this life. I'll step back….

Dan, the African, here to say, "Hi!"
I'm so happy we're going to France! It is where I prayed to love you so unconditionally. It is the place that we had our great, totally unrequited love. You refused to break your vows and touch me. Who knows? Maybe that's why I always denied you my hugs as Dan, the Brooklyn man.

Re: you and Sam? I don't know. He doesn't seem to like you at all anymore. I feel his annoyance with you when I'm with him. He's his mother's son. Let her have him. Let him go. He'll only take your energy and not appreciate it, just the way I did. But you should do it exactly like he proceeds. With kind words and no deeds.

I will keep flitting in and out. I'm pretty much connected with my next life and it will be very exciting, if I survive the first three years. But who knows? Things are pretty turbulent in the household where I live.

When you look at my picture, I see "us" and marvel at my own stupidity. If I could drain the pain from your body like draining a bathtub filled with dirty water, I would. Write the story of our life together. Maybe it'll help some other poor schlub like me, who sits in splendor and just doesn't realize it.

I wasted both of our lives! Don't waste another minute on people who don't like or value you. Life's too short. Especially yours. And you've done your time, Babe. You've done your time.

Forget my family. Go forward as yourself. You were so much better off without me. And you will be again. Good-bye my darling daughter, wife, mother. I've let you down more than once. That's why they were so mad at me. I hope I learn my lesson this time! I'm going to listen more carefully. To my teachers on earth and "up" there. Here.

My body hurts. Achy. Sad. I'm so tired.

Good-bye, my sweet Stephanie. Wife that I loved. I won't even remember your sweet kisses in a very short time, I know that. I'll have no "conscious" memory of anything at all. I just hope they let me be with you at Chartres. It is one of the places I loved you. But I think you had my number there. You wouldn't "engage" with me. But I worshiped you. And then when you worshiped me, and you did, I really couldn't have been meaner to you. End of story. And it's too sad for even me to think about. Just know that you will be fine in the world. And I'm sorry for all the "bag lady" jokes. They weren't funny. They were mean.

Bye, my Dan that was.

Cobalt Blue, back to clean up the circuits. But go and do some Qigong. Eat and come back and work. You are very fussy today, but it's the cold, the mourning, the anger from Lynn, and Sam's disappearance from your life that hurts your feelings so much.

Should I bother to work? Do you want to work on your book?

What do you want to do?

Run for the hills, hide my head in sand, and crawl up into a ball. Or I could work.

I chose to work. And that day, I made the final decision to go Paris. I booked tickets and found a place to stay, and then I called Sam and told him my plans, and he wasn't happy. In fact, he was downright furious.

Wednesday, November 27, 2002 – 5:59 a.m.
Wow! Time goes so fast. Woke up at 3:30, and simply refused to get up – I can't be that tired all day.
Paris!!!! I'm so excited. Paris, that's been calling to me since 1962. I'm slow to answer, but who cares? At this time next week, I'll be there. Advice for the day?

Cobalt Blue here, but later than we'd like. You need to set the alarm for 4:30. Your body is still in transition from sickness to health, and the heat that woke you at 3:00 wasn't us. Then you got cranky and defiant about getting up. Doesn't serve you and makes it harder for us to get through. We can only do this with your help. You can only "hear" if you listen. So tomorrow, which is your Thanksgiving, set the alarm for 4:30, get up, work, then nap. If you go to the late dinner, don't eat very much; when you leave, leave early. You may not choose to go, but you like wearing your pretty clothes.

We feel that advice might make you unhappy, in that all it concerns is your work, which simply must get done. Print out your story ("The Lopsided Little Christmas Tree") and send it off. Call your Amber agent just to see if you can fire up interest. Do it as a test. See if she has any ideas. Start taking the baby steps in the direction you want to go. Buy those two books. The brain book and the learned optimism book, and read them.

In France, if you can find an hour to sit and do your "left-handed" writing – which we can switch to the easier hand once we connect, then you will keep the "channel" open. Even though this seems simple to you, it's not simple in the least. The amount of coordination all this takes is as complicated as any semiconductor. Any computer. Between balancing your body, your own fussy emotions – since your body and soul are still in active mourning for the Dan that was – it is a balancing act for us. It is a team effort. But I think we've got your channel pretty open and it just needs to stay that way.

It is, I might say, such a luxury to be able to type. The directness of the connection makes it much more efficient. Your own dyslexia actually makes it possible. You can _feel_ the energy flitting back and forth inside your brain. We use one side and then can pull from information on the other. The brain is not the mind. The brain is finite. The mind, infinite.

Your mind, in particular, connects with, or can connect with so many coordinates; it's what makes you "spacey." That's why you need to focus on your work right now. Just stay focused.

When you come back from France, you will have the completion of your Dan book. Begin again from the beginning and _storm_ through it. Put yourself on a 5-page-a-day regimen and chart out the whole book. When you have three new chapters done, send it out. You need to work as hard as you can in the next few months, just to assuage your own concern. Leave it as concern. Don't let it go into anything besides that. Take action, based on a firm belief that all will work out for you.

For today? Just go for your walk. Do the Qigong. Plant your plants or ask the gardener to do it. Finally. Enjoy Lena and the babies – it drives your Dan nuts that you enjoy them. But he denied you Lily. Send Sam loving thoughts. Have no attitude when talking to him.

Get the money in order for your trip. Remember to read over today's advice. The reason you can't remember it is that you really don't hear it with the side of your brain that remembers.

Is my "dreaming" Stephanie back? Or do I need to call her again.

She's back. It's why you get so uppity. She's uppity because she knows how brave you are and she gets annoyed when you don't behave in ways that help you.

Do not diminish what you do. Do not diminish yourself at all, do not make yourself seem smaller to please anyone.

Anything else?

Follow Tracy's (my girl doc) suggestion from "Good Vibrations." (A website. Need I say more?) Your sexuality needs to get fired up again. Your husband, love of your life, died. You, my dear, did not. Reconnect with your own love of sex and let the last 13 years of torture go. He withheld from you so much of himself. We don't know who he was saving it for. Don't save yourself any longer.

Thank you.

Thursday, November 28, 2002 – 5:00 a.m.
It's Thanksgiving. I chose not to face the freeway and go to Mel's – I'll go to Lucille's instead. Yesterday I got a "howler" e-mail from Sam. He essentially divorced me because I'm going to France. His choice.
It's painful, but less so than I thought, since he's been so awful to me in the past year. As Dan said, "He's his mother's son."
Advice for today. Comments on Sam? On France?

Cobalt Blue, here. The e-mail that you got from Sam was written when he was essentially drunk. You could have figured that out by the time it was written. What you wrote in response came from the authentic you, and he doesn't recognize you as a force to be reckoned with. He does lump you together with all the "old ladies" he feels sort of orbit around him like the privileged "sun" that he is. Take yourself out of his "orbit." It is a complete waste of your finite energy. Let him work out his life in the ways he wants. They don't include you, because he resents you. He resents your ability to be fearless, because he, himself, is so afraid.

Just let him go so completely, that when people ask how he is, just smile and say, "He's fine." You don't need to share that he, too, is a "missing man." He's been "missing" from your life for the exact amount of time that your Dan has been "missing." You just didn't realize it fully. Now you understand. That is the only difference between today and yesterday – understanding.

Your love of both him and his father was so "unrequited" and wasted that it seems a shame. But it is what it is. Let him go completely. He's the one who will miss you. You won't miss him because you won't miss the pain. When you stop knocking your head against his "wall," you'll feel relief. And that's the authentic emotion.

The relief you feel from being "freed" from that "family" should settle in soon. You don't need to interact with them one tiny bit. Just smile and send them good wishes.

Go get the "Learned Optimism" book and read it. It will help you.

Anything else?

No. Just enjoy your Thanksgiving. Plant your poor plants. Plant your garden and begin to honor yourself in the same manner. The reason you don't look at the garden is that it reminds you too much of the "Dan" you loved. You loved your gardener. But you too could be a gardener, if you wanted.

Go eat, and come back and I'll work on my book. Then you _must_ work on yours.

Thank you.

November 29, 2002 – 4:57 a.m.
Went to Lucille's for Thanksgiving last night. Didn't get home until almost 11. Worked yesterday. Excited about Paris. I feel Dan wanting to talk to me. Advice for the day?

Cobalt Blue, here – We woke you earlier for a reason. Try to get up, even if it's "too early." You can make up the sleep and as we said, we have schedules "up here" too. Yes, your Dan, or whatever he thinks of himself now, did want to talk to you and you can choose to do it or not. The subject will be him and his son, whom he is visiting for the very last time. Their relationship is what keeps him here. He's still currying favor, a quality which sent you up the wall when he was alive and would still annoy you. He never showed his son the true "selfhood" he showed you, and consequently, when you said to Sam that your husband was not his father, you were 100% correct.

The sadness that you feel toward Sam has been with you all year – when you lost your husband, you lost his son. It's not as if you're not strong enough to "take the hit," as you like to say. You've actually already taken it. When you finally plant your "Sister Isabel," – your Dan – and all his manipulative, bad behaviors toward you on those cobblestones, just sit in the nave of that great cathedral and listen for us. You'll be able to hear your own sweet voice from all those years ago. You were a singer then, it's why those tapes from "The Anonymous Four" (a group that sings medieval music) fill you with such joy.

Just work on your book today, if only to re-read what you already have and · not be too judgmental.

You will have to blast through the book when you come home, otherwise you won't be able to finish in time. But for now, just enjoy the day. Keep showing up for yourself.

That is "your Dan" in your body. You stopped doing your "firewall" exercises. You can let him through if you want, but we need to clean up your circuits afterward. Do you feel how uncomfortable he makes you? He'll …

Dan, the baby African, here – I spend most of my time now scrunched inside "mother's" womb. Becoming a tight fit. The "Sister Isabel" incarnation I saw when I was "home," and it upset me no end. How I could have done that to you was such a betrayal. To agree, really request, a life with you and then so completely abandon you to my own self-obsession was well, pretty unforgivable. I'm so sorry for squandering your life the way I did. I squandered the time of our life together so deliberately that it defies my comprehension. But water under that bridge – and the bridges you'll be crossing soon will be in "our Paris." You'll know when I'm with you. I know you want to "drop me" off real fast, and I can't blame you. But maybe wait until Friday, next Friday to do it.

Don't harden your heart toward me. I loved you, in my fashion. I just didn't have it in me to really care about you. That's the nasty little reality of the situation. But deep down you knew it. You knew I didn't care about you and that's what you couldn't understand.

Re: Sam? Let him go completely. He's now turned all his anger toward you, as if you caused his present pain. Let him stew in it. Let him go. You've taken enough hits from him, too.

He doesn't care about you either, really. Chip off the old block, as it were. Let us both go. Good-bye my darling ex-wife. I hope when you remember our life together you can recall the love we shared when I let us, which was far too brief, in terms of what was possible.

I'll leave your body and won't be back. But I will be with you at Chartres, my love. I will miss you.

Impossible spirit that he/she was/is! May he learn something in this next go round – I, we, are not his guide, but we need to speak with them.

Re: your own anxiety? Just keep focused on your 15 second exercise. It will get you through. Don't plan anything beyond 15 seconds.

Saturday, November 30, 2002 – 6:03 a.m.

Yes, I know I'm here late, but I got caught by "Moulin Rouge" late last night. I watched the last 40 minutes again, so didn't get to sleep until after midnight.

Saw Dr. Bae yesterday and he showed me the front page of Newsweek – all about acupuncture. His friend's picture is on the front cover.

The utter aloneness of my life feels better than my "old" life. At yoga, Hilary DeVries told me she'd sold her book, "So Five Minutes Ago" for six figures. Amazing! Fabulous! I looked at the "Learned Optimism" book last night at Barnes and Noble Bookstore – all about developing habits of "good self-talk." Easier said than done!

Any advice for today?

(Cobalt Blue) – your fear that we will abandon you, too, is acknowledged yet not justified. We can't abandon you. You, on the other hand, can abandon "us." And most people with your kind of talent get bored with taking this much direction and begin to behave like recalcitrant children, which we feel you do only occasionally. It's why your ability to monitor your own body is so important.

The interconnection between body, brain and your core self is so exquisitely, so delicately balanced, that gaining a full "understanding" is simply impossible.

It is the "quest" of the species as a whole. Scientists try to decipher where the brain begins/ends and transmutes into the body. Or how the "mind" is different from the soul.

To simplify it so that you can visualize it and begin to use your own "power" (which you wanted more of), think of a gelatinous liquid suspended in that membrane we talked about over your head. Think of yourself as connected to the membrane by long flowing veins and arteries, just like your body is connected to your heart and all of its various parts by your own circulatory system.

But the give and take between the suspended liquid is completely at your control. You can choose to open valves and take in information or use the "shut off" valves and take in the cacophony that comes in from the five senses that belong exclusively to your body.

Once again, you choose how much information you want to take in. When you let yourself get exhausted, fussy and bombarded by external energy, you can't "hear" anything from us – your core being-ness.

You took a major hit in the past two days – you've acknowledged the loss of Sam. He's been gone from your life a long time, but you've just processed it. Let yourself understand it.

Spend today getting your house in order to be "abandoned" for 10 days. Plant your plants, otherwise they will die and you will be upset. Fix your stereo. You can do it yourself. Become the "man" in your own life.

Love your life, period. Embrace what is. Get on your own side so completely that it becomes second nature to you to do what is in your best interest. Stop currying favor – it's simply what killed your husband. His need to curry favor from the outside world – and especially from his "withholding" son is what drove you crazy while you lived with him. Don't do the same thing. Don't make the same mistake.

Dan and Sam's relationship goes back a long time. And with Sam, he fulfilled most of what he had planned with him, but he did it completely at your expense – both literally and figuratively. It cost you so dearly that their "combined" debt to you will remain "on the books" for a very long time.

But don't think you'll collect in this lifetime. Let the two of them go completely, but with love. They are the loves of your life and they both used and abused you in their own specific ways. Sam denigrates whatever you say to him now, principally because you feel like such a "loser" to him. Yes, I know you hate that term, but you have to understand that most people think of you just that way.

It just annoys them deeply that you don't share their belief about yourself. You are completely unsuccessful in the world at large, stunningly so, and yet you continue to persevere.

And that is the core of your strength. It is from this core that you will rise like a phoenix, if you can remain calm in the face of your own fear.

Develop your own skills of "keeping focused" so that you, too, can say, "I've just sold my book for six figures." How happy that would make all of us. See it happening for yourself. Do your own goddess ceremony everyday and speak those words out loud. When thoughts that are opposed to that reality flit in, know that they come from all the negativity that you chose to be saddled with.

You don't want to hear this, but you could have side-stepped this marriage if you'd listened to that migraine you had the night before you got married. You could have called off the whole thing, but that would have taken such amazingly "clear-sight" then, and you just didn't have it. You do now.

As we said, we cannot abandon you. You can choose to abandon us. But we know you won't now because we've got too much work to do together.

Thank you. Namaste.

As November came to a close, "Fly Girls" had crashed and burned. But what bothered me far more was that I had lost Sam. Slowly, I began to pay attention to the daily advice, and focus on what was good in my life. I tried not to fret about the past or worry about the future. Instead, I chose to fill my brain with excitement and joy, because I was going to Paris!

Still, I could feel something stealing my energy. What could it be?

Chapter Eighteen

"An American in Paris"

What else? It was Dan.

Sunday, December 1, 2002 – 6:08 a.m.

I'm feeling tired all the time. Maybe it's the sadness over losing Sam. Oh, well. I'm going to Paris and nothing's going to make me unhappy today, not even losing Sam. Advice for today?

Cobalt Blue here – later than we'd like, of course. But your grumpiness has to be contended with.
Firewall alert.

(Couldn't connect)

Here's the problem. Your Dan was blocking the circuits. Your "missing man" is not as missing as we'd like. Now you understand the betrayal of this lifetime. He's depleted your energy and still continues to steal from you.
He literally stole the time of your life and then squandered it so heartlessly that it defies imagination. On what? On the Giants? That's why Sam's so angry, because you put the finger on his own way of shutting out the world and manipulating all things around him.
Don't call Dan out. He's in the house. Let him go visit Bonnie (his sister), **who ignores him. Everyone else ignores him now because they can't hear him. You can, so he stays around you – and makes you so unhappy, I might add. Just like in life. He made you unhappy.**
He left you so completely exposed in the world, you may not survive. And if you choose not to, it will be a direct result of your having loved your "missing man." Nothing is a given. Nothing is preordained and if, when you return from France, you don't clean out all traces of your "missing man" from your house and get on with your life without him, he will

have prevailed and will have managed to completely destroy what is left of your life.

If you don't begin to honor your time, the only time you have left, you cannot make it up. There is no more time to give you.

The fatigue is your Dan draining you. Just like in life. He knows your coordinates. So just do your firewall exercises. Let him drain his son, who has far more energy to waste than you do. He wastes most of it anyway.

Vis-à-vis Sam's energy toward you right now? We wouldn't bother contacting him. He's so shut down because of all the strife up north [with his mother]; he is best left completely alone until he contacts you. And that may not be for a very long time. And if that's the way it will be, and it might be, then just let it alone.

Connect with your own creative energy and just be brave in the world. You really have no other options just now.

When you travel tomorrow, just do everything you can to take care of your body while you fly and when you're in Paris. Let Mel, who has a much stronger body, go and do what she wants. If you push yourself, which we know you'll want to, you will break down. Explain that to her and she will hear you.

Anything else?

Choose to connect with your own positive energy. When you let yourself sink into your own sorrow, your body takes the hit. And you don't have the luxury, quite frankly. Look at your life and just bless what you have. You live in splendor from your point of view. This is the best time of your life. Enjoy it.

Thank you. Namaste.

And to you. Go eat. Come back and we'll work on the book. Then you'll walk, pack and off to Paris.

So off to Paris we went. I had rented us a small, but pretty flat on the Left Bank, just off Place Monge. It was perfect, because it was close to two Metro lines and three days a week, a wonderful open-air farmer's market took over a tiny park nearby. The market drew all the locals, overflowed with vibrant, fresh vegetables, delicious honey cakes, and rich, creamy cheeses. The perfect place to practice my rusty French, so I loved it.

On Wednesday, we walked all over everywhere, so by day's end, both Melanie and I were completely exhausted. But while we sipped tea under the big clock at Musée d'Orsay, a charming old gentleman told us that the Louvre was open late, and that now would be the best time to go.

He pointed to the big buildings across the river, and so we went. It seemed as if no one else knew the secret of Wednesday nights at the Louvre – the museum was almost empty. So empty, in fact, that within minutes we were nose to nose with "The Mona Lisa." Then we wandered through the different wings and galleries, because I wanted to see every Caravaggio, David, and de LaTour that they owned.

Suddenly sheer exhaustion overtook me, and I said, "We have to find a place to sit down." So we walked into a side courtyard filled with classical statues. I saw a statue of Hercules wrestling a giant snake and I gasped – I recognized the body that I had seen that first night when Dan undressed for me. That amazing body, when I said to him, "I don't need to sleep with you. I should sculpt you. You look like Atlas." As I sat and stared at the statue, I just wanted to cry.

The following day, I was on the Metro, when I saw a woman who looked exactly like my sister Valrie, only she seemed so happy and fulfilled as she chatted with a man who obviously adored her.

The next two days flew by, as Melanie and I tried to enjoy as much of Paris as we could. By Saturday, I hadn't meditated, or even stopped long enough to say, "Hi," to the In Between.

Then just before 2 a.m., I woke with a jolt, knowing I had to put a pen in my left hand:

Sat., December 6, 2002 –1:39 a.m. (Paris)

Cobalt Blue, here. Thank you for getting up. We know how sad you feel losing your Dan, but he is now in final lock down. He will know you are at Chartres next week, but he cannot be with you.

He was with you at the Louvre. When you looked with such love at *his* body, he felt so much regret for his own stubborn refusal to enjoy the gifts he had, that he made a final decision to be locked down.

He tried to say good-bye again, but your body was too exhausted to be woken. Your sorrow yesterday was cellular. Let yourself cry it out.

Re: the woman on the train? She looked like your sister for a big reason. She is a part of your sister's probable selves – obviously *her* choices led her in a direction that supported her talent and she flourished.

Watch your thoughts carefully. When you feel them slipping into places that don't serve you, acknowledge them and choose to change them.

Vis-à-vis your next few days in Paris? Just enjoy every moment.

And we did. We went back to the Louvre three more times, Melly got mugged in the Metro by a threesome of Gypsies, and we managed to get lost in almost every part of Paris. But still, we had fun. Then on Tuesday, we took the train to Chartres.

Tuesday, December 10, 2002 – at Chartres

I did the tour with the old English gentleman who's been here at Chartres for 50 years. He talked about the beautiful blue and pink windows and who paid for what, and which statues were of which saints. But what he really said was that the administration at the cathedral was changing and they wanted to get rid of him. I felt so sad for him.

Then I looked around, and wondered where I could put the remainder of Dan's ashes, because the place is spotless. I sat in the chapel of the black Virgin Mary and lit a candle. I felt so sad, I wanted to just weep, but I refuse to cry in public. The feeling tone here evokes so much sorrow, longing and love in me.

Finally I saw the signs saying, "Visit the Bell Tower." I paid my four francs and climbed the winding, narrow stairway up to the top of the tower and out onto a landing. It was freezing up there, but so clear I could see to the horizon.

I sprinkled his ashes onto the old stones and then I saw the bell tower and the bells. Since Dan had been a blacksmith, this seemed perfect. I stood there throwing handful after handful of Dan at those big, iron bells. As the icy wind whipped my face, I turned to look out over the beautiful little town and out onto the French countryside. Then, as if by magic, the bells began to ring. And they rang and rang and rang. Finally, I burst into tears and I cried, but my tears stung my cheeks, as they froze to my face. So I stepped back inside the doorway, and looked out over the town at the horizon and listened to the bells. The bells tolled for more than ten solid minutes. It was as if they tolled for Sister Isabel and for Sister Bertrand, who loved her.

When I climbed back down the stairs, there was a real-life funeral in progress – the reason for those bells. I listened to the priest talk about life and how finite it is. I'm amazed at how much French I actually understood, and how much I didn't. Then that beautiful cathedral filled with music – organ music – and I'm so glad I got to send Dan off in style. I hope he feels the love I sent to help him in his new life…his life in Africa.

Advice?

Cobalt Blue – Dan is _finally_ completely gone. You have completed a dream of passion and love that began 401 years ago right here in this sacred place.

You can work, write the story of love lost, love found, love unappreciated
and yet…re-found because you came to Paris with your Dan – your Sister
Isabel – the love you waited for.

Come home now with the knowledge that the quest is over. You found your love.
And that was the task; you had no control over the outcome. Return with no
expectations. Your life is far from over – but this phase is through.

It was late in the afternoon by then. Melanie is incredibly psychic and she said
later that she "heard Dan" tell her to leave me alone. And so she took the train
back to Paris. But I had no idea where she'd gone. So I just headed back to Paris
myself. On the train, I put the pen in my hand and Barushe had a thing or two
to say:

*Barushe back. Now that Dan is finally gone. Quel un vieux rien! C'est
domage…(then he realized I didn't want to hear this in French)* **that he chose to
ignore everything positive in his life and chose to continually focus on what
wasn't – what wasn't his problem.**

*But enough of him. Your fear that you've lost Sam is real. But you never had
him. He needs to be let go of. He doesn't like you. He has no respect for who
you are. He is very single-minded, and his mind only sees life in terms of his
needs. You have no place in his life. Let him go.*

How much more do I have to let go?

**Let go until you stand alone – then you will fully understand your strength.
Hercules? Honey, who's still standing?**

Barushe seemed to be mad at both of them. When I got back home to Los
Angeles, I gave away the rest of Dan's clothes. Then I followed the advice, and got
rid of Dan's sorrow-filled desk. Such a relief!

Monday, December 23, 2002 – 6:33 a.m.
Advice for the day?

**Cobalt Blue, here – today we will just say a few words about your Dan, your
sadness, your final few days of active mourning, and your future, which is
bright, my dear shining warrior.**

**Re: your darling Dan? He is a memory to you, "he exists" as an energy form
but his main energy is bolted down – at his own request – in Africa. He
will have many challenges that will enable him to get over himself, in the**

vernacular. Because in your life together he was so mono-focused on himself, to the exclusion of all else, that it crippled him. Even his connection to Sam, was more about how he related to Sam, rather than about Sam. But you knew that.

Re: your final days of mourning. Stop blocking yourself from crying. You cried at Chartres but not fully. Go somewhere and – even in the car – and let it all go. If they begin to jackhammer on Monday, scream it out. (Workmen were about to pull up the concrete driveway next door.)

Stay focused on "us." Your mind is sometimes too flexible. Re: your future – entertain _no_ negative thoughts. Do not invite them in.

Re: your "warrior Stephanie," think of her as more a shining goddess warrior outfit you slip into – only you slip into her from inside out. Encourage her to come and stay with you. Look into the picture of you taken in Berkeley – you see her there. You see her in the eyes that look out from your wedding picture – it's only after you understood "the truth" of your relationship that your eyes lost their luster, their spark. And the spark is your warrior Stephanie.

You can reclaim her by doing just what you do every day. Show up for your life, and do the best you can – it's all a big chess game. And you can't know the next moves until the other "players" make theirs. And that's the fun of it.

Once again, you give yourself more trouble about your slowness than we feel. We would like you to jump out of bed at 4:30 and begin to work, but your body needs care and needs to move at its own pace. You don't like rushing. That's why you need to get up early. Last night when you tried to lie down and read, your body took the opportunity to sleep…it was tired. What you need to keep in mind is that you operate pretty much like a two-year-old. Your body goes and goes and goes, and then just needs to shut down. Next time just make sure you're in bed. You don't like falling asleep on the couch with the light on.

Embrace the joy of your life today – get whatever of the cleaning you can done without the music. You need music to clean. Fix the stereo yourself, if you want to. Don't wait for favors to be done for you.

Thank you. I'm ready to work. Namaste.

We salute the "you" in you.

Thursday, December 26, 2002 – 5:50 a.m.
I tried to give myself today off – but woke at 4:40 a.m., stayed in bed until 5, then got up. Christmas with Lynn's family was nice – how she does it – the work! She leaves

for Austin on Saturday? Sunday? Monday, I think? When I realized she was really going, I nearly burst into tears. Oh, well...

Advice for today?

Cobalt Blue – your fear that you will be all alone once Lynn leaves needs to be vacuumed out of your awareness. Completely. You need to be able to stand alone.

For today? Your Samuel made the choice to spend the holiday with you – he got your "message" without your doing any more than standing up for yourself with him, which was a good thing.

Your "Dan" wanted to connect with you today, but he's needed in his new life – there, of course, is an aspect of Enoch that still remembers Dan, but if truth be told, not fondly.

He chose challenges that he simply ignored once he got to "earth plane reality." He paid no attention, no matter how hard the cluster tried to communicate. He was even more obtuse than you were! And that says a lot, for it's taken us quite a long time to make you "pay attention."

But now that we have your attention, you are doing a bang-up job of it. Just continue to show up for your life. Show up for your work. Show up for your challenges. Know that you will be supported if you stay away from the petty demons in your environment.

Vis-à-vis your body – keep taking extra good care. The female symptoms are annoying to you, but will be resolved when you begin to have sex again. And you will – just don't let yourself get hooked again. You will keep in touch with us, and we will run a "search" on your perspective encounters.

After today, you are no longer a widow. You are single again.

Thank you. Ouch! My legs? Is that you or what?

Dan – the impish spirit, sneaking back to say a fond farewell to my darling Stephanie for the very last time. Yes, I know I've said it before, but this is the *last time*.

I set you free, my darling. I set you free. I loved you far more than I understood, but not nearly enough. You still long for me but not nearly as much as I still long for you. They want me to stay focused, and I will. But if truth be told, I don't have a great deal of affinity with this new life. At least yet.

There is nothing left for me to say except that in all my lives, you were my most devoted love. You nurtured me as Sister Isabel, and then you loved me as Dan. There are other incarnations where we share connections, but those two are "my personal" favorites. For you? I don't know, for in both of them I pretty much broke your heart. But if I could give you a magic needle and thread to sew up the gaping hole in your heart that I caused with my life, my living with you, I would. Just please, my darling Stephanie, I scream from this reality, to not ever let _fear_ get to you. That's the trick. That's the answer. No matter what happens, just look it in the eye and know that you have the skills to untangle any mess. You have the skill. It's what you're programmed to do. Just do it.

And when you see me again, please have the love you still have for me. Keep a candle burning in your heart, not just on my desk. Keep the candle burning every year for me. I will know about it. It will please us both.

There is no amount of tears that can be shed that will make up for my particular brand of treachery toward you. The insincerity with which I lived my life – the "great pretender!" You should have paid attention.

Pay attention, my shining, warrior goddess. Yes, you saw that body and I "fled." I agreed to final lock down, but slipping in and out is easy right now. It's birth that locks you in. _Birth_. And even then, it's easy to escape. My real bad habit. Always busy "elsewhere."

They are mad at me for breaking into your circuits again. Thank you for not doing your "firewall" exercises. Do them when I leave this morning, because I'm pulling energy, and they know it.

Go then. Say good-bye to me. Say good-bye to "us."

It's not as easy as that. But...thank you for sitting down. I have only a minute of two longer to be focused in with you. That's the discomfort in your legs...that is me, my energy.

Anything else?

Let me once again tell you how much I appreciate the elegance with which you've lived this past year of horrible, painful mourning for my used-to-be self. I wish I could have known what it would have been like while I lived – sort of "It's A Wonderful Life" (the movie) – for Dan, the man.

If I'd known the amount of "good" I could have been to the world by just "showing up," like you do, I might have stayed. Don't make the same mistake I did and underestimate your "good" in the world.

I saw you refused to make the same mistake I made with Samuel. I stand in awe of your ability to force his feet to the mat – to make him experience – make the choice – to keep the relationship.

I wish I could have been as authentic with him. I didn't have the courage. I lived in fear that he would withdraw his love from me, the way I had withdrawn my love and respect from my own father.

If I could I would sit and chat all day with you because it's lonely only dealing with these "new people" who aren't really "new" to me. The Third World is third for a reason, that's all they'll let me say right now. What a mess things are here!

I scream my love down through the centuries to you, my angel, my love, my wife. The thing so dear to me, and yet now so far away. Forgive me for the final time for stealing what was our life away from us. I stole it and then dropped it into the ocean like so much trash. What an idiot. But that's over.

Do the book. Get the passion for it. I know it takes energy, and that's a problem for you, and I'm not helping! Just taking this energy today – stealing it again from under Barushe's nose. Oh, he's mad! And so is…well, everyone in the cluster, because they needed you this morning. But they gave you the day off for me, so I thought I'd use it.

Good-bye, my Dan…

Cobalt Blue here to clean up your circuits – sit – he snuck in but you "enabled" him. You could have stopped him and yet we know this is his day. His last day, really. For next year he will not be able to get out. Unless he chooses not to stay in Africa.

What should I do today?

Leave the house. Hurry.

And so I did. Thus, the journey that had begun a year to the day before in the ICU, with my hand on Dan's heart as I felt it stop beating, yet hearing him yell, "Free at Last!" had now come full circle. Only now, I could finally say, "Free at Last, Free at Last, Thank God, Almighty, I'm Free at Last!"

I only heard from Dan one more time. It was Valentine's Day of 2003, and the "Day of Lovers" brought up in me the same longing to be loved that it brings up in everyone. I lit a fire in the fireplace and on an impulse, grabbed the beautiful quilt made from Dan's shirts and ties. I wrapped myself in it, and sat down on the couch. Then I felt that old familiar tug in my left hand, so I put a pen in it.

My pen drew a gigantic heart, and then a tiny little man with an enormous erection, somewhat like an African fertility symbol, with the words: "I miss you!

Joke!!" And I laughed out loud. It was "Dan the African," as he called himself, and then he began to complain about life in Africa, and I felt my own energy whoosh out of me, as if someone had pulled a plug.

So I put the pen down, and threw off the quilt from around my shoulders. I finally chose not to be depleted by my "missing man."

As that year passed, I tried to enjoy what each day brought, despite my precarious situation in the world. I read *The Power of Now*, by Eckhhart Tolle, then Deepak Chopra's *The Spontaneous Fulfillment of Desire*, and Wayne Dyer's *The Power of Intention*. I read anything I could find that encouraged me to continue towards my goal of finishing the book.

Samuel wrote to me toward the end of the year and said, "I could live my life without you, but I would rather have you in my life." And so, one of the true loves of my life returned, and we remain good buddies.

As I write these last words, it's November of 2005, and much has changed, yet much has stayed the same. Hurricanes have changed the landscapes of Louisiana and Texas, and many souls have journeyed back to the "In Between." I still work for Positive Changes in Beverly Hills, and whenever I get a new client who's lost a husband, a wife, a son, a daughter, mother or father, I always ask, "And did they come back to you?"

The answer is always, "Yes."

So, if you are reading this book, it will prove to you that I had the tenacity to finish it, no matter how long it took me. You've seen how many times I wanted to quit, but ultimately, I refused to give up. So, I urge you not to give up, even when everything seems lost. There's always hope.

If my story has helped you to believe in the magic of your own life, the sacredness of your own relationships, sexuality and connections, then I have done my job.

We are all made of stardust, and that's a fact.

– THE END –

FINDHORN PRESS

Books, Card Sets,
CDs & DVDs
that inspire and uplift

For a complete catalogue,
please contact:

Findhorn Press Ltd
305a The Park, Findhorn
Forres IV36 3TE
Scotland, UK

Telephone +44-(0)1309-690582
Fax +44-(0)1309-690036
eMail info@findhornpress.com

or consult our catalogue online
(with secure order facility) on
www.findhornpress.com